Guide to Cuba

THE BRADT STORY

In 1974, my former husband George Bradt and I spent three days sitting on a river barge in Bolivia writing our first guide for like-minded travellers: *Backpacking along Ancient Ways in Peru and Bolivia*. The 'little yellow book', as it became known, is now in its sixth edition and continues to sell to travellers throughout the world. Since 1980, with the establishment of Bradt Publications, I have continued to publish guides for the discerning traveller, covering more than 100 countries and all six continents, and winning the 1997 *Sunday Times* Small Publisher of the Year Award. *Guide to Cuba* is the 135th Bradt title to be published.

The company continues to develop new titles and new series, but in the forefront of my mind there remains our original ethos – responsible travel with an emphasis on the culture and natural history of the region. I hope that you will get the most out of your trip, and perhaps have the opportunity to give something in return.

Travel guides are by their nature continuously evolving. If you experience anything which you would like to share with us, or if you have any amendments to make to this guide, please write; all your letters are read and passed on to the author. Most importantly, do remember to travel with an open mind and to respect the customs of your hosts – it will add immeasurably to your enjoyment.

Happy travelling!

Hilary Bradt

41 Nortoft Road, Chalfont St Peter, Bucks SL9 0LA, England
Tel/fax: 01494 873478 Email: bradtpublications@compuserve.com

Guide to Cuba

2nd Edition

Stephen Fallon

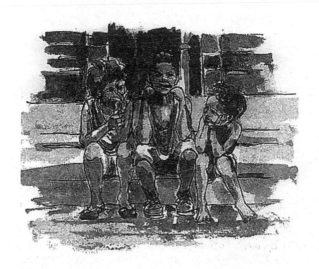

Bradt Publications, UK
The Globe Pequot Press Inc, USA

First published in 1995 by Bradt Publications.
This second edition published in 1997 by Bradt Publications,
41 Nortoft Road, Chalfont St Peter, Bucks SL9 0LA, England.
Published in the USA by The Globe Pequot Press Inc, 6 Business Park Road,
PO Box 833, Old Saybrook, Connecticut 06475-0833

The author and publishers have made every effort to ensure the accuracy of the information
in this book at the time of going to press. However, they cannot accept any
responsibility for any loss, injury or inconvenience resulting from
the use of information contained in this guide.

British Library Cataloguing in Publication Data
A catalogue record for this book is available from the British Library
ISBN 1 898323 62 3

Library of Congress Cataloging-in-Publication Data
Fallon, Stephen.
   Guide to Cuba / Stephen Fallon. — 2nd ed.
      p.   cm.
   Includes bibliographical references and index.
   ISBN 1-898323-62-3
   1. Cuba – Guidebooks.   I. Title.
   F1754.7.F35   1997
   917,29108'4–dc21   97-28199
                                          CIP

Cover photographs Christine Osborne Pictures
Front Traditional dolls and Che Guevara are popular souvenirs
Back Flower stall outside the Mercado in Havana
Photographs Stephen Fallon (SF), Chris Mattison (CM), Christine Osborne (CO)
Illustrations Isabel Fallow
Maps *Covers* Steve Munns   *Others* Hans van Well

Typeset from the author's disc by Wakewing Ltd, High Wycombe HP13 7QA
Printed and bound in Great Britain by The Guernsey Press Co Ltd

CONTENTS

LIST OF MAPS

Introduction

Put the question 'what is Cuba?' to a group of people and you are guaranteed a different response from each. The reality is that Cuba is a mixture of many different things. It is a Utopian experiment gone wrong; it is an island paradise with a culture as vibrant as anywhere on earth and it is a country of broken promises, thwarted dreams and lofty ideals. It is also one of the most misunderstood and maligned countries in the Caribbean and Latin America. Punished for choosing to adopt a different political outlook from its powerful neighbour, the USA, Cuba today is in the midst of an economic crisis – the *Período Especial* as it is euphemistically known. With the heavy subsidies of the Soviet Union now gone, Castro has chosen tourism as the new path to salvation for his country. The tourist infrastructure – good hotels, good roads and transport links – are already in place, while the dollar shops and tourist restaurants are well stocked. Life for the average Cuban, however, could not be more different. Shops are bare and food rationed as the wealth created by tourism only slowly trickles down to the man in the street. In the face of hardship, however, the innate optimism of the Cuban shines through. A walk along Calle Obispo in Havana or an evening in the Casa de la Trova in Santiago de Cuba will confirm this, for wherever you go on this lovely island the rhythms of Cuba are never far from earshot. Whether they emanate from the heated debates on topics ranging from politics to baseball around the plazas or from the Spanish guitars and African drums that beat out the hypnotic rhythms of the *salsa, son* and *rumba,* the passion and the vibrancy that is every Cuban's birthright are permanently on display.

Cuba today is a country undergoing a period of profound change. Old markets have gone and new ones need to be found and all the time the USA is tightening the economic screw. Paradoxically, this once closed society has been forced to open itself up and in doing so has revealed to the visitors who are now flocking to its shores its wealth of human spirit, natural beauty and architectural treasures. A troubled island? Perhaps. The jewel in the Caribbean? Undoubtedly. A visit to Cuba is a memorable and rewarding experience.

ABOUT THE AUTHOR

Stephen Fallon started serious travelling on a year-long tour of Asia in 1992 and is now a travel writer and photographer, speacialising in Asia, Latin America and the Caribbean. His passion for mountain biking has seen him undertake gruelling trips through Vietnam, Cuba, Indonesia and Venezuela. He lives in London.

ACKNOWLEDGEMENTS

I would like to thank the many friends I made in Cuba for the part they played in the making of this book. In particular I would like to express my appreciation to Dani and Rafael in Havana and to Brian in Santiago de Cuba. Thanks also to Sally Brock, my editor, for her skilful editing and sound advice, to Hans for his cartographic skills and to all at Bradt Publications for their support. For supplying the bike and equipment that enabled me to reach the more remote parts of Cuba, my thanks go to Graham Koster and Specialised Bikes (UK). My greatest debt, however, and the one which I could never begin to repay is to my wife, Christine, to whom I dedicate this book.

Part One

GENERAL INFORMATION

Chapter One

Background Information

HISTORY

The traumatic events in Cuba over the last four decades are only a small part of a colourful history that extends back well before the colonisation of the island by the Spanish during the 16th century. The key to Cuba's distant past is found in the area known as Oriente and, in particular, the city of Baracoa. It is here that you are most likely to encounter people who are the indirect descendants of the true indigenous inhabitants of the island, the Indians. It is estimated that there were once up to 500,000 Indians scattered across the island in various groups. The first are thought to have settled as early as 5000BC.

The three main aboriginal groups were the Ciboneys, the Guanahatabey and the Arawacks – or the Tainos as they were better known. The Tainos were the most advanced and sophisticated of the group and were skilled in fishing, agriculture, weaving and ceramics. They were also skilled builders, their homes being prototypes for the *bohío* – the traditional peasant huts common in the countryside of Cuba today. Sturdy constructions, they were built to withstand the force of hurricanes which still occasionally trouble the island.

The Indians were in general a friendly and peace-loving people, a fact acknowledged by Columbus who referred to them as 'gentle and without knowledge of what is evil... They love their neighbours as themselves.'

Spanish colonisation

The first European to land in Cuba was Columbus, who arrived on the island in 1492. Mistakenly, he believed that he had discovered the East Indies and it was not until another Spaniard, Sebastian de Ocampo, circumnavigated the island in 1508 that Columbus' mistake was realised.

Following Columbus' discovery, in 1493 the Pope decreed that Christianity should be taught to the Indians as part of the 'civilisation' process that Cuba was to undergo. Initially the Spanish paid scant attention to the island, preferring to concentrate on their colonial activities in neighbouring countries. It was nearly 20 years after Columbus' first landing that the Spanish finally arrived in force, bringing a bloody end to the Indians' idyllic lifestyle. In 1510 Diego Velázquez and an entourage of around 300 troops landed close to Guantánamo Bay. Within 50 years the Indian population had been virtually wiped out.

In the years between the landings of Columbus and Velázquez, Indian resistance to Spanish conquistadors had grown. By the time of Velázquez's arrival the principal leader of this resistance was an Indian named Hatuey. The wily Spanish realised that if they defeated this fearless fighter, they would break the back of the resistance and, within four months of Velázquez stepping ashore, they had captured their man. With a brutality typical of the time, Hatuey was tortured and then burned at the stake. The Spanish offered him salvation in exchange for his acceptance of Christianity but Hatuey refused. With Hatuey's death, Cuba had its first martyr, while the Indian fight against Spanish imperialism had been dealt a fatal blow.

Velázquez and his men swept across the country, enslaving many of the indigenous peoples in their quest for gold. Those he didn't take were usually killed. Many Indians, who had no natural immunity to the new diseases the Spanish brought with them, fell ill and died. Others, on hearing news of the Spaniards' ruthlessness, rather than face colonial genocide, took their own lives in mass suicide pacts.

The pace of development was initially slow under Spanish rule. After trying, and failing, to grow crops native to Spain, the settlers concentrated on the cultivation of more local crops, including tobacco. Forests were cleared to make way for cattle introduced from India and the wood was used in the export trade.

To facilitate the development of Cuba, Velázquez founded what are still known as the seven villas – Baracoa (1512), Bayamo (1513), Trinidad (1514), Sancti Spiritus (1514), Santiago de Cuba (1515), Havana (1515) and Camagüey (1515).

Slaves

Having killed off the Indian population, the Spanish were now obliged to bring in a replacement labour force to assist them in exploiting the riches of the island. In their search for gold (which as it turned out was a relatively fruitless one, Cuba not being rich in the metal) hundreds of slaves were brought across from Africa to work as forced labour. As attention was switched away from the excavation of gold to the cultivation of sugar and tobacco, so the hundreds of imported slaves became thousands.

Slaves, under Spanish law, were permitted to buy and sell their own homes, to marry and have children. They were also allowed, if they could afford it, to buy their own freedom. While it is true to say that their lifestyle was more favourable than that of slaves in other areas of the world (particularly America), the fact remains that they worked appallingly long hours in squalid and oppressive conditions which often resulted in misery and death. One explanation for the better treatment received is that slaves cost money and were an asset, as opposed to being an indigenous workforce capable of being exploited free of charge, as was the case with the Indian population. Although Cuba had fewer slaves than any other island in the West Indies, it remained, until 1886, the last Caribbean island to sanction the practice.

Nationalism

The fact that Cuba was relatively neglected in comparison with other colonies in the region partly explains the growth of a Cuban consciousness, of a national identity. The ascent of a new royal family to the Spanish throne at the beginning of the 18th century encouraged an increase in the cultural enrichment of Cuban society. In tandem with an increase in population, Cuba became a better educated and more refined country (for the affluent minority). In a more important sense, however, it remained backward, with most of the profits generated from its sugar and tobacco industries going directly to Spain.

There were several small but unsuccessful attempts to break free of the chains of Spanish monopoly during the first half of the 18th century, notably by the tobacco farmers. In spite of these mini insurrections, the reins of power remained firmly in Spain. However, as a population developed which was distinctly Cuban rather than Spanish, so resentment towards the colonists began to ferment.

Spanish power began to wane during the 18th century as England, France and Holland challenged for her overseas possessions. In 1762 the British navy captured Havana and occupied it for 11 months. In that time trade barriers were relaxed and contacts made with other colonies in North America. A further 10,000 slaves were drafted in to bolster the increase in sugar and tobacco production.

Havana reverted to Spanish control within the year, following Britain's decision to trade her in return for the Florida peninsula. As a result of this short, sharp shock, Spain made greater efforts to develop the Cuban economy and sugar and tobacco production was given a new lease of life. There was still the problem that the majority of the profits reaped as a result of these efforts found their way back to Spain.

Following the successful slave revolution in Haiti led by Toussaint l'Ouverture, the French Haitian slave masters fled *en masse* to the safety of Cuba, bringing with them their advanced knowledge of sugar production techniques. The sugar industry further expanded and more slaves were brought in to work the new plantations. Cuba replaced Haiti as the main sugar producer in the Caribbean. As the plantations expanded and the profits became greater, so the collective lot of the slave population deteriorated. This culminated in a series of slave revolts in 1844, when around 3,000 slaves lost their lives. Thousands more were imprisoned and countless numbers took to the hills. Some plantation owners, fearing for their future, called for Cuba to become a protectorate of the United States, seeing this as a guarantee against a Haitian-style revolt. Indeed, the American president, Thomas Jefferson, had suggested the same thing and had even sent an envoy to Madrid to enquire of the price Spain would accept for the sale of her colony. Meanwhile, sympathy for, and empathy with, the slave population continued to grow among the Cuban–Spanish and Creole population.

Ten-Year War of Independence

On 10 October 1868, Carlos Manuel de Cespedes, a wealthy plantation owner and lawyer from Bayamo, took a torch to his own sugar mill, 'La Demajagua', set free his slaves and declared Cuba independent. Thus began one of the most traumatic episodes in Cuban history. In his declaration, the *Grito de Yara* (Shout of Yara), he called for independence from Spain and the formation of a republic. His call to arms was taken up by many slaves and plantation owners, particularly in the east of the island, in Oriente. Cespedes was joined by Antonio Maceo and a Dominican, Máximo Gómez, who led the rebel military forces. The first battle of the war resulted in the brief capture of the town of Bayamo. Rather than return it to Spanish occupation, the rebels razed it to the ground.

The Spanish, determined to retain their possession, fortified the island with more than 250,000 troops and, despite certain brilliant tactical triumphs, the rebels, faced with such overwhelming superiority of both troops and firepower, were never able to gain the upper hand. In 1874 Cespedes was killed in battle and in 1878 the rebels agreed to call a halt to their insurrection in return for certain concessions and reforms. The Ten Year War had resulted in the deaths of around 250,000 Cubans and some 80,000 Spaniards. In addition, around 100,000 people fled the island to avoid the conflict.

José Martí

José Martí, writer, poet and lawyer, is the most revered figure in Cuban history – no mean feat given the number of candidates for the title. He is the founding father of independent Cuba and the number of streets, parks and monuments bearing his name pay testimony to his standing in modern-day Cuba. He was exiled for his outspoken views on independence; however, he continued his protests outside of the country, establishing the Cuban Revolutionary Party while in the United States. His work there brought him into contact with exiled Cuban tobacco workers who had left Cuba to find work. 'There is no danger of war between the races in Cuba,' he proclaimed. 'Man means more than white man, mulatto or black man. The souls of white men and negroes have risen together from the battlefield where they have fought and died for Cuba.' He led his party in an uprising against the Spanish in 1895 when, together with 6,000 rebels, he instigated landings at various points across the island. Sadly, Martí was killed during the ensuing battles but his rebels, with strong support from resident anti-colonialists, continued the struggle and in 1897 Spain agreed to grant Cuba autonomy. The rebels, feeling that total victory was within their grasp and unwilling to accept anything less than full independence, rejected the offer.

American intervention
It was at this juncture that the United States entered the fray. Having long courted Cuba, the USA had consistently failed in attempts to buy her from the Spanish, but the opportunity finally (and tragically) arose for the island to be annexed by force. As a result of the unrest following the rebel insurgence, America sent one of her warships, *The Maine*, to Havana, ostensibly to protect American citizens living there. For some reason, whether it was a bomb planted by the Spanish, or, as has been suggested, by the Americans themselves, simply as a result of pure accident, *The Maine* exploded, killing 258 sailors. The United States, egged on by its jingoistic media, seized the opportunity and declared war on Spain and, on 25 April 1898, battle commenced. The Cubans, sceptical about American motives and fearing the dawn of a new age of colonial power, nevertheless reluctantly accepted assurances that the United States was interested only in restoring peace and not in annexing the country.

Both America and Cuba combined quickly to topple the old Spanish regime and on 17 July 1898 the war was effectively over. Spain surrendered in the city of Santiago de Cuba. The Cubans, much to their chagrin, were barred from entering the city to take part in the celebrations despite the sacrifices they had made and the losses they had suffered. On 10 December 1898 the Paris Treaty was signed, bringing a formal end to the war between Spain and America. The United States effectively gained possession of Cuba. After more than three years of exercising its control, America finally granted Cuba its formal independence although, with the Platt Amendment giving the United States 'The right to intervene for the preservation of Cuban independence, the maintenance of a government adequate for the protection of life, property and individual liberty', independence came with strings attached. The amendment also gave the United States the right to have naval bases on the island and to this day one such establishment, the renowned Guantánamo Base, is still in operation.

The pre-Revolutionary years
After the war Cuba experienced an economic boom as American investors poured money into the sugar and tobacco industries. With the disruption to the world sugar supply and markets during World War I, Cuba

experienced a sugar boom that became known popularly as 'The Dance of Millions.' As investors, land barons and politicians reaped the rewards of prosperity, the majority of the population remained illiterate, undernourished and disillusioned. With the arrival of the age of prohibition in America, Havana became the decadent playground of the rich while the Mafia pumped money into brothel, casino and hotel businesses. The city discovered new dimensions to the phrase 'the sleaze factor'.

When the sugar boom began to wane and the Cuban economy took a turn for the worse, the government of Gerardo Machado, which had been elected on the back of a $500,000 election campaign paid for by an American-owned electrical company, watched the lights go out on its credibility. Following a general strike in the summer of 1933, Machado fled the country. During the chaos that ensued, Fulgencio Batista (a sergeant in the army) successfully staged a coup d'état. Modesty not being one of his more discernible traits, he announced himself as Colonel Batista before placing his considerable support behind Ramón Grau San Martín who became president. American President Roosevelt refused to do business with Grau and Batista's only option was to replace him with someone more acceptable. This he duly did by bringing in Colonel Carlos Mendieta. As successive presidents took office, giving the appearance of democracy, behind the scenes and with one eye always on America, Batista was pulling the strings. He was elected to office himself in 1940 but then his applecart was profoundly upset when, four years later, Ramón Grau San Martín was re-elected. Batista, so disillusioned by this, took off to Florida where he stayed until 1952, before returning to stage another successful military coup. One of the candidates for congress at the time, whose hopes for election were dashed, was a young man named Fidel Castro.

The Revolution

Repression and injustice were the hallmarks of the Batista government and before long the social and economic climate degenerated to the point where circumstances became ripe for revolution. Castro and his brother Raoul joined with a band of youthful dissidents in the area known as Oriente in the east and planned an attack on the Moncada barracks in Santiago de Cuba, hoping that this would spark off a popular revolt. The attack took place on 26 July 1953 and, militarily, was a disaster. Of the 134 who took part, three died during the attack and a further 68 were later tortured and executed. Castro was captured, tried and committed to 15 years' imprisonment. Following a public outcry, he was released from his detention on the Isla de Pinos (now called the Isle of Youth) and was exiled in Mexico. It was there that he met up with Ernesto 'Che' Guevara and, intent on returning to Cuba to try again to overthrow Batista, founded the July 26th Movement.

On 2 December 1956, Castro, Guevara and 80 other revolutionaries landed in Cuba on a small leaking cabin cruiser named *Granma*, bought, ironically, from a Texan. Again, disaster struck and most of the insurrectionists were either killed or captured by Batista's forces. Castro and Guevara managed to make their way into the hills around Santiago de Cuba and from here they were able to continue the Revolution, with the assistance of supporting movements in the cities. On 13 March 1957 around 40 students stormed the presidential palace in Havana, intent on killing Batista, while in July of that year a General Strike was called to protest against the killing of Frank Pais, the leader of the Santiago de Cuba uprising who had been incarcerated along with Fidel and Raoul on the Isla de Pinos. Similar protests continued throughout the country and Batista's only response was torture, murder and repression. In the face of this, support for Castro grew and it soon became apparent that Batista's days were numbered. On 1 January 1959, with millions of dollars appropriated through corruption stuffed into his suitcases, Batista fled the country.

After the Revolution
On his ascent to power, Castro promised to hold free elections within a year. He then set about tackling the problem of illiteracy by making education free and available to everyone. He introduced economic reforms aimed at assisting the more impoverished sectors of the population at the expense of the middle and upper classes. Much to the annoyance of the USA, he embarked on a huge nationalisation programme which directly affected American corporate interests. Although he did propose compensation, the Americans balked at his offers, considering them derisory. He also set about executing many of Batista's loyalists and ordering out all American military advisers whom he considered a potential counter-revolutionary threat. On 1 May 1960 Castro defaulted on his promise of elections within the year, declaring them unnecessary and fraudulent. Following his decision to expel 11 American diplomats from the country on 3 January 1961, the USA broke off all diplomatic relations.

The Bay of Pigs
Shortly after Castro's overthrow of Batista relations between the Castro government and the government of the United States began to deteriorate. The new Revolutionary government confiscated all privately owned property including that which belonged to US citizens. Castro dispatched his envoys to establish diplomatic relations with the world's leading socialist powers and became involved in the promotion and advocacy of revolution in other countries in Latin America.

Several US congressmen and senators denounced Castro and his actions and an anti-Castro lobby took root. This developed rapidly, leading to

Congress passing legislation in June 1959 enabling President Eisenhower to retaliate by cutting off sugar purchases from Cuba, followed by a complete embargo on all exports to Cuba with the exception of food and medicine. Relations between the countries continued to deteriorate and in January 1961 Eisenhower broke off diplomatic ties. Shortly after, Eisenhower was replaced by John F Kennedy as US president.

As early as May 1960, the CIA had been planning a US-backed invasion of Cuba. Initiated during the Eisenhower presidency but executed with Kennedy in power, the ill-fated Bay of Pigs invasion took place on 17 April 1961. On 15 April, three US-manufactured aeroplanes piloted by Cuban rebels bombed Cuban air bases. The intention was to soften up the Cuban military in readiness for the land assault, but the bombings acted as a warning signal to Castro who had time to prepare his forces for the invasion. Two days after the air attack, the 1,500 men of 2506 Brigade (the name given to those Cuban exiles who comprised the invading force, all of whom had been trained and armed by the United States) landed at several sites but mainly at Playa Girón in the province of Matanzas. The intention was to establish a beachhead and then fight their way inland. The rebel army were confident that once news spread of the invasion an uprising would take place and the overthrow of the Castro government would naturally follow.

The invaders were met by the overwhelming presence of the Cuban forces led by Raoul Castro, Fidel's brother, and within two days of the landing the exiles had been routed and 1,113 men captured. Kennedy refused to intervene with direct US military support and the proposed *coup d'état* was aborted.

The captured members of 2506 Brigade were all imprisoned while Castro and Kennedy haggled over the level of reparations required to secure their release. Castro finally agreed to release the prisoners in exchange for $53,000,000 worth of food and medicines. The humiliation of the United States was complete.

On 2 December 1961, with economic ties to the United States severed and with his country in need of a friend, Castro declared himself 'a Marxist–Leninist and shall be until the day I die'. The cry of *Liberdad o Muerte* which had echoed around Havana on 1 January 1959 was replaced by the slogan *Socialismo o Muerte* (Socialism or Death). Cuba became an ally of the Soviet Union.

The Cuban Missile Crisis

Relations between the two countries hit rock bottom on 22 October 1962. After obtaining the approval of Castro, the Soviet Union worked secretly to establish missile installations at strategic locations within Cuba. On 16 October, President Kennedy was presented with reconnaissance photographs taken by a United States U2 spy plane, one of many which regularly patrolled the area. The photographs clearly identified the construction work that was taking place. During a week of debate between the US and the Soviet Union, during which time the Soviets denied the existence of the bases, Kennedy addressed the nation to warn that any attack using nuclear weapons based in Cuba would be regarded as an attack by the Soviet Union and reciprocal action could be expected.

On 22 October 1961 Kennedy ordered the US navy to intercept all Soviet ships in the vicinity to ensure that there were no more shipments of military hardware entering Cuba. He threatened to blow out of the water any ships which did not turn around and return to the Soviet Union with their military cargoes. Khrushchev sent letters to Kennedy indicating that the missiles to be based in Cuba were merely deterrent in nature, followed by further letters indicating that the installations would be dismantled if an assurance was received from the United States that it would not invade Cuba and that US nuclear missile installations in Turkey were dismantled.

In a period of unprecedented cold war tension the world held its breath as the prospect of a third world war loomed large. Ultimately a deal was struck which led to the installations in Cuba and Turkey both being dismantled and a US conditional assurance not to invade the island of Cuba.

Cuba today

It is unimaginable to attempt to write about Cuba today without examining her paranoid relationship with the United States. With Key West only 90 miles to the north and with an estimated one and a half million people of Cuban origin living there, it is easy to understand the feeling of trepidation that Cuba or, more particularly, the Cuban authorities feel. A blockade lasting over 30 years and political philosophies diametrically at odds with each other combine to make a situation which is, on the one hand, potentially explosive and, on the other, farcical.

If the American blockade was designed to break Castro, then it has had almost the opposite effect, giving him reason to blame the USA for everything, from the shortages of food in the Cuban stores to the mass exodus of the Mariel Boat Lift in 1980 when 120,000 people fled to Miami. Blame for the raft exodus of the summer of 1994 was also firmly laid at the door of the USA. Nevertheless, there are signs that this policy might be beginning to work as dissent among some sections of the population has begun to grow. Following the collapse of the Soviet Union and, with no one around to bankroll Cuba any more (it is estimated that Cuba was receiving a financial subsidy equivalent to one dollar per day *per capita* from the USSR), the economic pressure exerted by the USA may be beginning to take its toll.

It had been hoped that, following the election of President Clinton, the United States would adopt a more liberal attitude towards Cuba. Following the lifting of the American embargo on Vietnam, hopes were raised even further that some sort of diplomatic breakthrough was in the offing. This was not to be. The war of words continued and America continues to turn the economic screw.

On 5 August 1994 the most serious outbreak of civil disorder since the 1959 Revolution took place on the Malecón, Havana's waterfront. Following the hijacking of three ferries the previous week, during which two police officers were killed, rumours spread that another Mariel-style exodus was to take place. Thousands gathered on the waterfront looking out to sea, waiting for the boats to arrive from America, but the boats never came. Attempts to clear the area resulted in clashes between the assembled crowd and the police and local guards, the *Blas Roca*, which continued into the early hours. Dollar shops were looted and a tourist hotel, the Deauville on the Malecón, was attacked. At first many thought a new revolution had begun but Castro's forces soon gained control and on 8 August around 200,000 people turned out in Havana's Plaza de la Revolution to show support for the beleaguered Fidel. Castro responded by threatening the USA with a repeat of the Mariel boat lift if they refused to stop what he considered to be incitements to riot, broadcast by the pirate Radio Martí from Miami. America responded to this threat by issuing a warning against Castro to stop trying to dictate American foreign policy. Paradoxically, both sides were desperate to ensure that a mass exodus didn't happen – Cuba because of the damage this would have caused to its already tarnished international image and America because of the financial burden of accommodating a new wave of refugees.

On 24 February 1996 the Cuban government shot down two Cessna light aircraft close to the beach area of Baracoa, west of Havana. These planes were piloted by members of a Cuban exile group based in Miami known as the 'Brothers To The Rescue'. Ostensibly established to provide a rescue service for Cubans fleeing the country by sea, the 'Brothers To The Rescue' had also carried out a leafleting campaign of Havana and other areas of Cuba in an attempt to increase instability on the island. Their links with the CIA and other exiled Cuban groups such as Alpha 66 have led many to question their underlying motives.

There is still a debate as to whether the aircraft, which had been given warning by the Cuban military to turn around, were actually shot down in Cuban or international airspace. Cuba and the USA have yet to agree on the matter.

The US accused Cuba of being 'scornful of international law' while Cuba countered that it was their right to 'interrupt the flights of aircraft which breached Cuban sovereignty and endangered the lives of Cuban citizens'.

Either way, the reaction of the powerful exiled Cuban lobby groups of Miami, allied to the opportunism of some of the more right-wing members of the Republican party who seized the opportunity to lash out at Cuba once again, gave birth to the Helms-Burton Bill which tightened the US embargo even further.

The Helms-Burton Bill

In a presidential election year and with Bill Clinton anxious to win in Florida where the exiled Cuban population had forged a powerful lobby, the smooth passage of the Helms-Burton Bill was all but assured. On 5 March 1996 the Senate was asked to vote on the following conference report:

> **The Cuban Liberty and Democratic Solidarity Act**
> 'To adopt the conference report (final version) of a bill to seek international sanctions against the Castro government in Cuba, and to plan for support of a transition government leading to a democratically elected government in Cuba. The bill codifies this and strengthens the US embargo of Cuba, requires additional US sanctions on countries that assist Cuba, denies visas to aliens who confiscate, convert or benefit from property confiscated from US nationals by the Cuban government, and allows US citizens with a claim to property confiscated by the Cuban government to take court action against any person who traffics in that property after August 1st 1996.'

The bill sailed through to legislation with only a handful of votes against (Senator Edward Kennedy being one of those who deemed it unjust).

There was (and still is) much international condemnation of the Helms-Burton Bill and what many saw as an unnecessary further step in the tightening of the US embargo. The European Parliament condemned the United States, accusing it of instigating a 'serious infringement of the GATT, World Trade Organisation rules and of international law'. Perhaps the most eloquent and heartfelt condemnation came from the American author Alice Walker. Her abridged letter is reproduced overleaf.

On 29 April 1997 the United Nations secretary-general Kofi Annan pronounced that he believed that the United States should reconsider its 30 year old economic embargo against Cuba. 'Let me say that the sanctions have been enforced for over 30 years and Cuba is still managing somehow. I would really hope that the time will come in the not-too-distant future when that embargo will be reconsidered.' Since 1992, the United Nations has voted every year in favour of a resolution calling for the lifting of the embargo. To date the resolution has been ignored.

Chronology of important events

1868–1878	The First War of Independence, led by Carlos Manuel de Cespedes, against the Spanish colonialists .
1895–1898	The Second War of Independence led by José Martí, Antonio Maceo and Máximo Gómez.
1901	In return for American troop withdrawal, Cuba agrees to the Platt Amendment which grants the USA the right to intervene in the affairs of Cuba.
1902 *May*	The Republic of Cuba is formed.

A LETTER TO PRESIDENT BILL CLINTON
from Alice Walker, poet and novelist, whose works include *The Color Purple*

13 March 1996

Dear President Clinton,

Thank you very much for the invitation to the White House while I was in Washington in January...

I love Cuba and its people including Fidel. The bill you have signed to further tighten the blockade hurts me deeply. I travel to Cuba whenever I can to take medicine and the small, perhaps insignificant comfort of my presence, to those whose courage and tenderness have inspired me practically my entire life. I have seen how the embargo hurts everyone in Cuba, but especially Cuban children, infants in particular. I spend some nights in utter sleeplessness worrying about them. Someone has said that when you give birth to a child – and perhaps I read this in Hillary's book, which I recently bought – you are really making a commitment to the agony of having your heart walking around outside your body. That is how I feel about Cuba...

I feel the suffering of each child in Cuba as if it were my own. The bill you have signed is wrong. Even if you despise Fidel and even if the Cubans should not have shot down the planes violating their air space... The bill is wrong, the embargo is wrong, because it punishes people, some of them unborn, for being who they are. Cubans cannot help being who they are. Given their long struggle for freedom, particularly from Spain and the United States, they cannot help taking understandable pride in who they are. They have chosen a way of life different from ours, and I must say that from my limited exposure to that different way of life, it has brought them, fundamentally, a deep inner certainty about the meaning of existence (to develop one's self and to help others) and an equally deep psychic peace. One endearing quality I've found in the Cubans I have met is that they can listen with as much heart as they speak.

I believe you and Fidel must speak to each other. Face to face. He is not the monster he has been portrayed; and in all the study you have done of Cuba surely it is apparent to you that he has reason for being the leader he is. Nor am I saying he is without flaw. We are all substantially flawed, wounded, angry, hurt, here on Earth. But this human condition, so painful to us, and in some ways shameful – because we feel we are weak when the reality of ourselves is exposed – is made much more bearable when it is shared, face to face, in words that heave expressive human eyes behind them. Beyond any other reason for talking with Fidel, I think you would enjoy it...

America at the moment is like a badly wounded parent, the aging, spent and scared offspring of all the dysfunctional families of the multitudes of tribes who settled here. It is the medicine of compassionate understanding that must be administered now, immediately, on a daily basis, indiscriminately. Not the poison of old patterns of punishment and despair. Harmlessness now! must be our peace cry.

I often disagree with you – your treatment of black women, of Lani Guinier and the wonderful Joclyn Elders in particular, has caused me to feel a regrettable distance – still, I care about you, Hillary and Chelsea, and wish you only good. I certainly would not deprive you of food in protest of anything you have done! Similarly, I will always love and respect the Cuban people, and help them whenever I can. Their way of caring for all humanity has made them my family. Whenever you hurt them, or help them, please think of me.

Sincerely, Alice Walker

1902	Cuba agrees to lease Guantánamo military base to the USA *ad infinitum*.
1924–1933	The era of the dictatorship of Gerardo Machado.
1934	Batista ousts the elected Dr Ramón Grau and remains in charge until 1944 when Grau is re-elected.
1952 *March*	Batista returns from the USA to overthrow the government of Carlos Prio Socarrás in a *coup d'état*.
1953 *July*	Castro and members of the July 26th Movement attack Moncada Barracks in Santiago de Cuba.
1956	Castro and Che Guevara sail from Mexico in the cabin cruiser *Granma* to spearhead an insurrection against Batista.
1959 *January*	Castro enters Havana and the victory of the Revolution is secured.
1960 *February*	A French ship bringing arms to Cuba is sabotaged. Castro uses the slogan *Patria o Muerte* for the first time during the burial of the victims.
May	Cuba restores diplomatic relations with the Soviet Union.
October	Cuba nationalises all major foreign banks. The USA imposes an embargo on all imports to Cuba.
December	Cuba establishes diplomatic relations with Vietnam.
1961 *January*	The US severs diplomatic relations with Cuba.
April	The Bay of Pigs invasion fails. Castro announces that Cuba is to become a socialist country.
1962 *January*	Cuba is expelled by the Organisation of American States.
October	'The Cuban Missile Crisis' – President Kennedy demands that Khrushchev withdraw Soviet nuclear weapons bound for Cuba. He imposes an American naval blockade of the island. Khrushchev backs down but secures a non-aggression pledge from the USA on behalf of Cuba.
November	The USA lifts its naval blockade but Kennedy indicates that the USA will pursue a policy of economic and political hostility against Cuba.
1963 *March*	In a speech given in Costa Rica, Kennedy declares that 'We will build a wall around Cuba.'
1964 *February*	The USA expels over 700 Cuban workers from the military base in Guantánamo.
1965 *March*	Cuba donates 10,000 tons of sugar to North Vietnam as a gesture of solidarity for its war against the USA.
1967 *October*	Che Guevara is executed while trying to foment a revolution in Bolivia.
1972 *July*	Cuba becomes a member of COMECON (Council for Mutual Economic Assistance).

1973 *March*	Statistics are published that reveal Cuba to have the lowest infant mortality rate in Latin America.
1974 *January*	Soviet President Brezhnev visits Cuba.
1975 *January*	Cuba re-establishes diplomatic relations with the Federal Republic of Germany. Cuba sends the first of its troops to Angola.
1976 *April*	Bombs explode in the Cuban Embassy in Lisbon and the Cuban Mission to the United Nations.
1977	Jimmy Carter lifts the ban on American citizens travelling to Cuba.
1978 *April*	Cuba signs a protocol on commercial co-operation with the Soviet Union.
1979 *June*	Cuban Americans are allowed to visit their families in Cuba.
1980 *April*	The Mariel Boat Lift. Twelve people crash a mini-bus through the security gates of the Peruvian Embassy and claim political asylum. Castro invites anyone wishing to leave Cuba to exit from the port of Mariel and 120,000 Cubans take up his offer.
1981 *August*	Cuba sends more troops to Angola following the invasion of that country by South African forces.
1983 *October*	The USA invades Grenada and 24 Cuban construction workers are killed fighting with American soldiers.
1984 *June*	Cuba decides to boycott the Los Angeles Olympics.
December	Cuba agrees to take back 2,700 'undesirables' who left Cuba for the USA during the Mariel Boat Lift. The USA signs an accord agreeing to accept 20,000 Cuban immigrants per year.
1985	Radio Martí is launched in Miami, broadcasting anti-Castro propaganda into Cuba. Cuba suspends the immigration accord in protest.
1988	Cuban and Angolan troops defeat South African forces in the battle of Cuito Cuanavale. South Africa agrees to negotiations over its role in Angola. Later both Cuba and South Africa sign a treaty agreeing to withdraw all troops from the country and establish a timetable for independence in Angola.
1989	General Arnaldo Ochoa Sánchez, military hero of the Angolan war, is executed by the Cuban authorities for drug-trafficking. This incident was a big blow to the Cuban psyche as he was highly regarded by the Cuban people and was considered one of the most honest and trustworthy of military figures.
1989–1992	The Soviet Union and the eastern bloc disintegrate and Cuba loses its estimated $500 million a year subsidy.

1994 *August*	Havana witnesses its first street riot since 1958 following the hijacking of three ferries and the killing of two policemen. Castro goes onto the streets to try to pacify the people. An estimated 40,000 Cubans attempt to cross the Florida Straits to get to Miami. The USA repeals its policy of granting asylum to all those fleeing Cuba and those picked up at sea are taken to Guantánamo military base.
September	Castro announces that farmers may sell any surplus stock on the open market once they have met their government quotas.
1996 *February*	Cuban airforce shoots down two civilian planes flown by the Miami-based organisation 'Brothers to the Rescue'. There is disagreement as to whether the incident took place in Cuban or international airspace.
March	The US Senate approves the Helms-Burton Bill which further tightens the US economic embargo on Cuba.
1997 *June*	Che Guevara's remains are discovered in a shallow grave in Vallegrande, Bolivia. They are later flown back to Havana.

POLITICS

The official line is that Cuba is an independent, socialist, non-sectarian state. The elected representatives of the Assemblies of People's Power exercise power on behalf of the people of Cuba, a united and democratic republic. The assemblies are constituted on a municipal, provincial and national basis with the national assembly being the equivalent of parliament. Municipal elections are held, by secret ballot, every two and a half years and provincial and national elections every five.

The reality is that Cuban politics are dominated by one figure, Fidel Castro – El Commandante. Lionised by those who regard him as a charismatic leader of great principal and dignity (one of his more unusual admirers is the Argentinian footballer Diego Maradona who referred to him as 'My idol ... The one man in the world who has been true to himself.'), he is loathed by others who see him as the last of the world's great dictators, a man no longer of his time. Whatever your opinion of him, there is no doubt that Castro is one of the most important and influential figures ever to emerge from Caribbean and Latin American history.

Castro is extremely proud of the fact that, to date, he has managed to see off eight American presidents despite constant predictions of his impending demise. Questions about his well-being are regularly invoked but he currently appears to be in good health – no doubt his decision to quit smoking cigars has helped in this respect. He is often seen and heard in public, his recent visit to the Malecón in Havana to give encouragement to his supporters after the disturbances of August 1994 being a prime example of his willingness to lead from the front. He appears regularly on Cuban television, usually to deride the 'Yanquis' for their attempts at destabilisation. His speeches, delivered usually without notes, can, and often do, go on for hours. Despite failed assassination attempts and plots to overthrow him, it seems likely that Castro will be around for a few years yet, although the harshness of the *Período Especial* ('Special Period'), the euphemism he has given to the post Soviet Union era, has left its mark on the Cuban people and many are now more prepared to voice their dissent and challenge his omnipotence in Cuban political life. If he survives the next few years then it is quite likely he will chalk up a ninth American president on his scoreboard.

Political opposition

The most effective political opposition to the Castro regime is based in Miami (see separate section). At home, opposition is limited to the voices of dissent on the streets of the cities. Cubans these days are quite prepared to express their opposition to the failings of their political system (individually rather than collectively). The hardship experienced during the *Período Especial* seems to have bred a new confidence in them to speak out. Nevertheless, dissidents who are regarded as damaging or potentially damaging are often imprisoned or, if the authorities are feeling charitable, given a cautionary beating. As with all totalitarian regimes, political opposition is suppressed if there is a danger of it becoming effective or challenging and consequently there is no acknowledged opposition leader or grouping. This makes it almost impossible for political change to occur.

By way of a supplement to the police force, the Cuban authorities set up what is known as the CDR (the Committee for the Defence of the Revolution). Although membership of the CDR is not compulsory, it is expected that all Cubans will participate. Set up in the early 1960s, ostensibly to combat terrorism and the threat of a counter-revolution, most people dedicate one night per month to patrolling the streets of their neighbourhood, reporting to the authorities on anything suspicious. More disturbingly, the CDRs have been augmented by the recently formed *Blas Roca*, a rapid response crew of vigilantes. It was the *Blas Roca* who were seen patrolling the streets of Havana, wielding baseball bats and spiked staves, after the disturbances of 5 August 1994.

Cubans in Miami

An estimated one and a half million Cubans live in Florida, the vast majority in Miami. Their numbers were swelled by some 120,000 following the Mariel Boat Lift in 1980 when Castro allowed boats crewed by Cuban exiles in America to pick up, from the port of Mariel, their compatriots who wanted to leave Cuba. Castro also took the opportunity to empty his prisons of many hardened criminals who seem to have prospered in Miami, developing their criminal interests in a way unimaginable under an authoritarian regime. It is interesting that Castro threatened the USA with a repeat of this mass exodus following the August 1994 disturbances, obviously regarding the option as a potential safety valve should the pressures of his *Período Especial* become potentially explosive. It seems that he regards this as a useful threat against attempts of overt destabilisation by the USA.

Since the Revolution, when many Cubans fled to Miami, a large sector of the expatriate population have been planning for the day when they can return. Many do not consider themselves emigrants but rather are *en exillo*, waiting for the day when they can return home. Some are happy to bide their time until the death of Castro, when they feel Cuba will fall into line, like the majority of Latin American and Caribbean countries. A more substantial proportion would like to see an American-backed invasion, although the possibility is extremely unlikely. Others have taken a more pro-active role themselves, believing that Castro needs to be thrown out by force and, if the USA won't do it, then the ex-pat community will have to do it themselves. As a result, two prominent paramilitary style groups have been set up. One is called Alpha 66, the other Commando F4. Both groups are inheritors of the mantle carried by those failed exiles who took part in the defeat at the Bay of Pigs in 1961. In the summer of 1994, the Federal Bureau of Investigation stepped up its surveillance of these groups, as it was reported that they were hoping to stage some sort of publicity coup, possibly through a terrorist strike at a tourist destination in Cuba itself. There were reports that shots were fired at a tourist hotel in Camagüey early in 1994, but their influence and depth of support on the island is highly questionable and many doubt whether they have the strength and organisational skills to stage anything remotely effective.

Probably the most influential tool the anti-Castro exiles have at their disposal is Radio Martí, a pirate radio station which broadcasts anti-Castro propaganda into the heart of Cuba. On 5 August 1994 Castro largely blamed such propaganda as 'incitement to riot'. Broadcasts from Radio Martí informed Cubans that a flotilla of boats was on its way from Key West in Florida to whisk them off to America. No boats came, but in the days just before and after 5 August three vessels were hijacked in Havana (resulting in the death of two policemen) as attempts were made to flee to Florida. It was reported that in the first half of 1994, 5,163 people had crossed the straits from Cuba to Florida on boats and rafts, the highest recorded number since the Mariel Boat Lift. Another 40,000 were estimated to have attempted the crossing in August and September. Those who survived the journey were to find that the American 'Open Door' policy had been reversed and, despite the enormous risks they had taken, the gates to their dream world had been closed.

THE ECONOMY

The Cuban economy is on the verge of collapse. Life under a 30-year-old American economic embargo was only made bearable because of the huge subsidy Cuba received from the former Soviet Union. Since the demise of communism in eastern Europe, Cuba finds herself with nobody to bail her out. These days there is barely enough food to sustain the population. Cuba exports the bulk of what she produces in order to obtain much-needed hard currency to repay her crippling foreign debts. Sugar cane and sugar production are the twin mainstays of the Cuban economy, while tobacco, coffee, citrus fruits, vegetables and grains are also important cash crops. Many Cubans have taken to cultivating smallholdings in an attempt to supplement their meagre rations (rations being the operative word, for ration books have been in existence in the country since the early 1960s).

Cuba was a founder member of the Council for Mutual Economic Assistance (COMECON) and grew to be regarded as the spoiled child of that organisation. At the height of Soviet assistance, Cuba was receiving the equivalent of one dollar per day for every one of its inhabitants. Sugar and nickel were exchanged with the Soviet Union on extremely favourable terms. In one sense this alliance was inevitable, as its natural trading partner, the USA, who prior to the Revolution accounted for 80% of Cuba's export market, erected an iron curtain of its own in the form of a total economic blockade. With both the Soviet Union and COMECON gone, these days Cuba is trying to establish new markets for its produce, especially in Latin America.

As with most state-regulated economies, there has developed a vital and burgeoning black market. The black market has long been in operation but it was given a new lease of life by Castro's decision on 26 July 1993 to allow Cubans to possess American dollars (previously anyone caught holding dollars faced a jail sentence of up to five years). This was an inevitability given that Cuba desperately needs hard currency and that Cubans living in Miami were, and are, keen to send dollar remittances to their families back home. Thus you will find dollar shops not only for tourists in Cuba but also for the Cubans themselves. The darker side of this, however, is that there has been a fairly dramatic rise in crime and prostitution, primarily in the major cities and in key resorts (prostitution in Varadero is a big problem). You are also likely to be hassled by people trying to sell you cut-price cigars and rum and, in Havana and Santiago de Cuba, children will openly ask you for dollars. Although begging (previously an unknown phenomenon) is not a problem in the way that it is in many other Latin American countries, these days you are likely to experience it – especially in Havana around the Plaza de Armas.

TOURISM IN CUBA

A relatively new and important building-block for the Cuban economy is tourism. With the assistance of foreign investment, particularly in Havana and the beach resort of Varadero, a tourist infrastructure is already in place.

The number of foreign visitors arriving in Cuba during 1996 increased by 30% (in real terms 250,000) topping the much-coveted figure of 1 million (1,001,739 according to official statistics). The countries supplying the most visitors were Italy (185,000), Canada (156,000), Spain (113,000), Germany (75,000), France (61,000), Mexico (36,000), England (28,000) and Colombia (24,000). The dramatic rise in the number of visitors now arriving from Europe testifies to the fact that Cuba as a tourist destination has become high profile, offering much more than just a beach holiday. Cuban Ministry of Tourism officials confidently predict that the number of visitors for 1997 will top the 1.2 million mark.

Although still lagging behind other Caribbean islands such as Jamaica and the Bahamas it is fair to say that the majority of islands in the area fear Cuba's tourist potential and the impact the development of tourism in Cuba will inevitably have on their own economies. For Cuba the reinvention of itself as a holiday destination could hardly have come at a better time. Needing to generate revenues to replace the lost subsidies of the Soviet Union and in the light of the tightening of the US embargo under the Helms-Burton Bill, the success of the Cuban tourist initiative was (and still is) critical.

RELIGION

The official line on religion in Cuba is that there is freedom of belief without any sectarian bias. Compared with the former socialist states of eastern Europe, it is reasonably accurate to say that religious oppression was never as great a problem on the island as it was in those other countries. Indeed, Castro had many admirers among, and developed close links with, the Catholic libertarian theologists of Latin America during the 1980s. Nevertheless Castro would never approve of the church playing an active role in political life unless it was an advocate of the Revolution, and has always closely monitored the role of religion (particularly the Catholic Church) to ensure that it does not do anything that would adversely affect the course of the Revolution. Castro also abolished the Christmas holiday, replacing it and other key religious dates with holidays celebrating the success of the Revolution.

In what is regarded as something of a coup for Castro it was announced in 1996 that Pope John Paul II was to visit the island. In 1991 Castro, mindful of the tensions which were prevalent on the island at the beginning of the *Período Especial*, decided not to allow the Pope to proceed with a planned visit. In more recent years, however, Castro has repeatedly invited Pope John Paul II to visit Cuba and reiterated the invitation when he was received by the Pope in the Vatican in November 1996. During the visit, scheduled to begin on 21 January 1998, the Pope is expected to visit the cities of Havana, Santa Clara, Camagüey and Santiago de Cuba. The Cuban government has promised to give the Pope free reign to travel to whatever part of the island he wishes and to address whomever he desires. In a country where Catholicism had previously been suppressed but is now tolerated (though not actively encouraged), it is not simply the country's pious who await the visit in a state of expectation. The Cuban people see this as a further example of the opening up of the country to external influences and also demonstrating Castro's confidence in his own position.

Santería
A derivative of the Catholic creed, essentially a mixture of that faith and the religious practices and beliefs brought to Cuba by African slaves, has given birth to the most fascinating religion in Cuba: Santería (or Regla de Ocha as it is sometimes called). African slaves identified their deities (orishas) with colours as opposed to figures and under Santería Christian saints have amalgamated with African orishas to produce a religious synthesis that sees Our Lady of Mercy (dressed in white) become Obatala; Our Lady of Regla (patron saint of the ports of Havana and Matanzas and wearing blue) become Yemaya; Saint Anthony (Messenger of the Orishas and wearing red) become Ellegua; and the most famous saint of all, Our Lady of Charity (the yellow-clad patron saint of Cuba), become known as Oshún. In Santería, when joining the faith each follower identifies with a particular orisha during the initiation period. It is usually possible to identify followers of Santería and their chosen saint by the coloured beads they often wear around their wrist or neck. Santerían saints are worshipped through a variety of rituals including dancing, music, chanting and occasionally animal sacrifice. There is also an element of voodoo and it is common, during Santería ceremonies to witness the use of black voodoo dolls as part of the ritual. During Santería carnivals you are quite likely to witness people falling into trances during the height of the celebrations.

It is possible to find small pockets of communities who practise the Protestant, Muslim, Methodist and Baptist faiths and two other Afro–Cuban religions, Palo Monte and Abakud, also have their followers (the latter consisting entirely of men – women are not allowed to practise).

GEOGRAPHY

The island of Cuba is situated in the west of the Antilles range some 144km off the coast of Florida. Its shape is long and narrow and its general appearance has been described as 'a freestyle swimmer's arm about to submerge' or 'a large alligator'. It comprises the island of Cuba, the Isle of Youth (formerly Isla de Pinos) and 4,195 keys and islets. There are 14 provinces – Pinar del Río, La Habana, Ciudad de la Habana, Matanzas, Cienfuegos, Villa Clara, Sancti Spiritus, Ciego de Avila, Camagüey, Las Tunas, Holguin, Granma, Santiago de Cuba and Guantánamo. There is also the special municipality of the Isle of Youth.

In total the island measures 1,200km in length and has three mountainous regions – the Organos in the west, the Escambray in the central area and the Sierra Maestra in the east. Cuba has nearly 6,000km of coast line and boasts over 280 beaches and some 200 bays. The capital city of Cuba is Havana (La Habana) which is located on the northern coast of the west region. The population of Havana is approximately 2.7 million. Cuba, at over 114,000km², is just slightly smaller than England.

Climate
Cuba is a tropical country with an average of 330 days of sunshine per annum. The average temperature is 25.5°C. There is no summer or winter as such, although the coldest month tends to be January (21°C) and the hottest July (30°C). The average relative humidity is high at around 78% and average rainfall per annum is 1,515mm. The driest months are December and August. Hurricanes are a potential hazard, notably between August and November, but these are uncommon. The best time to visit Cuba is in April or May, when there is an average of over seven hours of sunshine per day. The wettest months are September and October (140mm per month). There are no great climatic differences between regions although the east of the island (Santiago de Cuba, Guantánamo and Baracoa) tend to record the highest temperatures during July and August.

Population
The population of Cuba currently stands at around 11.2 million. Since the Revolution, life expectancy has increased dramatically from an average of 52 years to 72 years. Infant mortality has fallen to 11 per 1,000 live born, which is the lowest infant mortality rate in Latin America. Cuba has sophisticated family-planning initiatives and contraception and condoms are widely available.

NATURAL HISTORY
Chris Mattison

Although wildlife is unlikely to be the main reason for a visit to Cuba, the island does have a unique and interesting flora and fauna. It must be stressed, however, that much of it is hard to find because it occurs in some of the more remote regions, notably the Sierra Escambray and the Sierra Maestra, in the eastern part of the country. More easily accessible regions that can be productive, though, include the Zapata peninsula, centred on Playa Girón, and the Sierra del Rosario Biosphere Reserve, which can be easily explored from Soroa or Las Terrazas.

Plants
The most conspicuous plants in Cuba are the trees, and the most majestic of these is the royal palm. This is one of the few species that has been largely spared during the destructive agricultural clearances in the lowlands – isolated trees and small groves are a prominent feature of many landscapes, perhaps most notably in the Viñales valley and on the Zapata peninsula, but also to be seen in and around the capital and alongside many roads throughout the country. Royal palms are legally protected and are held in high esteem by the Cubans, both for their grace and, in former times at least, for their usefulness, providing food (its seeds are edible as is its 'heart') as well as materials for building, thatching and weaving. Other prominent trees include the giant figs, many of which have cable-like roots that grip rocks and cliffsides and long trailing aerial roots. Others are stranglers, first climbing, then surrounding and finally choking their hosts, often royal and other palms. Hardwoods, such as ebony and mahogany still thrive in the more remote forests and have been re-introduced to other parts, such as the Sierra del Rosario. Finally, along the dry and rocky south coast the dominant shrub is *Coccoloba uvifera*, easily identified by its huge glossy green leaves.

The most conspicuous of the smaller plants are the bromeliads, or air plants, which are nearly all epiphytes – plants that grow on other plants. Many Cuban trees are festooned with a variety of species, mostly belonging to the genus *Tillandsia*, which look rather like shuttlecocks. They are not parasites but merely use the branches of their hosts as 'perches' to get nearer to the sunlight. Old forest trees in humid regions, such as the edges of the Zapata swamp, tend to support the most luxuriant colonies of these plants, which are restricted to the New World. Then there are about 300 species of orchids, including a small number of endemic ones. Finding wild orchids is quite difficult unless they are in flower but you can see a good selection of species (including some introduced species) in the orchid gardens near Soroa.

Perhaps surprisingly, Cuba is the home of many species of cacti. Many occur only in the drier regions to the far east of the island and these include several species of *Melocactus*, distinctive cacti found only in the Caribbean with what look like woolly hats – correctly known as *cephalia* – growing from the top of their barrel-shaped bodies. Other cacti are not always immediately obvious, though. Epiphytic cacti, which are well represented in Cuba (even in Havana), grow among the branches of larger trees and have long, trailing stems. Close inspection will reveal the small clusters of spines spaced along their stems. Some species produce large, showy flowers, usually white in colour, and strongly scented, which open only at night, earning one species, *Selenicereus grandiflora*, the well-deserved common name of 'Queen of the Night'.

A good introduction to Cuban flora can be had by visiting the Botanical Gardens, near Lenin Park, where a large area is laid out systematically to show representative trees and shrubs from the various regions. Guides (often teachers or university professors) can be hired for a small fee and the information they provide greatly increases the value of such a visit. Some of them are especially knowledgeable about the uses of the various species.

Animals

Land mammals are rare in Cuba, most having been hunted out long ago or driven to extinction by loss of habitat. Arboreal rodents, known as hutías, represent an endemic group and can sometimes be seen scuttling about in the forests, usually in the evening. Otherwise the visitor will have to be content with a variety of 'small game'.

Being a tropical island, Cuba supports large numbers of invertebrates, not all of them welcome! The butterflies, however, can be dazzling at certain times of the year; most are on the wing in mid-summer although you should be able to find some species in any month provided the weather is warm and sunny. Over 150 species occur on the island, not counting vagrants, and many are found nowhere else. Swallowtails, of which there are 13 species, are worth looking out for, although there is one that may cause confusion if you are trying to identify it. This species is black and emerald green, and a strong flyer. It is especially common in the Viñales valley and it comes as some surprise to learn that it is not a butterfly at all, but a day-flying moth.

Other invertebrates include large hairy spiders of the type commonly known as 'tarantulas', which are numerous but unlikely to be seen unless you search for them under rocks and forest debris. Land crabs swarm over the forest floor around the fringe of the Zapata swamp, and often crawl out on to the gravel coastal road in the evening, when they are most active. Beware. When they hear an approaching car they stop and raise their claws in defence. If you run over one there is a very good chance that it will puncture a tyre.

Fish are more likely to be of interest to the sportsman or the scuba diver than the average naturalist. The coastal waters are home to a wide variety of Caribbean species, including marlin, swordfish, tuna and barracuda, while the reefs around the coast provide refuges for shoals of small, colourful species. There are reefs around the Isle of Youth and the smaller coral cays that surround Cuba. Dolphins, which are not fish but mammals, of course, are commonly seen offshore and whales are sometimes sighted off the north coast.

There are between 150 and 200 species of reptiles and amphibians in Cuba, of which well over half are endemic. Many are small, brown frogs and lizards, which are easily overlooked and of little interest except to the specialist, but a few are spectacular. These include the Cuban crocodile, *Crocodylus rhombifer*, an endangered species, which lives in the Zapata swamp and on the Isle of Youth. The easiest place to see it, however, is in the crocodile farm between Playa Larga and Jagüey Grande. The Cuban iguana, *Cyclura nubila*, also classed as endangered, a large, knobbly-headed lizard that is common on Cayo Larga and Cayo Iguana but which also lives along the south coast. Small anolis lizards are everywhere throughout the island and some species are associated with buildings. The walls of La Hermita Hotel in Viñales, for instance, are often hopping with a bright green species while caves in the *mogotes*, in the same region, are the home of a specialised species which lives on vertical and overhanging rock faces. The squeamish visitor will no doubt be pleased to learn that none of the 22 snake species are dangerous. The two extremes of size are represented by the tiny blind snake, which lives in the earth and looks more like an earthworm than a snake, and the Cuban boa, which can grow to over 3m in length. This species occurs only on Cuba and has suffered great habitat loss through the clearance of forests for sugarcane. It enjoys international protection.

It is the Cuban birdlife that will draw most naturalists to the island. Of the 350 or so species that have been recorded, 20 are endemic to the island. The prime birdwatching region is the Zapata peninsula, where 170 species occur, and which is the only place to find three imaginatively named species – the Zapata rail, Zapata sparrow and Zapata wren. To be truthful, none of these birds is very colourful and their secretive habits make them all but impossible to find without the aid of a good guide and a lot of luck. Another endemic, Fernadina's flicker, a type of ground-feeding woodpecker, is more common here than in other parts of Cuba but can also be hard to find. The Cuban trogon lives in forests throughout the island and was chosen as the national bird because its colours – white, blue and red - are the same as those on the Cuban flag. The bee hummingbird is the world's smallest species and is found, though not that easily, in forest clearings and gardens but you should be able to find a larger hummingbird, the Cuban emerald, known locally as 'zunzún' (which describes the noise that it makes when it whizzes by). Perhaps the most engaging bird in the whole country, however, is the Cuban tody, a small, rotund bird with a long bill, bright green back, red throat and pink flanks. It seems to be quite common around Soroa and is very inquisitive, approaching quite closely and flitting from branch to branch along forest paths. Of the birds that even the most casual visitor is almost bound to see, the endemic Cuban blackbird, known locally as 'totí', is very common everywhere, as is the rather similar Antillean grackle. They are distinguished by the shape of their tail, that of the grackle being V-shaped while the blackbird holds its tail horizontally in the more conventional manner. Grackles are also rather raucous and often hang together in small flocks, sometimes with one or two Cuban blackbirds in attendance. Finally, the turkey vulture is ubiquitous, often associated with villages and frequently seen doing a useful job of picking clean the carcasses of dogs and other roadkills along every road and track.

In summary, Cuban wildlife has suffered greatly over the last few decades through pollution and, especially, the side-effects of intensive agriculture. New policies, that promote sustainable farming through organic and environmentally friendly techniques can only help to reverse the process. Although there is still some way to go, Cuba could eventually realise its potential as one of the most important centres for eco-tourism in the Caribbean region.

THE CUBAN PEOPLE

Cubans are a nationalistic, industrious and creative people who are proud of their achievements over the last 30 years (regardless of how they currently feel about Cuba's future in a changed political universe). Theirs is a vibrant and expressive culture most typified by their music which resonates in all corners of the island. This, however, is the era of the *Período Especial*, the time when Cubans have been asked to make even greater sacrifices for the sake of the Revolution. As visitors to the island, tourists are largely shielded from the harsh realities that most Cubans take for granted as part of their daily lives. What most visitors regard as essentials – things such as soap, toothpaste, clothing, some foodstuffs (it has been officially acknowledged that there is a lack of protein in the Cuban diet) – are barely available except in the dollar shops which have proliferated during the last four years. Since most Cubans do not possess dollars, these items are largely unobtainable or are subject to rationing, a practice which has been in operation since the birth of the Revolution.

Many of the younger generation who have no recollection of the pre-Castro years, look enviously towards the consumer society of the USA; they are disgruntled and will express their dissatisfaction openly in conversation. Some of the older generation who began to grow weary of the Revolution in the face of hardship have witnessed an upturn in the economy in comparison with the particularly difficult years of the early 1990s; they feel that the decision to push tourism has paid great dividends and offers some hope of a more prosperous future. Given the hardships that most Cubans have experienced and are still experiencing, it is remarkable that they are able to retain their lust for life. But they do, and when you witness the young couples strutting their stuff on the streets of Habana Vieja, or the older men debating passionately their love of baseball in Parque Central, you begin to feel that the innate spirit of the Cuban people will once again pull the country through.

Cubans are a hybrid of many different races and cultures. Traces of French, Chinese and North American ancestry can be found among the more prominent African and Spanish heritage. The black population, which accounts for 30% of Cuban citizens, is invariably the result of a fusion between European and African people. They are known as mulattos. A substantial proportion of black people in Cuba are pure descendants of the slaves brought during the colonial era from countries such as Nigeria, Senegal and the Gambia. Despite what you might read in the government tourist information brochures, racism has not been eradicated from Cuban society. The vast majority of senior positions in all walks of Cuban life are occupied by those of European descent. It is very rare to find a black face at managerial level, even in hotels and restaurants. Black people tend to be employed in the less prestigious jobs, as waiters, porters and receptionists.

Around 60% of the population is of European descent. In contrast to the black community, these people, known as crillos, tend to occupy positions of authority and higher status. That said, with opportunities for advancement during the *Período Especial* restricted, the crillo population is experiencing a hard time in much the same way as the mulatto minority. Recession has become a great social leveller.

Cuban women

The position of women in Cuban society has been greatly enhanced since the Revolution. Women play an important role in the functioning of both industry and the military. Current figures show that almost half the workforce is made up of women and they are expected to participate in the sort of manual labour from which they would ordinarily be excluded in most capitalist countries. Probably the biggest problem faced by Cuban women is one inherent in their culture. While the Revolution may have advanced their status in society, it has yet to do away with the Latin macho who still, unfortunately, thrives in the country and the culture.

Gay Cuba

If the Latin macho can be a problem for women in Cuba, he can cause a bigger headache for the gay and lesbian population. It is still illegal to display homosexuality in public in Cuba and, while gay men and lesbians are generally tolerated, they, especially gay men, are often verbally abused and ridiculed. After the Revolution, the government set up 'Units for Military Aid to Production', institutions which were charged with rehabilitating those who were deemed unsuitable to be integrated into the army. Among the target group was Cuba's gay community, particularly the men. The institutions soon established for themselves a loathsome reputation and when Graham Greene visited Cuba in 1965, he criticised them vehemently. Castro, obviously stung by Greene's (and other) criticism, abolished them in 1966. Since then, however, it can hardly be said that the gay and lesbian population has made great strides towards acceptance and integration. At present there is little or no gay scene in any of the major towns or cities.

LANGUAGE

The official language of Cuba is Spanish. The Cuban people are very well educated and in the major cities many people have some, if only a limited, grasp of English. Prior to the break up of the Soviet Union, Russian was the language most taught in schools but that has now been superseded by English and there is a tangible desire to learn and practise the language. On your walkabout in the cities, you will constantly be approached by people who want to practise their English-language skills with you. If you intend to venture outside the major cities it is useful to go armed with at least a smidgen of Spanish. Many Cubans have studied abroad, often in the old East Germany. It is not unusual to come across people who are virtually fluent in English and German as well as their own language. A list of useful words and phrases appears in *Appendix One*, page 250.

CULTURE

Without question the most vibrant element of Cuban culture is its music. *Salsa,* a consequence of the fusion between Spanish guitar and African drum, is perhaps the best known of the genre. Although not unique to the country – *salsa* reverberates around most of the countries of Latin America – Cuban *salsa* has a heavier reliance on the acoustic guitar and percussion, distinguishing it from the more brassy sound of other Latin American *salsa.*

At the height of its musical prowess, midway through the 20th century, many Cuban musicians were hired to play in the United States where their Afro-Spanish rhythms gelled with the American jazz sound to give rise to a music called Cubop which in turn evolved into Layini jazz. This era also gave rise to the dance – the *mambo* which, together with the *cha-cha-cha* (another Cuban invention), became popular throughout the world. During the 1960s Cuba developed four new dance rhythms, the *pachanga,* the *mozambique,* the *paca* and the *pilón.* Today, Cuban music is undergoing something of an international resurgence. Old troopers like Pablito Milanes and Silvio Rodríguez are finding new markets for their records, while perhaps the most famous Cuban-American in the pop world, Gloria Estefan, has recorded and released, in collaboration with her husband Emilio, a celebration of Cuban music entitled *Mi Tierra* (My Homeland) which has become an international best seller.

No section on Cuban music would be complete without mention of the most famous song to come out of Cuba, a song that has spawned a thousand chants on the football terraces of Britain and a song from which it is difficult to escape in Cuba – *Guantanamera.* The tune, composed in 1929 by Joseito Fernández, was supplemented by the words of José Martí's *Versos Sencillos,* a combination put together by the Cuban musician Hector Angulo towards the end of the 1950s. American folk singer Pete Seeger sang it at his concert in New York's Carnegie Hall in 1963 as a gesture of solidarity with the Cuban people.

Model Prison, Isle of Youth

Chapter Two

Practical Information

GETTING THERE AND AWAY

Cuba sees tourism as a key building-block in its new economy and great efforts have been made over recent years to promote the island internationally. Luckily for Cuba many airlines and tour operators are fast cottoning on to the fact that the country, better known for its leader and its political system than anything else, is in fact one of the jewels of the Caribbean. With year-long sunshine, an abundance of beaches, a vibrant culture and surrounded by the clear waters of the Caribbean Sea and the Atlantic, Cuba's tourist potential is boundless. Getting there has never been easier. There are several tour operators offering both package deals and flight-only options or, alternatively, you can book direct with one of several airlines who fly there.

Getting there from the UK and Ireland
At present Cubana Airlines the Cuban national carrier runs four flights per week (from London Gatwick airport). Flights take around nine hours, some going direct to Havana and some stopping en route at Varadero or Santiago. A weekly flight from Manchester will start in December 1997, out every Friday, in every Thursday. In-flight service has improved greatly in recent years and the DC10s, which Cubana lease from the French Airline AOM, are more reliable than the old Ilyushins previously in use. Return fares can be booked for between £375 and £425 depending upon the season. Cubana has a good international safety record. The best way to book a flight with Cubana is through one of the tour operators listed below.

KLM, the Dutch airline, flies to Havana via Amsterdam. The cost of a return fare ranges from £550 to £625.

Iberia, the Spanish airline, flies to Havana for a cost of between £555 and £635 while Martinair, the other Dutch airline to fly to Cuba, offer a service via Amsterdam to either Holguin or Varadero. Prices range seasonally from £510 to £610 and a stopover in Amsterdam is permitted on either the outward or return journey.

Getting there from Europe

As well as those European operators listed above, the German airline, LTU, operates several flights a week from Düsseldorf to both Havana and Holguin. Again these are aimed at package tourists, but they do offer flight-only deals. At present there is no through-fare deal and you must arrange to make your own way to Düsseldorf to pick up the connection.

Cubana Airlines operates services to Havana from Barcelona (Saturdays), Berlin (Sundays), Brussels (Saturdays), Frankfurt (Saturdays and Sundays), Lisbon (Tuesdays and Saturdays), Madrid (Mondays, Wednesdays and Fridays), Moscow (Tuesdays), Paris (Saturdays and Sundays), Rome (Mondays).

Getting there from the USA

The strict economic embargo the USA still rigidly enforces against Cuba means that it is difficult to make your way from America to the island. The US Treasury Department's Trading with the Enemy Act does not make it illegal for US citizens to travel to Cuba but does forbid them from spending US dollars once they get there. There are no scheduled flights operating between the two countries, although special charter flights operate from Miami to Havana (although these are even more restricted following the implementation of the Helms-Burton Bill). These are mainly used by expatriate Cubans returning to visit relatives. They are also used by accredited journalists or officials who have specific reasons to visit Cuba. Professionals engaged in research projects are also entitled to visit the island, as are members of organised tours whose purpose is educational or research related.

Individual travellers usually circumvent the restrictions by travelling to Canada or Mexico before flying on to Cuba. On arrival, the Cuban immigration authorities will not stamp your passport (unless you specifically request them to do so) thus ensuring that, if you so wish, nobody back home need ever know you've even visited the country, let alone contravened a directive of the US Treasury Department.

The Center for Cuban Studies is a good source of current information about the country. It publishes a bi-monthly magazine called *Cuba Update* which is informative and well researched. You can obtain a copy or take out a subscription by writing to 124 West 23rd Street, New York, NY 10011; tel: 212 242 0559.

Getting there from Canada

Cuba is a popular tourist destination for Canadians and there are frequent direct flights from the major cities – Toronto, Montreal and Quebec – to Havana, Varadero, Holguin and Santiago de Cuba. Most of these flights ferry package tourists on organised tours but it is possible to obtain a seat-only booking.

Getting there from Latin America

There are several flights daily to Havana from South and Central America. The most frequent services are operated by Mexicana Airlines and TAESA from Mexico City and Cancun while Viasa and Aeropostal Airlines operate daily from Caracas and Merida, Venezuela. Lacsa Airlines operates flights from Costa Rica. Cubana flies regularly to Lima, Peru; Buenos Aires, Argentina and to Panama City.

Getting there from the Caribbean

Cubana Airlines has connecting flights to Jamaica, Barbados and the Dominican Republic. Viasa also flies from Havana to the Dominican Republic.

Tour operators and agencies

Regent Holidays, 15 John Street, Bristol BS1 2HR; tel: 0117 921 1711; fax: 0117 925 4866

Interchange, 27 Stafford Road, Croydon, Surrey CR0 4NG; tel: 0181 681 3612; fax: 0181 760 0031.

Journey Latin America, 16 Devonshire Road, London W4 2HD; tel: 0181 747 3108; fax: 0181 742 1312

South American Experience, 47 Causton Street, London SW1P 4AT; tel: 0171 976 5511; fax: 0171 976 6908

Hayes and Jarvis, 152 King Street, London W6 0QU; tel: 0181 748 0088; fax: 0181 741 0299

VE Tours, 37–39 Great Marlborough Street, London W1V 1HA; tel: 0171 437 7534

Cox & Kings, 45 Buckingham Gate, London SW1E 6AF; tel: 0171 873 5001

Bike Tours, PO Box 75, Bath, Avon BA1 1BX; tel: 01225 480130

Trips Worldwide, 9 Byron Place, Clifton, Bristol BS8 1JT; tel: 0117 987 2626; fax: 0117 987 2627

Cosmos, Tourama House, 17 Homesdale Road, Bromley, Kent BR2 9LX; tel: 0181 464 3444

Cubanacán UK Ltd, Skylines, Unit 49, Limeharbour Docklands, London E14 9TS; tel: 0171 537 7909

Progressive Tours, 12 Porchester Place, Marble Arch, London W2 2BS; tel: 0171 262 1676; fax: 0171 724 6941

Sunworld (Iberotravel Ltd), 71 Hough Side Road, Pudsey, LS28 9BR; tel: 0113 2393020

Red tape

Visa and entry requirements

Unless you are a citizen of a country having a visa exemption agreement with Cuba you will require a full ten-year passport to get in. This must be accompanied by a tourist card, which can be obtained from the Cuban Embassy or, more easily, from a tour operator or agency. The current cost is £10 and the card can usually be issued on the spot (no photographs are required, just your passport details). If you do not have a tourist card, you will not be allowed entry as a tourist. If you arrive in Cuba as a transit or transfer passenger you may remain in the country for up to 72 hours without a tourist card. The tourist card is valid for one entry only and expires 30 days after arrival. If you wish to remain in the country longer it is easy to extend your tourist card (either at your hotel or any tourist office) for an additional month up to a maximum of six months.

If you are visiting Cuba for business purposes or with the intention of working or studying you will require a visa. This is best obtained from the Cuban Embassy or Consulate at a current cost of around £30.

Cuban Embassies/Consulates

UK (Embassy) 167 High Holborn, London WC1V 6PA; tel: 0171 240 2488

UK (Consulate) 15 Grape Street, London WC2H 8DR; tel: 0171 240 2488

France 16 Rue de Presles, 75015 Paris; tel: 1 4567 5535; fax: 1 4566 4635

Germany Kennedy Allee 22–24, 5300 Bonn 2 Godesberg; tel: 228 885 733

Netherlands Prins Mauritslaan 6, 2582 LRR, The Hague; tel: 2 371 5766

Italy Via Licinia 7, 00153 Roma; tel: 6 575 5984

Spain Paseo de la Habana 194, Madrid; tel: 1 458 2500

Australia 9–15 Bronte Road, Suite 804, Bondi Junction, Sydney, NSW 2026; tel: 70 354 1417

Canada 388 Main Street, Ottawa K1S 1E3; tel: 613 563 0141

Immigration

The majority of tourists arrive in Cuba at Havana's José Martí international airport although many, particularly those on package tours, fly into either Varadero or Holguin. On arrival, provided you have your documents in order (passport and tourist card/visa), getting in is relatively hassle free. The immigration official will not stamp your passport unless asked. Your tourist card is stamped and you will be given a portion of it to retain until departure. Look after this as it can cause complications if lost. You will be expected to have hotel accommodation pre-booked although, provided you have an address to hand, you will be allowed to pass unhindered. Having said that, Havana is not the sort of place you can stroll around looking for cheap guesthouses or checking out the traveller's scene, although if you do take a chance you may well be approached by somebody offering you a room or apartment. This sort of black-market accommodation is illegal although quite prevalent. The going rate starts from around $10 per day for a room with a fan. There is a Cubatur tourism desk at the airport which exists especially to assist independent tourists. They will be able to provide you with a list of hotels and prices and can book accommodation on your behalf (you'll be issued with an accommodation voucher to give to your hotel on arrival).

Arrival by sea

As with arrival by air, you should be in possession of a passport and tourist card/visa. You are also obliged to give 72 hours' notice of arrival and all ships/boats must submit a full passenger list (including crew) detailing date of birth, occupation and passport number. Entry must be either through Havana (Marina Hemingway), Varadero or Cayo Largo.

Customs regulations

You will be given (usually on your flight) a form to complete on which you must detail all valuable items you are bringing into the country. You will also need to detail how much currency you have with you. Having completed the form the chances are nobody will be interested in looking at it. Along with those personal belongings that you reasonably require for the duration of your stay, you are entitled to bring the following:

- One camera with five rolls of film (note that the airport's X-ray machine is film-safe)
- Personal jewellery
- One pair of binoculars
- One video camera with five cassettes
- One portable musical instrument
- One portable record player with ten records
- One portable tape recorder
- One portable TV set
- One portable typewriter
- One portable PC
- One baby pram
- One tent and camping equipment
- Sports equipment (eg: fishing gear, bicycle, canoe or kayak less than 5m long, two tennis rackets and other similar articles)

Duty free allowances

You may bring into the country a duty free allowance of 200 cigarettes or 50 cigars or 250 grams of pipe tobacco or an assortment of all three provided they do not exceed 250 grams in weight; two bottles of spirits, 250ml of perfume or toilet water and a reasonable amount of cosmetics and toiletries.

Exports

If you buy durable goods in Cuba it is a good idea to keep the receipt as this may save complications upon departure. Do not try to export any products made out of endangered species as you will fall foul of the international agreement aimed at preventing this type of odious trade. During your stay you may well be offered the chance to buy black coral, usually from some undesirable-looking street vendor. As pretty as it may look, black coral is on the protection list and you should therefore decline the offer.

There is a limit of 200 cigars which you are allowed to take out of Cuba, but this will almost certainly exceed the limit you are allowed to bring into your country of residence. You should check to see what this is or else be prepared to sacrifice at least half your stock should you be singled out for inspection by a diligent customs officer back home.

Like the cigars, Cuban rum is among the world's finest. It is also very cheap – $6 for a bottle of seven-year-old Havana Club. The maximum amount you can usually bring into your own country is one litre, although the Cuban authorities will have no objections if you set off with more.

Do not try to export any Cubans even though they may try to convince you to take them with you. Any attempt at this is guaranteed to land you in hot water with the authorities.

MONEY

Cuban currency

The Cuban currency is the peso. One peso is made up of 100 centavos. Banknotes currently in circulation are 50, 20, 10, 3 and 1 peso. Coins in circulation are 3 and 1 peso, 40, 20, 5, 2 and 1 centavos. As far as the tourist is concerned the peso might as well not exist. For tourists in Cuba there is a parallel currency – the US dollar. You will be required to pay for your hotel, your food, your transport (local buses excepted) and your souvenirs in US dollars. It has always been difficult for a tourist to spend Cuban currency but it has never been as difficult as it is now. Anything of real worth is no longer available in Cuban pesos. The US dollar is now the main currency. Since July 1993, Cubans have been allowed to have and to spend dollars. Prior to this, a Cuban caught in possession of a dollar was liable to a lengthy jail sentence. Since July 1993, dollar shops have opened up in almost all of Cuba's major cities, giving those Cubans who receive dollar remittances from relatives living in the USA the chance to buy 'luxury items' such as soap, toothpaste, Coca Cola etc, while at the same time putting much-needed hard currency into Castro's coffers.

If you are tempted to exchange money on the black market the current rate on the streets is $1 = 40 pesos; the bank rate, should you wish to change money legally, is $1 = 0.85 peso. A huge difference, but either way the chances are you will get little or no opportunity to spend your Cuban currency.

Travellers cheques and credit cards

It is best to take travellers cheques in US dollar denominations. Almost all tourist hotels will cash these for you at a commission rate of 3–4%. It is much easier to change money at a tourist hotel than a bank (although some hotels do occasionally run short of dollars), particularly if you are trying to cash cheques of $100 and over. Some hotels insist that you are a resident before cashing although the majority are happy to oblige and take their commission. Do not take travellers cheques drawn on an American bank as these will not be acceptable (in order to avoid the effect of the American embargo, these cheques have to be negotiated through third countries and the problems involved in doing this make them prohibitive).

The situation is similar with credit cards – American Express won't do nicely. Mastercard, Visa, Diners Club and JCB are widely accepted in tourist-related establishments.

Tourist money

Cuba has also developed its own special tourist currency known as B certificates. If you hand in a $10 note as payment for something you are likely to get some of the change in B certificates. Effectively, these are Cuba's equivalent to the US dollar. You will be able to use these as the equivalent dollar payment wherever you go. Even black-market traders are happy to accept them as they can be spent in the dollar shops. If you have any left over at the end of your trip they can be freely converted back into dollars.

The black market

The black market is a key element of the Cuban economy. Prior to the demise of the Soviet Union and the end of its huge subsidies to Cuba, the black market existed primarily to manage the supply of luxury consumer items such as TVs, fridges etc. These days, during the *Período Especial*, even essentials such as soap, toothpaste and deodorant can only freely be bought for dollars on the black market. With the Cuban peso becoming ever more worthless and the barest of essentials rationed almost out of circulation, Cubans are becoming ever more dependent on the black market to survive.

During your stay in Cuba you may well be offered the chance to exchange money on the black market. Only a few years ago it was almost impossible to walk down a street without being accosted by a shady-looking youth with a fistful of pesos offering you a favourable exchange rate. Today there are far fewer one-man *bureau de change* merchants in operation. This is not because there is no demand for dollars, on the contrary, they have never been so sought after; rather, it is the common knowledge that, for the tourist, the peso is a worthless currency. Everything you will need to spend money on in Cuba will be charged in dollars. Many tourists have walked away from a deal where they have negotiated a rate of 120 pesos per dollar and found that at the end of their trip they have 120 pesos left in their pockets.

If you do feel the need to change money on the black market it is better to avoid transactions on the streets where you are more likely either to be ripped off or be caught by the authorities. The punishment can be imprisonment although you are more likely to escape with just a fine. Cubans who are caught are more often than not imprisoned. Your best bet is to speak to a friendly waiter or barman. They will usually be able to advise you on rates etc and may well conduct the transaction for you. A safer option is to stick with paying for everything in dollars. You will usually find that this is the only option open to you anyway.

Paladares

In 1995 the Cuban government legalised the existence of what were previously referred to as black-market restaurants. This was in part a response to pressure from legitimate hotels and restaurants who hoped that the taxes that these new establishments would be subject to would drive them out of business, and in part the realisation of the authorities that if you can't close them down, you may as well generate some revenue from them.

These restaurants are known as *paladares*. Essentially they are partially converted homes where entrepreneurial families have sectioned off part of their living accommodation for the specific use of feeding tourists (and well-heeled Cubans). These establishments are allowed to seat a maximum number of twelve people. In Havana you are likely to be charged between $8 and $10 for a three/four-course meal plus fruit and coffee. Beer or soft drinks are usually $1 extra. Some of the more exclusive *paladares* (notably in Miramar and Nuevo Vedado, Havana) sell wine. Prices are a little cheaper outside of Havana. The quality of the food is often of a higher standard than that available in the hotels and restaurants and the portions more generous. Some of these restaurants have written menus, but most don't. While they are not usually clearly identified it is relatively easy to find a *paladar*. Tourists are often approached by Cubans eager to obtain the commission available for escorting them to the premises. Simply by asking around, you will be told where the *paladares* are situated and recommended as to which are the best.

Although many private restaurants are now legal some still operate in clandestine circumstances in order to avoid paying tax. These places are known as *casa particulars*. They are usually cheaper than the *paladares* but the food is generally as good.

Gifts for Cubans

All gifts will be generously accepted by Cubans. If you wander around the streets of Havana people will ask you for soap, chocolates and chewing gum (Chiclets). If you are going to take gifts, take soap. The meagre ration of one small bar a household per month is patently insufficient. Toiletries in general are in extremely short supply and are very welcome. Clothing, especially T-shirts and training shoes, are much in demand and the Cuban woman's passion for cycling shorts and lycra in general is evident throughout the country. People, especially young children, will ask you for dollars. It's up to you whether you give them. As it is more than likely that they will be spent on items such as soap, it is probably best to take a stock of the stuff with you to dispense. Whatever else you bring, don't bring cigars or rum!

TOURIST INFORMATION

The Palacio del Turismo office on Obispo Street in Havana has moved a little closer to Parque Central but the information obtainable from there is not what it once was. The best places for information on travel within Cuba is usually from the tour operator desks within the main hotels. Those operated by the Rumbos group, notably in the Hotel Inglaterra, are particularly helpful.

There are four main tour operators in Cuba: Havanatur, Cubatur, Cubanacán and Gaviota. Havanatur is the largest international operator and is a subsidiary of CIMEX SA, the largest business concern in Cuba. It owns a substantial number of hotels in the country and is largely responsible for the promotion of package tours to Cuba. It works with agencies and operators internationally to promote Cuba as a holiday destination and the majority of people arriving on organised tours will have had them organised by Havanatur. The head office in Cuba is at Calle 2 No 17 entre 1ra and 3re, Miramar, Municipio Playa, Ciudad de La Habana; tel: 7 332273. It is a useful source of tourist information although you should remember that its prime aim is to sell tours and not give out free advice.

Cubatur is largely responsible for the operation of tours and tour-related programmes for visitors. It owns the majority of tourist hotels and also a large number of restaurants, nightclubs and shops. It is useful when it comes to booking flights and train tickets etc and you will find Cubatur bureaux in most of the tourist hotels. The central office is at Casa Central, Calle F No 157, between 9th and Calzado, Vedado; tel: 7 327075/321702/333683/334116/334117; fax: 7 334037/333104/333330/333529.

Cubanacán (Corporación de Turismo y Comercio Internacional) was founded in 1987 with the specific intention of promoting Cuba as an international tourist destination. It was also given the responsibility of establishing links with foreign companies wishing to invest in joint ventures in the Cuban tourist sector. It also operates an extensive network of hotels, villas, and fishing and hunting reserves and, like the other agencies, offers tours and related services.

Gaviota was founded in 1988, again with the aim of establishing and developing tourist facilities for foreign visitors. It has also set up an international network to promote tours to Cuba. Gaviota, like the other organisations, has a growing chain of nationwide hotels and has branched out into the tour and excursion markets.

In a country where state involvement in all economic activity is a fact of life, there is surprisingly little co-ordination between these different tourist organisations, even though they are all ultimately answerable to the government.

Business hours and holidays

Public offices are generally open from Monday to Friday, 08.30–12.30 and 13.30–17.30. Post offices work longer hours, 08.00–18.00. Restaurants usually close at around 23.00, although if you are prepared to carry on spending you may well find that they stay open a lot longer. Similarly cafés, particularly in Havana, will remain open until you decide to stop spending dollars. It is quite common to see people eating and drinking in the cafés of Calle Obispo until well after four in the morning. Check-out time at hotels is almost always 14.00, later than in most other countries. Chemists are open from Monday to Saturday, 08.00–17.00. Emergency chemists are open 24 hours – whether you will find any medicine in them these days is another matter.

Cuba commemorates the following days as national holidays:

1 January	Anniversary of the Revolution – Liberation Day
1 May	International Workers' Day – Labour Day
26 July	National Rebellion Day – Anniversary of the Attack on Moncada Barracks, 1953
10 October	Anniversary of the Beginning of the Wars For Independence

After the Revolution religious holidays such as Christmas and Easter were scrapped. All public holidays currently celebrate some aspect of the Revolution.

Time

Cuba uses Eastern Standard Time during the winter and Eastern Daylight Time (one hour later) from May to October. Cuban time is five hours behind British time.

Electricity

Cuba's electricity supply is 110 volts at 60hz. Outlets take flat blade plugs, so if you are thinking of taking a hair drier, travel iron etc, you will need an adaptor. Electricity black-outs are common, although the tourist hotels tend to be spared the more lengthy cuts most Cubans have to endure. This may change as the Cuban economy becomes more hard-pressed and the resources necessary to keep up a satisfactory level of supply diminish. The safety levels of electrical sockets and fittings, even in the better hotels, is well below what you would expect in Europe. Bare wires and badly fitted plugs are the norm. Take care when using these facilities.

Weights and measures

Cuba uses the metric system and weights and distances are quantified in terms of kilograms and metres. You will occasionally come across references to pounds, ounces, quintals, etc – a throwback to Cuba's pre-metric days.

Maps

You are strongly advised to buy a map of Cuba prior to your departure. There are several excellent ones available including those published by Hildebrand and Freytag & Berndt which both cost around £6. They are also useful for providing a brief résumé of the country as well as having reasonably good street maps of the major cities and tourist spots.

In Havana you can buy more specific maps dealing with a particular city or region. A specialist map shop called Tienda El Navegante can be found at Mercaderes No 115, entrance on Obispo and Obrapia, La Habana Vieja, Ciudad de La Habana; tel: 7 61 3625; fax: 332869. As well as stocking marine charts and information, they do a good range of city and provincial maps.

Map shops in the UK and North America

London

Daunt Books, 83 Marylebone High Street, London W1 4DE; tel: 0171 224 2295; fax: 0171 224 6893

Stanfords, 12–14 Long Acre, London WC2E 9LP; tel: 0171 836 1321 and 29 Corn Street, Bristol BS1 1HT; tel: 0117 929 9966; fax: 0117 929 9966

Travellers Bookshop, 25 Cecil Court, London WC2; tel: 0171 836 9132

Travel Bookshop, 13 Blenheim Crescent, London W11 2EE; tel: 0171 229 5260

London Map Centre, 22–24 Caxton Street, London SW1; tel: 0171 222 4945

New York

The Complete Traveler Bookstore, 199 Madison Avenue, NY 10016; tel: 212 685 9007

Rand McNally, 150 East 52nd Street, NY 10022; tel: 212 758 7488

Traveler's Bookstore, 22 West 52nd Street, NY 10019; tel: 212 664 0995

California

The Complete Traveler Bookstore, 3207 Filmore St, San Francisco, CA 92123

Rand McNally, 595 Market Street, San Francisco, CA 94105; tel: 415 777 3131

Map Link, 25E Mason Street, Santa Barbara, CA 93101; tel: 805 965 4402

World Journeys, 971-C Lomas Santa Fe Drive, Solana Beach, CA 92075; tel: 619 481 4158

Chicago

Rand McNally, 444 North Michigan Avenue, IL 60611; tel: 312 321 1751

The Savvy Traveller, 50 E Washington Street, IL 60602; tel: 312 263 2100

Canada

Open Air Books and Maps, 25 Toronto Street, Toronto, M5R 2C1; tel: 416 363 0719

World Wide Books and Maps, 1247 Granville Street, Vancouver

Ulysses Travel Bookshop, 4176 Saint-Denis, Montreal H2W 2M5; tel: 514 843 9447 (also branches in Toronto and Quebec)

Film and photography
Airports and X-ray machines
Fortunately all Cuba's airport X-ray machines are film-safe, despite their archaic appearance. This comes as a huge relief as not only is your baggage X-rayed on departure at José Martí Airport but also on arrival. Your baggage will also be X-rayed prior to departure at all airports on domestic flights as well as international ones.

Film and developing
Fresh Kodacolor print film is widely available in most dollar shops and it is even possible to find slide film such as Kodak Ektachrome, especially in Havana. There are several places to have your print film developed and most tourist hotels offer a film-processing facility. It is more difficult to get hold of batteries, so come well stocked with a sufficient supply to get you through your trip. If you do require specialist batteries or film, the best place to obtain them is at the Prensa Internacional on Calle 23 (La Rampa) in Vedado, Havana.

The best times to photograph
Invariably the best time to take photographs is between 09.30 and 11.30, or late in the afternoon from around 16.00 onwards. At these times the sunlight is best for colour photography. Between the hours of 12 noon and 16.00 the sunlight can be exceptionally strong and photographs taken during this time are more likely to develop with a washed-out appearance. One way of protecting against this is to use a polarising filter.

Most Cubans are eager to pose for the camera, so expect to be asked to take a multitude of family shots and photographs of children. In a country as poor as Cuba most people don't have access to cameras and you will more than likely be asked to send copies of your photographs back to the country once you have had them developed. This is a gesture much appreciated. As with every country, there will always be those who do not want to be photographed for whatever reason. You should be careful to respect their wishes.

Apart from militarily sensitive areas or buildings, you are generally free to photograph anywhere in Cuba without hindrance, although some museums do have special regulations on photography.

MEDIA AND COMMUNICATIONS
Media
The press
As you would anticipate, there is no free press in Cuba and all publications are state owned and wholly uncritical of the party. The official daily is the *Granma* which reflects the party's pre-occupation with the Revolution and with world communism. The fact that these days the paper tends to be little

more than half a dozen pages thick is as much a reflection on the demise of international communism as the scarcity of resources required to operate the paper. *Granma,* so named after the boat in which Castro and Che Guevara set sail from Mexico in 1956 prior to toppling the Batista regime, publishes an *International Weekly Review* in English, Spanish, French and Portuguese which is essentially a summary of the preceding week's reportage in *Granma.* The daily trade unions' paper, *Trabajadores,* toes the party line in the same way *Granma* does. There is no independent trade union movement in Cuba as this was abolished shortly after the Revolution. Other provinces have their own newspapers which are as follows:

Havana	*Tribuna de la Habana*
Santiago de Cuba	*Sierra Maestra*
Isle of Youth	*Victoria*
Pinar del Río	*Guerrillero*
Matanzas	*Girón*
Cienfuegos	*5 de Septiembre*
Villa Clara	*Vanguardia*
Camagüey	*Adelante*
Holguin	*Ahora*

Television

Cuba has two national TV stations, Cubavision and Tele Rebelde. In terms of quality and variety, Cuban television is a vast improvement on Cuban newspapers. Surprisingly, both TV stations broadcast old American and European films, soaps and cartoons. The national obsession with sport, particularly baseball, is satisfied by a liberal dose of sports coverage. The World Cup in the USA made for popular viewing with most Cubans giving a passionate allegiance to the eventual champions, Brazil, their Latin American brothers. Political propaganda features less heavily than in the papers although Castro's speeches (unedited versions) are still broadcast and news film of international affairs is very selective. Very little that challenges the party or the system is broadcast.

In many of the tourist hotels a special channel for tourists, called Canal del Sol, runs foreign film and Cuban tourist information. In many hotels satellite television is also available (CNN and MTV are represented). If you walk around the streets of Habana Vieja (Havana Old Town) you will notice many home-made satellite dishes hanging precariously from the walls. The authorities conduct occasional purges, tearing down these dishes, but they are quickly re-erected. In the area around Guantánamo, many households are able to pick up the American forces TV, while a more direct and deliberate form of anti-Castro propaganda is beamed in from Miami by TV Martí, a station set up by Cuban exiles with the aim of sending pro-democracy messages into the heart of their former homeland.

When walking the streets of Cuban cities you will always be able to obtain your directional bearings by looking up at the TV aerials. These are pointed towards the United States in an attempt to pick up signals emanating from Florida and beyond.

Radio

The main national radio station, called Radio Taino, broadcasts nationwide in both Spanish and English. The best stations tend to be the ones you can pick up from Florida. These are particularly popular with Cuba's youth who seem to be developing more of an empathy with hip hop than *salsa*. The most famous, or perhaps infamous, radio station is Radio Martí which, like its TV counterpart, broadcasts anti-Castro propaganda from Miami. Castro blamed Radio Martí for the mass raft exodus of August 1994, claiming that the station had been promoting the idea that a flotilla of boats (like the one dispatched during the 1980 Mariel Boat Lift) was on its way from Florida to pick up Cubans wanting to flee the country. As well as broadcasting anti-government sentiments, Radio Martí promotes American culture through American pop music and advertisements for consumer goods.

It is a good idea to take a shortwave radio to enable you to pick up the BBC World Service.

Post and telecommunications

Cuba has a national post office system that handles domestic and international communications. Its motto should be 'we're getting there, slowly' particularly when it comes to sending a letter or postcard. If it arrives at all, it is guaranteed to have taken so long that you will have beaten it home by at least a month. Even Cubans don't trust their postal system and you may be asked to take letters with you to post from your home country which they automatically assume is more reliable. You can buy stamps for your postcards and letters in most dollar shops where, by definition, you must pay in dollars. If you want to take advantage of that fistful of Cuban pesos you obtained on the black market but can't get rid of, now's your chance. If you are prepared to brave the queues at the post office you can pay in Cuban currency. If not, the current dollar prices are:

Destination	Cost (US$)	Destination	Cost (US$)
Europe	0.30	North America	0.50
Asia	0.50	South America	0.25
Africa	0.50	Central America	0.20
Australia	0.55	Cuba	0.05

The Cuban telecommunications system is very dated. It was set up prior to the Revolution and has had little by way of an overhaul since. It is much easier to make a call, either locally or internationally, from your hotel although, if you like a challenge, street payphones are available. They accept Cuban currency (centavos), but even if they are operational there is no guarantee that you will get through. If you do need to make an international call, costs can be very high (for a European call from Havana it costs around $8 for three minutes).

The post and telegraph office also offers the following services – telex, telegrams, fax, cables and DHL international courier service.

Telephone

When telephoning Cuba you will need to use the appropriate international dialing code which varies depending on which country you are calling from. The country code for Cuba is 53. The city codes are as follows:

Bayamo	23	Holguin	24	Sancti Spiritus	41
Camagüey	32	Las Tunas	31	Santa Clara	422
Ciego de Avila	33	Matanzas	52	Santiago de Cuba	226
Cienfuegos	432	Nueva Gerona	61	Trinidad	419
Guantánamo	21	Pinar del Río	59	Varadero	5
Havana	7	Playa Girón	59	Viñales	8

HEALTH AND SAFETY
with Dr Jane Wilson-Howarth

Cuba's national health system is the envy of Latin America. Following the Revolution, over 50 new hospitals were built as Castro declared a health-care system that would look after his people from the cradle to the grave. Health-care facilities such as dental clinics, blood banks and epidemiology laboratories were established. These measures dramatically reduced the incidence of polio, malaria, diphtheria and tuberculosis which were common in Cuba. There are currently around 42,000 doctors in the country (approximately one for every 260 persons). Cuba's infant mortality rate also fell dramatically after 1959 and, at 10.7 per 1,000, it is the lowest in Latin America. Life expectancy has increased from around 59 years to approximately 75.

The major dilemma the health-care system faces is an acute lack of basic resources – a typical problem in modern-day Cuba. As a result of the economic collapse, medicines and medical provisions are becoming increasingly scarce and if the problem is allowed to continue the impressive health-care statistics will begin to suffer.

As a tourist you could find yourself in a worse place to fall ill. Barring accident, the most distressing experience you are likely to suffer is a touch of diarrhoea brought on by a different type of diet. Another potential danger is the hangover brought on by copious amounts of Cuban rum. For this, however, you have only yourself to blame.

Pre-departure vaccinations

There are no obligatory inoculations required for entry into Cuba but you should heed your doctor's advice and have the standard ones anyway. Visit your GP or travel clinic at least six weeks before departure to ensure you can be adequately immunised in time. Typhoid injections are a sensible precaution and hepatitis A (Havrix or gammaglobulin) is a must. Check with your doctor to make sure you are up-to-date with immunisation against polio and tetanus. Your doctor or travel clinic will also be able to tell you if there are any new ailments common to the area against which you will need to be immunised. As Cuba is non-malarial (see below) you can dispense with inconvenient chloroquine tablets, but dengue is a risk so it is best to avoid bites of mosquitoes, especially during the day.

Illness and diseases
Diarrhoea

Often a problem for a traveller or a tourist, this is caused by enterotoxigenic forms of the bacteria which everyone has in their bowel: *Escherichia coli*. Each geographical area has its own strains of the bacteria and it is these alien strains which cause inflammation of the intestine and diarrhoea. Don't panic, diarrhoea rarely lasts more than a couple of days. If possible you should try to rest up for a couple of days to allow your body the opportunity to rid itself of the toxins. If the problem persists for more than three days treat yourself with ciprofloxacin, or visit one of the island's numerous polyclinics for treatment. Diarrhoea coupled with fever should also be treated with ciprofloxacin.

Either way, it is important to keep yourself hydrated, as an inevitable consequence of diarrhoea is dehydration. This is best achieved by taking water mixed with oral-rehydration salts and glucose. The body's capacity for absorbing fluids and salts is greatly increased by taking sugar at the same time. An electrolyte replacement (half a litre of water, half a teaspoon of salt, half a teaspoon of baking soda, quarter of a teaspoon of potassium chloride and four heaped teaspoons of sugar or dextrose) should prove a great pick-me-up. Although many people are shy of taking antibiotics, a three-day course of ciprofloxacin (500mg twice a day) will make you feel better faster. It is wise to include ciprofloxacin as part of your medical kit as such treatments are scarce in Cuba. You are best advised to steer clear of rich and spicy foods and stick to a plain diet (boiled rice, bananas etc). Looking on the bright side, you are in a country where the food is bland anyway and where you would be hard-pressed to find rich or spicy food if you walked the length and breadth of the island.

Dysentery

If you start to experience severe stomach cramps while you are suffering from diarrhoea and if you begin to pass blood in your faeces, then you have dysentery. You should visit a doctor or a hospital where your problem will be clinically diagnosed. If confirmed then you will require medication. Flagyl is usually an effective cure for amoebic dysentery, as is tinidazole. For bacilliary dysentery ciprofloxacin, norfloxacin, or nalidixii acid for three days should do the trick. These antibiotics are usually effective if you complete the course.

Effects of the sun

Cuba is a hot country all year round and in the months of July and August the temperature often soars into the high 90s (35–37°C). Exposing yourself to too much sun can cause headache, sunburn, nausea, chills and vomiting. Use a good suncream (factor 15) and a lipsalve to prevent your lips from cracking. Give your skin enough time to acclimatise and cover yourself up with long-sleeved and long-legged clothing if your skin starts to feel raw. Wearing a hat or a cap is also recommended. Make sure that you keep yourself topped up with fluids and bear in mind that alcohol dehydrates. If the lure of Cuban rum proves irresistible, have an adequate supply of water to hand to rehydrate yourself. Take extra salt on your food if your taste for salt increases to compensate for the loss of body salts caused by perspiration.

Dengue fever

This is a mosquito-borne disease which, although resembling malaria, is not fatal and is not recurrent once the illness has passed. Although endemic in Cuba, epidemics are quite rare despite the large presence of mosquitoes in the country. The symptoms include high fever, pains in the joints and severe headaches. If you are unlucky enough to contract dengue fever the only treatment is absolute rest allied with paracetamol and codeine to relieve the symptoms and an intravenous drip to stop you from dehydrating. The curious may wish to know that the mosquito is a day-biter which has black and white stripy legs!

Hepatitis A

This disease, which affects the liver, is most often found in countries which have poor sanitation. Thankfully this description doesn't apply to Cuba, but that is no reason to be complacent and immunisation is strongly recommended. The disease is usually contracted via infected food or water. The most notable symptoms are fever, loss of appetite and lethargy. Your skin will adopt a yellowy hue as will the whites of your eyes. Your urine will also betray symptoms as it turns a deep orange colour. Again, the best cure is complete rest. You will need to ensure a healthy diet and lay off the booze and the cigarettes. Hepatitis A is definitely an illness to avoid and this can largely be accomplished by having a Havrix immunisation prior to your departure. Two injections give protection for ten years. You should speak to your local GP if you are interested.

Hepatitis B

This disease is spread in an identical fashion to the AIDS virus – ie: through sexual intercourse, through use of a contaminated needle or congenitally at birth. The vaccine which protects against hepatitis B is expensive and you will be required to have a blood test before it is given. More common precautions are to avoid unprotected sex (take your own condoms), and to take your own supply of sterilised needles for use in an emergency (remember – medical supplies are running short in Cuba) and steer clear of acupuncture, ear-piercing or anything that may involve the use of unsterilised needles.

Rabies
Rabies is a viral infection transmitted from infected animals. It is fatal once contracted. If you find yourself in the unfortunate position of having been bitten by a suspect animal, then take the following course of action:

1 Immediately scrub the bite for five minutes under running water using soap followed by iodine or, failing that, with a local spirit. Experiments have shown that this in itself reduces the risk of contracting rabies by around 90%.
2 Get an anti-rabies injection as soon as possible. Once symptoms appear, this is a sign that the disease has travelled slowly along the nerves to the brain and the disease is incurable. Before this, the anti-rabies injection is effective. Be sure not to delay – having the injection is a matter of urgency. Immunised people should still get a booster, but have more time.

This disease is rare in Cuba but it is wise to guard against it. Avoid stroking and petting any stray dogs you come across. The likelihood is that you will resist this anyway, as Cuban dogs err on the skinny and unkempt side and even avowed dog lovers will find their sympathy for mutts tested by these unsavoury specimens.

AIDS
It is difficult to gauge the level of Acquired Immune Deficiency Syndrome (AIDS) in Cuba as the government is reluctant to reveal statistics to illustrate the problem. The boom in tourism and the legalisation of (and subsequent clamour for) US dollars have resulted in a huge increase in prostitution, which is bound to have a detrimental effect on AIDS figures. Castro's way of dealing with the problem was to isolate anyone diagnosed as HIV positive in one of the island's infamous AIDS sanatoriums. This practice was halted as a result of international and economic pressure, the cost of running the sanatoriums proving prohibitive in an era when cuts to the country's health service budget were inevitable. The authorities hold regular publicity campaigns, warning of the dangers of the disease and on how best to protect oneself from it. Condoms are available, although their quality is dubious and, as with almost everything else, supply has been affected during the *Período Especial*. Men should carry their favourites from home. It should be remembered that AIDS can also be spread by the use of infected needles and contaminated blood transfusions. If you are unlucky enough to have an accident while in Cuba, make sure (if you can) that any medical equipment used on you is freshly sterilised or taken from a sealed bag and have medical treatment only if absolutely necessary. If you need a blood transfusion, ask for screened blood. Having your own supply of sterilised needles is a wise

and worthy precaution. Better still, ask your GP or pharmacist to make up a travel medical kit for you or buy one from a specialist such as Nomad or MASTA (see *Useful addresses*, page 50). As mentioned earlier, it is wise to avoid any activity which involves skin puncturing.

Mosquitoes and other hazards
Mosquitoes
Thankfully Cuba is a non-malarial island, despite the ubiquitous presence of the mosquito. Unfortunately, as anywhere else, the insect is still a pest and likes nothing better than to feast off the blood of a newly arrived tourist. The worst place in the whole of Cuba for these irritants is probably the Isle of Youth. For a few hours around sunset the mosquitoes seem to undergo a severe hormonal imbalance and, swollen to the size of footballs, dive Stuka-like from the skies, proboscis erect, penetrating through even the thickest shield a can of Autan spray provides.

Fortunately the rest of Cuba is not nearly so bad and repellents such as Autan and Jungle Formula (sometimes available in the dollar shops but better purchased prior to leaving) do the job. The most powerful insect repellent is DEET, so check the percentage of DEET on the product label. Sleeping in an air-conditioned room helps avoid bites, but so does a fan to some extent. In the evening it is worth wearing long trousers and a long-sleeved T-shirt to give added protection against the mozzies' wrath.

Sharks
Sadly, Autan have yet to come up with a convenient spray to protect you from these fellows! Sharks are present in the waters around Cuba, just as they are throughout the Caribbean. They also tend to feature prominently in the news as there is often someone who has recently fallen foul of shark attentions, usually when trying to swim to Guantánamo base or else when making an ill-advised attempt to get to Florida the hard way. There is no need to feel paranoid about sharks. They very rarely attack close to shore and sensible swimmers should not venture too far from the shore. With a healthy respect and a little common sense, the closest you are likely to get to a Cuban shark is when agonising over the decision whether to have one grilled or fried for your dinner.

Medical kit
- Water purifiers (the best is iodine which can also be used as an antiseptic to clean wounds)
- Vaseline for cracked lips/skin
- Moleskin and adhesive-backed foam rubber (for blisters and sore feet)
- Butterfly closures or steristrips
- Crepe bandages
- Fabric Elastoplast/Bandaids
- Ciprofloxacin and rehydration sachets
- Paracetamol or aspirins

- Amoxycillin or other broad spectrum antibiotics (take tetracycline or erythromycin if allergic to penicillin)
- Decongestants (eg: Actifed) if you suffer while flying
- Cough and throat pills
- Antifungal cream and powder

Useful addresses

British Airways Travel Clinics; tel: 01276 685040 for the nearest one to you. Inoculations, travel supplies.

Dental Projects Ltd, Blakesley Lodge, 2 Green Street, Sunbury-on-Thames, Middlesex TW16 6RN

Centers for Disease Control, Atlanta, GA3033, USA; tel: (404) 332 4559. This organisation publishes annually the *Health Information for International Travel Bulletin* which is also available from the US Government Printing Office, Washington DC 20402, USA.

International Association for Medical Assistance to Travellers (IAMET), 735 Center Street, Lewiston, NY 14092, USA; tel: 716 754 4883. They provide lists of English-speaking doctors as well as health information.

MASTA (Medical Advisory Services for Travellers) at the London School of Hygiene and Tropical Medicine, Keppel St, London WC1 7HT; tel: 0171 631 4408.

Nomad Travel Pharmacy and Vaccination Centre, 3–4 Wellington Terrace, Turnpike Lane, London N8 0PX; tel: 0181 889 7014; fax: 0181 889 9529.

Crime
Theft
With tourism a key building-block in the new post Soviet Union Cuban economy, woe betide any Cuban caught committing a crime against a tourist. Punishment is harsh and jail sentences lengthy but, despite this, there has been a sharp increase in the level of crime of all types. This can largely be put down to two main factors: the chronic shortages brought about by the collapse of the Cuban economy and the legalisation of possession of dollars in July 1993. The materialistic culture which is promoted via the pirate radio and TV stations of Miami also needs to be taken into account.

Given the level of material deprivation in Cuba, it is surprising that theft, and crime in general, isn't an even greater problem in the country. If you do fall foul of robbers you are most likely to do so in Havana or in one of the other major cities and you will more often than not be a victim of robbery by stealth rather than by force. Sadly, bag snatching has begun to be regarded as a lucrative pastime, especially among the more unsavoury characters of Habana Vieja. The narrow streets of the old town lend themselves to this sort of crime and you should guard against the possibility by leaving your valuables in the hotel safe. If you must go out laden with cash, travellers cheques and other rich pickings, put them in a money belt and tuck it under your T-shirt. Be alert to the fact that, in a Cuban's eyes, you are a multi-millionaire and use your common sense.

If you choose to deal on the black market then you are inevitably increasing the likelihood of becoming a victim of crime. If you exchange money this way, treat the dealer with a combination of caution, respect and suspicion and try to conduct the transaction in as public a place as possible without actually risking arrest. Similarly, if you buy cigars or rum on the black market the chances are you will end up with counterfeit goods. A popular scam is for a Cuban to sell inferior quality rum in a sealed Havana Club bottle or cheap cigars cunningly disguised as premier Cohibas or Monte Cristos. Be warned and use your common sense. A bottle of Havana Club is only $6 in the tourist shop and a box of Cohibas (at $250 for 25) is bad for your health!

Violence

Mugging and violent crime against tourists are relatively uncommon in Cuba although you should always be alert to the danger. Again, Havana is the place where you are most likely to experience this sort of crime. At the moment, however, there has yet to develop the sort of violent criminal culture that exists in other parts of the Caribbean and Latin America, but this could change as the economic crisis deepens. During the Mariel Boat Lift of 1980 Castro took the opportunity to rid his prisons of the more hardened criminals and this undoubtedly helped to stem the development of a criminal culture. It was reported that he repeated the exercise during the 1994 raft exodus. The best way to guard against muggings is not to make yourself an obvious target. Leave your valuables in a safe deposit box back at your hotel and carry as little money as possible. Dressing down when walking the streets at night is a good idea as flash and expensive jewellery can attract unwanted attention. In Habana Vieja stick to the more populated areas like Calle Obispo and don't venture too far off the beaten track. The same can be said for Santiago de Cuba and other big cities. It is always worth seeking advice from local people as to which areas are best avoided.

Women travellers

Latin machismo is very much a part of Cuban culture and, despite the recent progress of women within Cuban society, there is little evidence that this cultural characteristic is on the wane. That said, the sort of harassment a woman can expect is usually confined to comments on the street. It is up to you whether you choose to ignore the comments or whether you decide to make a few of your own. If you hear a Cuban hiss at you this is not necessarily an insult. Cubans hiss to attract attention. The direct English translation of the Cuban hiss is 'excuse me'.

As a foreign woman you will invariably attract attention – not all of it wanted – wherever you go. The majority of people will simply be curious or keen to practise their language skills. The Cuban people are an extremely hospitable lot and as a woman traveller you are likely to be well looked after with people always prepared to help out if you do happen to find yourself in any difficulty. Travelling in Cuba, even alone, you are likely to feel much more secure and at ease than you would in any other country in Latin America or the Caribbean.

ACCOMMODATION
Hotels
Prior to the Revolution, Havana in particular and Cuba in general were home to some of the most stylish and luxurious hotels in the world. With prohibition in the United States limiting the opportunities for revelry, many affluent Americans in search of a spot of decadence came to Havana, only a short hop across the Florida Straits, to satisfy their needs. The American Mafia invested heavily in the hotel and casino industry and for a time Havana became the fun capital of the world. All this ended with the ascent of Castro and many of the hotels were converted into accommodation for the Cuban poor.

With the resurgence of tourism, many former hotels are undergoing restoration and repair. New ones have been built, especially in the beach resorts of Varadero, Cayo Largo and Santa Lucía, with the assistance of foreign investment.

This is not usually the case outside of Havana although the policy of accommodating tourists away from city centres seems to be on the wane. It is now possible to stay in the centres of Santiago de Cuba and Camaguey amongst others, when up until recent years, the hotels situated there were open only to Cubans.

Accommodation is comparatively expensive in Cuba, with Havana, as you would expect, being one of the more costly places to stay. Most tourist hotels have excellent facilities, including swimming pools, and rival those found in the rest of the Caribbean.

When describing hotels I have categorised them according to price as follows:

	In Havana and Varadero	Elsewhere
Category 1	US$15–20	US$10–20
Category 2	US$20–50	US$20–30
Category 3	US$50–80	US$30–50
Category 4	US$80–100	US$50–60
Category 5	US$100 plus	US$60–80

Peso hotels
If you venture to some of the more remote parts of the country, it is possible that you will come across some peso hotels which will take you in, but in most cases you will politely be refused entry and referred to an establishment that will be happy to take your dollars. If you are really stuck, people may also offer you the opportunity to stay with them in their

own homes. This is a good way to sample Cuban life but you should remember that these are hard times for the Cuban people and although they would like to be able to share with you a good meal or a cup of coffee, often their rations do not stretch that far.

Black-market accommodation

A fairly recent innovation for the dollar-hungry Cuban is to offer black-market accommodation. You may well be approached during your stay, especially in Havana, to take advantage of someone's flat or room at a much lower cost than you would pay for hotel accommodation. It is possible to hire a flat in central Havana for around $15 per day. Again, if you deal on the black market you are vulnerable to being ripped off. Only get involved in this if you have established a strong level of trust with the person who is making the offer. If you slip the suggestion of black-market accommodation into your conversation with one of the waiters at your most favoured café, this will usually elicit some sound advice and recommendations.

Camping

Camping is popular in Cuba although the majority of those opting to camp out are Cuban rather than foreign. Most campsites are situated well out of town, but they do offer a cheap alternative to hotels. Cubamar situated at Paseo No 306 at 15, Vedado, Havana (tel: 7 305536) is a good place for information about camping facilities in Cuba. On most sites tents are pre-erected or the accommodation consists of basic chalets. Prices range from between $6 and $10 per night.

EATING, DRINKING AND SMOKING

Food

The tourist literature published by the Cuban government will try to convince you that Cuban food is a mouth-watering synthesis of Spanish and African influences. The time was when it may have been and no doubt the time will come again when it is. This, you must remember, is the *Período Especial* and, although tourists are largely spared the sharp end of its thrust, the overall blandness of Cuban food is testimony to the fact that even the simplest ingredients for traditional Cuban cuisine are in short supply.

Historically, Cuban cuisine did develop as a result of the cultural influences of these two countries. The Spanish colonists brought with them citrus fruits, such as oranges and lemons, along with rice and vegetables, while the African slaves (who for obvious reasons were unable to bring anything with them bar their culture) developed a penchant for local produce such as cassava, maize and okra. The two gradually fused in time to give rise to dishes such as *arroz congri* (rice and beans – sometimes known as Moors and Christians), *tostones* (pieces of plantain lightly fried, beaten with the fist then fried again) and *ajiaco criollo* (a meat and vegetable stew).

One of the mysteries of life in Cuba is the comparative lack of availability of fresh fish. There are two reasons for this. The first is historical: Cubans have never been great fish eaters which is surprising given that Cuba is the largest island in the Caribbean. Their taste has always been for meat (pork being a particular favourite) with fish and seafood trailing in a poor second. The second reason is that the Castro regime does not allow private fishing boats. All fishing boats have to be licensed with the state and are subject to its control. This practice is the result of a combination of two things: the fact that Cuba's economy is controlled and regulated by the state and, more influentially, that a Cuban with a private boat is unlikely to take it fishing, choosing instead to load it full of family and friends and sail it to Key West in Florida.

Another mystery is the scarcity of fruit but the reason for this is more straightforward. As with much of its produce, Cuba exports the bulk of its fruits, especially citrus fruits, to obtain much-needed hard currency. The majority of Cuba's crops are cash crops although some are reserved for the tourists. The average Cuban is unlikely to receive much in the way of fresh fruit as part of his or her monthly ration and you should bear this in mind when you are tempted to moan about the absence of fruit from the hotel menu. Thankfully, the Cubans knock up a mean ice-cream which should satisfy anyone with a sweet tooth (though don't expect much in the way of vitamin C from the fruit-flavoured ones).

In some cities, notably Havana, you will find restaurants that cater for the more cosmopolitan taste-bud, serving French, Italian, Spanish, Arab and Chinese food. These are detailed in the restaurant sections later in the book.

The legalisation of and growth in the numbers of *paladares* has had a significant effect on the availability of good food in Cuba. The complacency which was evident in hotels and restaurants has been undermined by the competition these new establishments provides. The result has been better quality food, more attentive service and a more realistic pricing of food and drink in hotels and restaurants. This competition has been of great benefit to the tourist.

Drink

If Cubans are somewhat lacking in imagination when it comes to cooking, then they more than make up for this when it comes to creating cocktails. They are aided and abetted by the presence of some of the world's finest rum which is thankfully produced in sufficient quantity to ensure that, even when they have satisfied the large export market, there is enough left over to keep both the tourist and the Cuban relatively happy. The best rum is undoubtedly the seven-year-old Havana Club which is delicious drunk on the rocks. For cocktails, a lighter rum (usually three-years-old) is used. Other excellent brands include Caribbean Club, Bucanero, Caney and Legendario. At an average price of $2 a cocktail they also represent good value for money.

Cuba Libre	Light dry rum, cola, lemon juice and ice, garnished with a slice of lemon.
Mojito	Light dry rum, lemon juice, sugar, crushed mint leaves and ice.
Daiquiri	Light dry rum, lemon juice, sugar, crushed ice. This is mixed in a blender before being served.
Havana Special	Light dry rum, maraschino, lemon juice, pineapple juice and ice.
Pina Colada	Light dry rum, coconut cream, pineapple juice. Mixed in a blender then served.
Manhattan	Old Gold dry rum, Angostura, red vermouth, ice.
Cuba Bella	Light dry rum, extra aged dry rum, crème de menthe, grenadine, lemon juice and ice.
Isla de Pinos	Light dry rum, grapefruit juice, red vermouth, ice.
Cubanito	Same ingredients as a Bloody Mary (vodka and tomato juice) but substituting vodka with light dry rum.

Apart from a vast array of wondrous cocktails, most restaurants and cafés stock a wide variety of imported beers such as Heineken, Carlsberg, Molsen and Labatts, as well as selling pretty good Cuban beer. The best known are Hatuey, named after the rebel Indian, Cristal and Bucanero. All these beers are around 5% in alcoholic volume and are very good. The Hatuey, which comes in bottles, is weaker, cheaper and tastes on the flat side. Expect to pay $1–2 for a beer (bottle or can).

Tobacco
Cigars
Cuba is home to the world's finest tobacco. The province of Pinar del Río and in particular the area known as San Juan y Martinez, is where the top grade leaf is grown. The tobacco is planted in November in phases to ensure that the leaf will be ready for harvest at different times. When it is ready to be harvested the plant, containing around 15 leaves, is hand picked, with the farmer careful to ensure that leaves from the base, middle and top section of the plant are separated. This is crucial as the position of the leaf on the plant has a bearing on the quality and strength of the cigar. Generally, the higher leaves are stronger than those closer to the stem. Once the leaves have been dried out they are stacked in a warehouse and allowed to ferment. This helps to dispel some of the impurities. The spine of each leaf is stripped and the leaves are then fermented again before being taken to the cigar factories where they are processed into the finished article. There are many different steps involved in making a good cigar, although it is fair to say that not all Cuban cigars live up to the standards appreciated by *aficionados*. If you get the opportunity to sample the sort of cigar a Cuban receives as part of his monthly ration you will appreciate this fact.

The best cigars money can buy are Cohibas. Most cigars undergo the sort of fermentation process described above, but the Cohiba is given a third fermentation lasting two years. For a box of Cohibas you should expect to pay around $250 for 25. It is possible to buy them on the black market for around $40. A box of Cohibas retails at around £400 in England. They are not for sale in the USA as a result of the trade embargo. If you dabble in the cigar black market you should beware, as some of Cuba's biggest rip-off artists operate in this area. A box of Cohibas should always be sealed and if, after close inspection, it shows any sign of having been tampered with, then the cigars inside are almost certainly fake.

Other premium brands for sale include Romeo y Julieta, H Upmann and Monte Cristo. All can be bought in the dollar shops for $100 and upwards.

On 1 March 1997 Fidel Castro presided over a celebration to mark the 30th anniversary of the Cohiba cigar, Cuba's finest. Invitations to the $500 per head gala were sent to cigar-smoking *aficionados* all over the world. Many attended, although invited celebrities such as Arnold Schwarzenegger, Jack Nicholson, Danny DeVito and Demi Moore did not show up. Although many Americans were amongst the audience not many would have returned to the USA with a box of Cohibas; it was not the price that deterred these high rollers, but the prospect of a ten-year jail sentence under the Trading With The Enemy Act.

Cigarettes

It is possible to buy well-known brands such as Marlboro, Camel and Winston in most dollar shops and many cafés, especially in Havana. The cost is usually $1.50–2.00 per packet. If you are desperate for a smoke and run out of western cigarettes or, alternatively, if you would simply like to shave a couple of years off your life expectancy, then you should try a Cuban cigarette. For a country capable of churning out the world's best cigars, Cuba also deserves the accolade of producing some of the world's worst and most lethal cigarettes. Untipped and guaranteed to send you into a rage of coughing, even the hardened smoker will balk at the crudity of the quality of these fags. Cubans smoke them like there is no tomorrow and indeed, at an average rate of ten a day per person, perhaps, in due course, there won't be! You can buy these cigarettes at most cafés for $1 a box. To save money you should place your mouth over the exhaust pipe of an old 1950s Buick and inhale!

THINGS TO BUY

Many of the tourist hotels have their own craft shops which take (surprise, surprise) US dollars only. Sadly, the Cuban seems to have little conception

Above: *Cuban tree frog* (Osteopilus septentrionalis) (CM)

Below: *Mygalomorph (tarantula) spider* (CM)

TRADITIONAL…
Above: *Ploughing with oxen, Pinar del Río* (CM)
Below: *Public transport, downtown Trinidad* (SF)

...AND MODERN

Above: *Cojímar, east of Havana* (CO)

Below: *Public telephone* (CO)

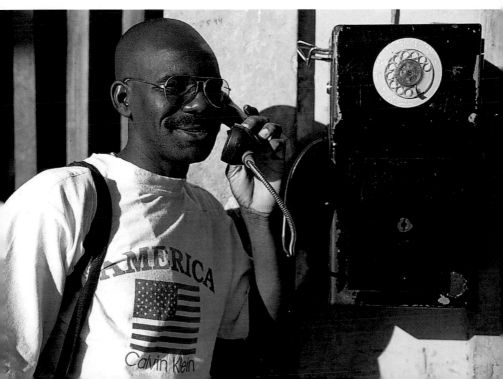

Gran Teatro and Capitolio, Havana (SF)

as to what constitutes a good gift and the shops are generally stocked with things like wall-mounted crabs, Che Guevara mirrors and styleless glass artefacts designed to smash in your hand luggage the moment the plane home hits a spot of turbulence. Some shops stock Cuban dolls wearing national costume which are not only good value at $6–10 but are also typically Cuban and therefore a nice memento of your stay. Stalwarts such as booze and cigars represent the best value for money and it is difficult to complain when you have access to both the world's finest tobacco and its rum. CDs of Cuban music are widely sold and the chances are that the group you have been listening to every night at your café or hotel will have offered you a tape of their music. Sadly, whether it is a result of poor tape quality, the lack of rum in your bloodstream or a combination of both, the music never sounds as good played on your £600 mini system back home. Nevertheless, you may be lucky and buy a tape that remains intact after a few plays and, if so, you should have paid around $5 for it. Clothes are generally scarce, unfashionable and of poor quality.

American cars

Cuba is a classic car buff's paradise. 1950s American cars, including Buicks and Chevrolets, are still in circulation and many of them, especially in Havana, are maintained in excellent condition. The Cuban government has not been slow to recognise the commercial potential of these cars and has been exporting them to foreign collectors in return for hard currency. If you are interested in buying one of these beauties and shipping it home you should make enquiries with the authorities in Havana (the Corporation Cimex SA will be able to help you).

ARTS AND ENTERTAINMENT

Since the Revolution Cuba has invested a great deal of time, money and effort in promoting the arts. The National Culture Council was founded in 1961 with the intention of preserving and developing Cuba's cultural heritage and since then there has been a vast increase in the number of cinemas, theatres and galleries and other cultural facilities. The National School of Art (ENA) was also set up to work in collaboration with the school network to promote art and to train artists and art tutors. If there are a multitude of other things for which Castro can be criticised, he deserves some recognition for his role in making Cuban society artistically expressive (although critics of the Revolution tend not to be given a platform to express themselves unless they leave the country). Admittance to the cinema, the theatre and most other cultural centres is normally free for Cubans, but tourists will be expected to pay in dollars. Charges, even for Cubans, are beginning to be phased in as it becomes more difficult for the state to continue with its 100% subsidy.

Cinema

Cuba invariably receives foreign films for screening long after they have been released. Cubans will tell you that a foreign film is shown in every country in the world and when there is nobody left who wants to see it they send it to Cuba. While this is a little unfair, it is true that most films are dated. However, given the amount of dross emanating from Hollywood these days, this is not necessarily a bad thing. Cuba does have its own small but active film industry and although the majority of films are commissioned to promote the party line, there is a critical strain running through the industry and the most popular films are those which explore anti-establishment themes. Cuba is also home to a yearly Latin American Film Festival and the New Latin American Film Foundation sponsors a TV and video school in Havana.

Cuba's most prominent film director of recent years is Tomás Gutiérrez Alea who sadly died in 1996. His film *Fresa y Chocolate* (Strawberry and Chocolate) won the jury's special prize at the 1994 Berlin Film Festival and was an international box office success. The film examined the relationship of a committed socialist and a homosexual working at the Coppelia in Havana. Its underlying message of tolerance and understanding struck a chord with Cubans as well as international audiences.

Theatre

The theatre received no financial support prior to the Revolution but has flourished since. There are many theatre groups throughout the country but the plays that tend to be performed are ones which do not call into question the authority of the state. Havana is still the centre of Cuba's theatrical world with the National Lyric Theatre having the highest reputation for innovation and originality. Santiago de Cuba also boasts fine theatrical traditions. Tourists are required in almost all instances to pay for tickets in dollars.

Dance

The National School of Cuban Ballet has an international reputation of the highest order. It is directed by the country's universally acclaimed prima ballerina, Alicia Alonzo, whose fame has transcended Cuba. Cuba's close association with the former Soviet Union made it possible for Cuban ballet to have access to the expertise of Moscow's Bolshoi Ballet, which greatly enhanced its standing.

Both the Cuban National Dance Ensemble and the National Folk Ensemble were founded in 1959 and these too have won widespread critical acclaim.

Music

The music of Cuba reflects the cultural heritage of the people of Cuba. 'A love affair between the African drum and Spanish guitar' (Fernando Ortiz), the many distinct styles emanating from the island have had a profound influence on world music in general. The most notable rhythms are:

Son: Music which emanated from the mountains of Cuba particularly the Sierra Maestra. The instrumentation is simple, comprising a *tres* (a guitar with three sets of double strings), bongo, maracas, clave, trumpet and vocals.

Salsa: A unique style of Afro-Cuban music which incorporates jazz-influenced horn-based ensembles. The genre received widespread acclaim in New York during the early 1960s. Eddie Palmieri and Celia Cruz are amongst its two most eminent exponents.

Mambo: Invented by the brothers Orestes and Israel Lopez in Havana in 1939, this genre swept through Latin America in the 1940s and 1950s. The *mambo* sound usually involves a large ensemble of horns, rhythm section, vocals and woodwind.

Cha-cha-cha: Invented in 1951 by the Cuban composer Enrique Jorrin who gave name to the genre after listening to the sound of dancers' feet on the dance floor. Cha-cha-cha swept the music world in the 1950s.

Charanga: Similar to cha-cha-cha only with the addition of violins and flutes.

Musicians who are exponents of most of these style can be found in the clubs and cafés of most large towns and cities (particularly Havana). Almost all cities in Cuba have their own *casa de la trova* where both *trova* (traditional ballads) and *nueva trova* (post-revolutionary ballads) can be heard. Perhaps the most famous *casa de la trova* is the one in Santiago de Cuba.

Sport

One of the most remarkable advancements Cuba has made since the Revolution is in sport. Castro invested heavily in sports facilities and in the coaching of sports. Like the Soviet Union, Castro viewed Cuban sporting prowess on the international stage as an ideal advertisement for the promotion of communism. The National Institute for Sports, Physical Education and Recreation (NDER) was established in 1961 with the aim of promoting all sporting activities nationwide. Professional sports were abolished and Cuban sport across the board adopted amateur status. In 1991 Cuba hosted the Pan American games in which they came first. The commitment to hold the games was made prior to the collapse of the Soviet Union and although by 1991 the country was well into the *Período Especial*, Castro decided to honour the commitment to go ahead with the games. New stadiums were built and sports facilities upgraded and it is no coincidence that many Cubans look back at the games with mixed feelings, wondering if they were actually worth the colossal amount that was spent on hosting them.

A sign of the changing times can be identified in the recent establishment of an organisation called Cuba Deportes. This is a sports management company based in Havana which has been set up to handle the professionalisation of Cuban sport. The star attraction on the books of Cuba

Deportes is the world high-jump champion, Javier Sotomayor, but there are many other athletes, boxers and baseball stars who are also registered. 1994 saw the first professional tennis tournament in Cuba since the Revolution with the event jointly sponsored by Benetton, DHL and Heineken, while in November of the same year the first ever cross-island car rally took place.

Baseball

The most popular sport in Cuba is baseball. Many Cubans will argue that the sport, rather than being founded in the USA, actually has its origins in Cuba where it was initially played by the Taino Indians under the name *batey*. The Cuban national team habitually dominates the world championships and in the Barcelona Olympics romped home to gold. Scouts from the National and American leagues are frequent visitors to Cuban stadiums, regularly monitoring the progress of the country's top players, hoping to lure them into the professional leagues of the USA with the temptation of big money. Baseball is one of the most unifying aspects of Cuban culture with the game not only played in major city stadiums but also in the squares of Habana Vieja, Santiago de Cuba and throughout the country. People of both sexes and all ages share a passion for the sport and debate about the game is a common feature of Cuban conversation. It is accurate to describe baseball as being as important to Cubans as soccer is to Brazilians. For Cubans it has always been possible to gain entrance to baseball matches free of charge, but recently the introduction of admission fees has started to creep in.

Much to the chagrin of the USA, the Cuban national baseball team took the gold medal in the 1996 Olympic Games in Atlanta.

Boxing

The success of the Cuban boxer, Teofilo Stevenson, three times Olympic and world amateur super heavyweight champion, ensured that the tradition of boxing in the country was not only maintained but also set a new level of excellence for others to follow. Cuban boxers have built up a fearsome international reputation and boxing has developed into the second most popular sport in Cuba behind baseball. Many coaches and trainers from other countries come to Cuba to study and learn from Cuba's pugilistic training methods and in successive Olympics the country has done remarkably well, taking medals in a host of different divisions.

The current rising star of the Cuban boxing world is another heavyweight named Felix Savon. In the 1994 Goodwill Games in St Petersburg, Savon was a convincing winner and earned himself the reputation of being the world's most outstanding heavyweight prospect. He confirmed this by easily winning the gold medal at the 1996 Olympic Games in Atlanta. In addition, Cuba won a further three gold medals in the boxing tournament, although this was seen as something of a disappointment back home as Cuba was hoping to sweep the board.

Basketball

Basketball is a particularly popular game among Cuba's black community. Many black Cubans are familiar with the names of Michael Jordan and Magic Johnson and these and other basketball stars act as role models. Although the vast majority of people don't have access to televised basketball games, they are surprisingly clued up on what is going on in American basketball and, as you would expect, they are great admirers of basketball fashion although most cannot afford a bar of soap, let alone a $100 pair of Air Jordan basketball boots. The game itself is taught and played at school and there is a multitude of courts in all cities. When you walk down the Prado in Habana Vieja you will see a host of impromptu basketball games being played with Coke tins used as basketballs and wire attached to tree branches replacing basketball nets.

Soccer

The sport of soccer (or football as it is better known outside the USA) is growing in popularity in Cuba, although it is hard to imagine it ever rivalling baseball as the number one pastime. The 1994 World Cup Finals in America were given extensive coverage both on the TV and in the press and the Cubans lined up squarely behind their Latin American cousins Brazil in terms of allegiance. Nigeria also attracted a great following and there was tremendous disappointment when they eventually lost out to Italy. The sport is currently being promoted heavily at grass-roots level and no doubt Brazil's victory will have given the game a shot in the arm. The Cuban authorities would dearly like to see football take root as it would assist them in their ambition to steer the country towards a common cultural identity with Latin America. It is hard to imagine, however, the Cubans doing anywhere near as well in football as they do in many other sports.

Athletics

Cuba has developed into an athletics power out of all proportion to its population of little over 11 million people. In addition to Sotomayor, Ana Fidelia Quirot and Marisa Marten are world leaders in their disciplines, while the most famous of them all is Alberto Juantorena, former Olympic 400m and 800m gold medal winner. Athletics is still an integral part of schools' sporting curriculums.

By Cuban standards, the 1996 Olympics in Atlanta were a disappointment. Sotomayor competed despite being injured but could not claim a medal and Quirot could only finish in second spot in her discipline.

Chapter Three

Getting Around

BY AIR

There are two airlines currently operating internal flights, but the vast majority are operated by Cubana, the national airline. Aerocaribbean, the other carrier, operates charter flights to the more popular tourist destinations. Cuba is a deceptively large island and flying is an easy way of getting around, especially if you want to see as many places as possible but haven't the time to use the road or rail network. The Cubans regard flying as the most reliable method of transportation as the planes are generally on time and have a better safety record than you would expect, given the ageing nature of the fleet.

The Cubana domestic aircraft fleet is an all-Russian line-up. Tupolevs, Antonovs and twin-propellered 32-seater YAK 40s are used to fly passengers internally, while for international travel leased DC10s and Ilyushins are employed.

Do not expect too much in the way of in-flight entertainment or service. Most flights are less than an hour anyway and you will invariably have to make do with a boiled sweet and a small mouthful of coffee. If you are flying on a YAK 40 (which cover the short journeys, eg Havana to the Isle of Youth) you will undergo an experience similar to an appearance on *Top of the Pops* in the 1970s, as what looks like dry ice pours through the aircraft's ventilation system limiting visibility to around 1m. Don't panic as this soon clears, although if you opt for a window seat the levels of condensation can leave you feeling rather damp at the end of your short trip.

Aerocaribbean operates charter flights for tourists, principally to Cayo Largo. It is possible to get a flight-only deal if you sweet talk one of the tourist representatives or one of the staff at the Palacio del Turismo who will make a booking on your behalf. This largely depends on how full the flights are at the time and during peak seasons the chances of getting on an Aerocaribbean flight without paying the full excursion price are slim.

It is possible (but expensive) to charter flights or helicopters for individuals or parties through Aerocaribbean and Aero Gaviota, who provide services in association with Cubana Airlines.

Reservations

Although the domestic air service experiences the same sort of supply and demand problems that mark out Cuban life, things have definitely improved since the bleak period of the early 1990s. Cubana is now able to operate more domestic services and to more destinations than before. It is still, however, a sensible idea to try to book your flights at least a week in advance (allow even more time if possible). That said, Cubana seems to have an unwritten policy of allowing foreigners to jump waiting lists for economically logical reasons. As a foreigner has to pay for a flight in dollars, two or three foreigners on the same plane can heavily subsidise the flight for the rest of the Cuban passengers. It is unwise to attempt a telephone booking when trying to secure a ticket on a domestic flight. Your best bet is to visit a Cubatur, Havanatur or Cubanacán office which will be able to book your ticket and in most cases issue it within minutes. Alternatively you can pay a visit to the Cubana Airlines office and obtain your ticket direct.

Timetable

All information is subject to change. You should check with the airline for verification (fares quoted are all one way).

From Havana:

To	Day	Price
Baracoa	Tue, Fri, Sun	$80
Bayamo	Tue, Thu, Sun	$52
Camagüey	Daily except Sat & Sun	$58
Cayo Coco	Tue, Thu, Sat, Sun	$48
Ciego de Avila	Wed, Fri	$48
Guantanamo	Daily	$80
Holguin	Daily except Friday	$70
Isle of Youth (Nueva Gerona)	Daily	$20
Las Tunas	Mon, Wed, Fri	$64
Manzanillo	Mon, Wed, Fri	$66
Moa	Mon, Wed, Fri	$80
Santiago de Cuba	Daily	$76
Varadero	Daily	$22

BY TRAIN

Although the train service in Cuba is a painfully slow mode of transport – journeys by bus are quicker – it does offer the opportunity for you to become acquainted not only with the Cuban landscape but also with the Cuban people. The rolling stock is in need of modernisation and, with the exception of luxury class, journeys of any reasonable distance are guaranteed to leave you with a rick in your neck and a pain in your backside. That said, you are generally well looked after on the trains and in luxury class, as part of the price of your ticket, you will be given something to eat and drink (usually a cheese sandwich and cola). If you are making a long journey (eg Havana to Santiago de Cuba) it is a good idea to stock up on crisps, nuts and other provisions to sustain you through the trip. Bear in mind that, although a rail journey in Cuba may be advertised as taking ten hours, the chances are it will take longer, sometimes a lot longer.

An important point to consider when booking your train ticket is the estimated arrival time of the train at your intended destination. Arriving in a city at four in the morning and trying to find a hotel room can be a daunting prospect.

The rail line that links Havana with Santiago de Cuba meanders its way via Matanzas, Santa Clara and the central cities of Camagüey and Las Tunas before dipping down to Santiago, the final destination. The distance between the two major cities is 860km and the journey, on the fastest type of service, the *especial,* takes around 16 hours at an average speed of 54km an hour.

Classes
Segunda
On short journeys made on branch lines there is likely to be only the one class available – this one. *Segunda* means second class. A more accurate definition would be cattle truck. These trains are for the hardy and committed travellers. On the positive side they are very cheap and they do get you there, eventually.

Primera
Marginally more luxurious than *segunda,* this class is still very cheap, although you can still expect an uncomfortable level of overcrowding on most services.

Primera especial
More padding on your seat, less people in your carriage and worth paying the extra if the class is available on your route. Sometimes you are given a small but typically unappetising snack to help you through the day.

Especial
These trains are easily the best and consequently seats get booked up quickly. The seats on the *especial* are capable of reclining so far back that you almost have to be a contortionist to take full advantage of the facility. This is the closest thing you will find to sleeper class, which is an innovation Cuba seems to have overlooked. Allow yourself at least four days when making a reservation (it should be noted that this service is available only on the train from Havana to Santiago de Cuba). Despite being the élite class, sitting in an *especial* seat does not exempt you from

the possibility of getting soaked due to a leaking carriage roof in the event of a heavy shower. Leaking roofs are a common feature of Cuban trains and tropical rainfall does not discriminate between classes. Even the rain in Cuba tows the party line!

Reservations

Officina Ladis is the organisation now responsible for issuing rail tickets to tourists, having taken over from Ferrotur. All of the main railway stations now have a Ladis office from which you are required to purchase tickets in dollars. In Havana, the Officina Ladis is at Calle Arsenal (as was Ferrotur) behind the main railway station.

If you are travelling with a bicycle you will be required to pay a small surcharge. This is payable in Cuban pesos almost always at the end of your trip. Unscrupulous guardsmen may try to rip you off by insisting that payment be made in dollars. If you have some pesos which you have changed on the black market, now's your chance to use some of them. Such an opportunity doesn't arise too often.

There is no segregation between smokers and non-smokers on Cuban trains. This can be a problem for those who object to breathing in other people's cigarettes, particularly when the cigarettes in question are the particularly nasty Cuban brand.

Timetable

This is the *especial* timetable. Fares quoted are one way and are payable in US dollars.

Departs	Arrives	Departure time	Arrival time	Cost (from Havana)
Havana	Matanzas	16.25	17.55	$8
Matanzas	Santa Clara	18.00	20.25	$14
Santa Clara	Guayos	20.30	21.55	$17
Guayos	Ciego de Avila	22.00	22.55	$19
Ciego de Avila	Camagüey	23.00	00.55	$22
Camagüey	Las Tunas	01.00	02.55	$26
Las Tunas	Cacocum	03.00	03.55	$30
Cacocum	Santiago de Cuba	04.00	06.45	$38

The Santiago de Cuba–Havana *especial* departs from Santiago at 16.35 arriving in Havana at 07.05. The service stops at those stations given above.

BY BUS

Buses would be an excellent way to travel around if it were not for the fact that trying to get a ticket for one is nigh on impossible. Buses go to the parts of Cuba most other modes of transportation do not reach. Services are heavily in demand and often your best bet is to book yourself on to a tour bus rather than attempt the challenge of getting aboard a typical Cuban interprovincial service – usually booked up weeks in advance. If you do manage to obtain a ticket for one of these then you can expect a third-world ride sharing a wildly entertaining experience not only with other Cubans but also with their livestock, their farm produce and their goods and chattels in general. At the end of a long distance you will emerge either with the happy feeling of belonging to a new and loving family or, alternatively, like death warmed up.

Most towns have two separate bus stations catering for local and municipal services (Terminal de Omnibus Intermunicipales) and for long-distance journeys (Terminal de Omnibus Interprovinciales).

The *intermunicipal* bus services require no advance reservations. Instead you must turn up early and queue like everybody else. Invariably you will be given a slip of paper which means you can get on the bus. Fares are collected once you are aboard. You should remain patient, tolerant and good-humoured in the face of all this mayhem; if this is beyond you you should consider another mode of travel. Chaos is the order of the day at the majority of intermunicipal bus stations and displays of petulance or bad temper are not going to change that. If you do finally get aboard you will find that services are, almost without exception, overcrowded and slow and just when you think you have hit a stretch of road and your driver is building up speed, someone will want to alight and the bus will turn sharply into a series of small crumbling roads which will add even more time to your journey. In defence of intermunicipal bus services, they are generally eventful and, on an anthropological level, they are a microcosm of Cuban society.

The *interprovincial* services are run by the government enterprise, Omnibus de Cuba. They are extremely popular as not only do they offer a more extensive service network than trains, but they are also faster. Most Cubans have to book a month in advance to stand any chance of getting on one of these buses. If you want to travel on a long-distance bus you will need to go to the bus station where you will most likely be put on a waiting list. Foreigners are often pushed up the list as a tourist equals hard currency, but such is the demand that you will still have to wait an average of 10 to 14 days before getting a seat. Some employees of Omnibus de Cuba may offer you the opportunity of paying over the odds (in dollars) for a ticket which could drastically reduce your waiting time. It is worth checking with the tourist authorities to see what the likelihood is of getting a ticket on one of these services. If you do travel long-distance remember to stock up on food and water for the trip. Although long-distance bus journeys are broken up every three or four hours by rest breaks, it is unlikely that you will find any edible provisions en route.

Tourist buses, although generally quite expensive, at least offer the opportunity of comfortable, hassle-free travel. You can book these through the state-owned Transtur agency; other companies such as

Gaviota and Cubanacán offer similar services. Alternatively you can try to talk your way on to one of the organised excursion buses. It is sometimes possible to strike up an arrangement with the tour leader who is not averse to a little hard currency bonus.

BY CAR

Driving

Probably the best way to travel around is by car. There are two main roads: the National Southern Expressway is an eight-lane highway (some of it still under construction) that links Havana with Sancti Spiritus in the central region and Pinar del Río in the west (it also links Las Tunas with Bayamo); the other main route is the Central Highway which has less lanes and is in poorer condition than the Expressway but does link the country from almost one end to the other. The Vía Blanca Expressway, which links the key tourist destinations of Havana and Varadero, was actually built by American engineers when the two countries were on more convivial terms.

Driving along these expressways (known as *autopistas*) can be an eerie experience as traffic, especially away from the main cities, is almost non-existent. Roads in general, and the *autopistas* in particular, are in good condition although parts of the surface are broken up. Wear and tear in recent years has become less of a problem due to petrol shortages and the decline in the number of cars using the roads. The vast majority of roads are paved and, although fuel is expensive (almost $1 per litre), tourist cars are adequately catered for and finding petrol shouldn't be too much of a problem. There are a reasonable number of 24-hour petrol stations on the expressways (run by Servicupet or Servicentro) and the Rumbos organisation operate 24-hour motorway cafés which sell food, soft drinks and alcohol! It is a good idea to fill up with fuel in and around the major cities as running out in the middle of nowhere can be disheartening. Some petrol stations (usually called Diplo stations) serve foreigners only.

Driving offers unrivalled freedom to roam and, with traffic sparse even in the major cities, getting around by car is certainly an option worth considering.

Car rental

There are two rent-a-car services for tourists in Cuba – Havanautos and Transautos. Havanautos is by far the larger and if you do decide to rent a set of wheels it will most likely be through them.

Remember to take your driving licence as it will not be possible to rent a car without it. If you do happen to forget it, a copy faxed by a friend at home will often be acceptable. The minimum age for car hire in Cuba is 21.

When renting a car it is advisable to ensure that all the necessary equipment is not only present but also in working order. Tyres in particular take a battering on Cuban roads and it is worth checking that the condition of those on your car is acceptable. You should also check the spare tyre; if you intend to rent a car for more than a couple of days you will probably need it. It is wise to ensure that the tool kit, in particular the jack, is present and works.

Havanautos have offices throughout the island with the main office being in Havana at Calle 36 no 505 at the junction of 5a Avenida, Miramar; (tel: 7 225891). Other places where you can find Havanauto offices are listed below.

Havanautos have a wide range of vehicles for hire including Nissan Sunnys, Daihatsu Jeeps and even Mercedes Benz 190Es. If you want the

HAVANAUTOS OFFICES

Havana
José Martí International Airport
(tel: 7 335197/335215)
Hotel Capri (tel: 7 333483)
Hotel Nacional (tel: 7 333192)
Hotel Habana Libre (tel: 7 305011)
Hotel Triton (tel: 7 332921)
Hotel Riviera (tel: 7 333577)
Hotel Plaza (tel: 7 622906 ex 510)
Hotel Presidente (tel: 7 327521)
Hotel Deauville (tel: 7 628051/59)
Hotel Copacabana (tel: 7 332846)

Playas del Este
Hotel Tropicoco
(tel: 687 2351)
Hotel Itabo (tel: 687 2581)
Villa Panamericana (tel: 7 338113)
Villa Tropico (tel: 5692 83612)
Villa Tarara (tel: 7 814267/335071)

Pinar del Río
Hotel Pinar del Río (82 5071)

Isle of Youth
Hotel Colony (tel: 61 98181/98282)

Cayo Largo
Hotel Isla del Sur (tel: 333156)

Varadero
Varadero International Airport
(tel: 5 64185)
Hotel Internacional (tel: 5 663011)
Hotel Villa Tortuga (tel: 5 63653)
Hotel Siboney (tel: 337094)
Hotel Paradiso (tel: 5 63971)
Varadero Gaviota (tel: 5 63625)

Santa Clara
Motel Los Caneyes (tel: 422 4512/15)

Cienfuegos
Hotel Rancho Luna (tel: 43 48120/24)

Trinidad
Hotel Ancon (tel: 41 4011)

Camagüey
Hotel Camagüey (tel: 31 72015)
Cayo Guillermo (tel: 33 30184/30143)

Ciego de Avila
Hotel Ciego de Avila (tel: 33 28013)

Holguin
Motel El Bosque
(tel: 24 481012/481895)
Hotel Río Luna Gaviota
(tel: 24 30102/30202)

Santiago de Cuba
Santiago de Cuba Airport
(tel: 226 91014)
Hotel Las Américas (tel: 226 42011)
Hotel San Juan
(formerly Motel Leningrado)
(tel: 226 41121)

Baracoa
Hotel Porto Santo (tel: 21 43511–12)

cheapest car, you can rent a 0.8 litre Daewoo Tico for around $45 per day. The Nissan Sunny LX will set you back approximately $49 per day, the Jeep around $50 and the flash Mercedes $150. Rates are reduced if you rent for longer than six days. However, the cost doesn't stop there. On top of the daily rate you will have to pay an additional fee (usually 30¢) for every kilometre you do over the first, free, 100. This can have a drastic effect on your overall bill, especially if you are intending to clock up quite a few kilometres. You can opt for unlimited mileage at an increased initial outlay and it is worthwhile working out roughly how many kilometres you are going to do and weighing up the cost of both options. You will be required to pay in advance, including a deposit of around $200. The cost includes maintenance and repairs, but it is worth considering taking out collision insurance which is extra. Be sure to study the small print of the contract before you sign it.

All told, car hire is quite an expensive option although, if you can arrange to hire a vehicle as part of a group, the costs can be shared, making it a much more attractive proposition. Sadly, as everything is regulated by the state, Havanautos have an almost captive market which they milk to its full extent. Charging $20 over the odds for a full tank of petrol when you take over the car is one particularly infuriating scam.

Long-distance taxi

This is an expensive method of getting around the country but the costs can be substantially reduced if you can assemble a small group to share the costs. A long-distance taxi service is provided by Taxis Cubalse (tel: 7 33 6568), Transtur (tel: 7 41 3906) and Transgaviota (7 23 7000). The approximate costs are as follows:

From	To	Distance		Fare	
		one way	return	one way	return
Havana	Pinar del Río	172km	344km	$78	$144
Havana	Viñales	197km	394km	$89	$164
Havana	Soroa	70km	140km	$40	$80
Havana	Matanzas	103km	206km	$60	$109
Havana	Varadero	150km	300km	$80	$120
Havana	Cienfuegos	254km	508km	$115	$212
Havana	Trinidad	337km	674km	$171	$299

Hitchhiking

One of the most striking things about Cuba is the number of people standing by the roadsides trying to thumb a lift. The practice is known as *bottela,* which translated means 'bottle', and it is not confined to hitching lifts solely in cars; cycles too are targets and it's not uncommon to see three people precariously balanced on a bike meandering along the road.

The shortage of petrol and the lack of buses means that hitching is an integral part of Cuban life. So much so that the government have intervened to ensure that all state vehicles must stop and pick up as many passengers as possible without creating a dangerous level of overcrowding. Officials are actually employed to carry out the task of stopping vehicles (usually lorries and trucks) and organising lifts. Most cities have designated hitching points, often close to major road intersections, to make the practice easier and more regulated. If you want to try hitching you should join the fray at one of these hitching points. As well as causing great amusement among those gathered, you are also likely to be given preferential treatment when the first truck comes along. Hitching lifts outside of the main towns is more difficult as the number of vehicles is greatly reduced. Nevertheless, if one does come by, the chances are it will stop to pick you up. Hitching is a way of life in Cuba and people have a habit of pulling together when times are hard.

BY BICYCLE

Cuba is an excellent country in which to have a bike. With the exception of the areas around Pinar del Río, Trinidad, Santiago de Cuba and Baracoa, the land is relatively flat and it is possible to zip around at a good speed. Also, the lack of major traffic makes the roads user-friendly for the cyclist.

As a result of the fuel shortage Cuba has become a nation of cyclists. Imported Chinese bikes, with names like the Flying Pigeon and the Rooster, vastly outnumber motor vehicles in all cities. These bikes are crude but sturdy contraptions which have only one gear and questionable braking systems. Cubans somehow manage to coax great speed out of them. As you climb a steep hill on your 21-gear $800 mountain bike, don't be too surprised if a young Cuban flies past you with barely a cursory glance, pedalling furiously but effectively and leaving you trailing behind within moments. Bicycles are usually dispensed by the state to those who are regarded as key workers, although there is now a thriving black market that deals in both legitimate and stolen bikes. Bike theft is a major problem in Cuba, especially in Havana, and if you do take your own be sure to take a good 'D' lock.

If you are intent on long-distance cycling you should plan the trip carefully and come well supplied with replacement parts as they will be hard to obtain once you're in the country. A good tool kit, comprising an adjustable spanner, a set of Allen keys, a chain breaker, tyre levers and a screwdriver with a Phillips attachment, should be sufficient. Packing a small assortment of nuts and bolts may also prove a good move. It may also be worthwhile investing in a set of puncture-proof inner tubes as these can save you a lot of hassle. For normal inner tubes you can now buy a special sealant (Slime is one of the main brands) which, once pumped into the inner tubes, automatically seals punctures up to one third of a centimetre in diameter. If the puncture is any bigger than this you will have to repair it in the conventional manner. Fortunately there is an abundance of puncture repair outlets in all towns and cities.

If you tire of travelling on your bike or if you are running short of time, you always have the option of putting it on board a plane, a train, a bus or even a lorry. Cycling, if only in the cities and the surrounding countryside, is probably the best way to get to know an area intimately.

Cuba has its own Federation of Cycling which is well worth contacting for information on cycling conditions, routes and events in the country (tel: 7 683776 or 683661). Other good sources of information are the mountain biking magazines, *Mountain Biking UK* and *Mountain Biker International,* both of which carry articles on cycling in far-off places. Both magazines are published monthly and are widely available in most UK newsagents. In the USA there are several equivalent magazines.

ON FOOT

It is unlikely that you will want to do too much long-distance walking. This is a tropical country and a tropical climate does not as a rule make for good walking conditions. There are, however, some excellent and manageable walks in the mountainous areas around Pinar del Río (Viñales), Trinidad and Santiago de Cuba. If you intend to go hiking it is best to leave early in the morning before the heat becomes too unbearable and it is important to stock up with water and enough provisions to get you through the day. Luckily Cuba's diet is heavily carbohydrate-based which means you should have plenty of energy for those steep climbs.

AROUND TOWN
Horse-drawn cabs

One of the most popular forms of transport in the smaller towns is the horse-drawn cart. The Cuban name for this is the *coche*. With petrol so scarce, this form of transport has become an integral one, although in cities like Havana and Santiago de Cuba the *coche* is retained largely for the tourists. The horses pulling these carts are poorly treated and emaciated and, while it is understandable that they should function as a working necessity for Cubans, there is little to recommend them as a mode of transport for the visitor.

Bicytaxis

A relatively new transport phenomenon, particularly in Havana, is the dawn of the *bicytaxi*. Anyone who has travelled to the Far East will recognise them as *samlors* or *cyclos*. These three-wheeled bicycles are the cheapest, slowest and perhaps most enjoyable mode of transport in Cuban cities. They normally carry a maximum of two people and the going rate for tourists is around $1 per two kilometres.

Part Two

THE GUIDE

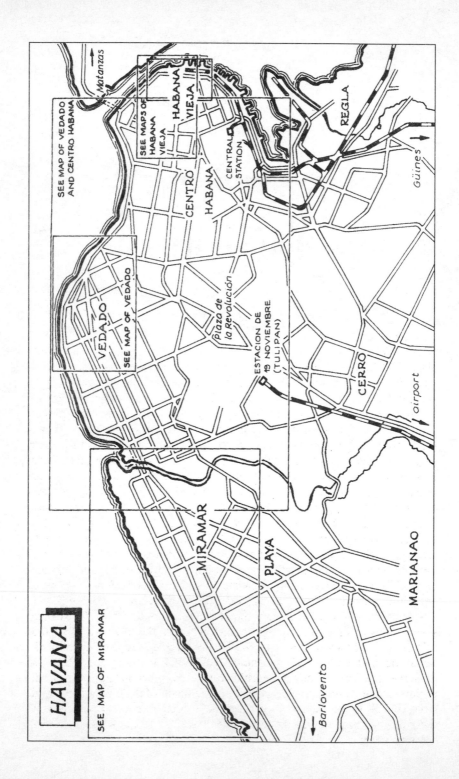

HAVANA

SEE MAP OF MIRAMAR

SEE MAP OF VEDADO AND CENTRO HABANA

SEE MAPS OF HABANA VIEJA

SEE MAP OF VEDADO

MIRAMAR

VEDADO

CENTRO HABANA

HABANA VIEJA

REGLA

PLAYA

Plaza de la Revolución

ESTACION DE 19 NOVIEMBRE (TULIPAN)

CENTRAL STATION

CERRO

MARIANAO

← Matanzas

Güines →

airport →

Barlovento →

Chapter Four

Havana

HISTORY AND ORIENTATION

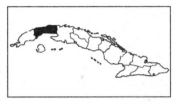

Havana, the capital of Cuba, was founded
in 1514 by Diego Velázquez. It was
initially known as Villa de San Cristobal
de la Habana and occupied an entirely
unsuitable position in the middle of a
swamp. For obvious reasons it was moved from its original site (not once
but twice) before it came to occupy its current position on a broad and
sweeping bay on Cuba's northern coast. To the east lies the narrow and
well-protected harbour entrance and to the west the Almendares river.

Havana owes its growth and prosperity to the almost natural perfection
of its harbour. The Spanish, in the course of their conquest of Central and
Latin America, earmarked the city as the ideal stopping-off point for their
ships. In order to protect their vessels from English, French and Dutch
attack (not to mention the attentions of the ubiquitous pirate fleets that
operated in the surrounding waters), the Spanish built a wall around the
city and constructed huge fortresses at the entrance to the harbour. Both
the Castillo de la Real Fuerza (completed in 1577) and the Castillo de los
Tres Reyes del Morro (completed in 1610) are still standing today and,
together with the wall, constitute the perimeter of the old town. Those
parts of the wall which are still intact but largely buried during the passage
of time are currently being excavated by the Cuban authorities who
recognise both their historical significance and their tourist potential.

The heart and soul of Havana is the old town, **Habana Vieja**. One of the
seven townships founded by the Spanish in Cuba, the town was declared
a Heritage of Mankind Site in 1982 by the United Nations Educational,
Scientific and Cultural Organisation (UNESCO) which was keen to
preserve the beauty of its architecture and promote the historical
importance of its role within the region. As a result of the funding received
from UNESCO the Cuban government have been able to restore many of
the buildings around and including the Plaza de Armas to their former
colonial glory.

As with many old Spanish colonial cities, the residential quarters of Habana Vieja were once a mixture of different social and economic classes. Walking down these streets in colonial times you would have passed through neighbourhoods made up of slave owners living in quarters above their slaves, and merchants and entrepreneurs living above their warehouses or stores. Gentrification of particular areas, apart from the houses surrounding the plazas, was rare and you were just as likely to see a well-dressed member of the Spanish bourgeoisie enter and exit through the same door as the worker on whom he depended. This socio-economic intermingling owed more to economic practicalities than any desire to foster inter-class harmony, but the fact that this was how it used to be is reflected in the architectural juxtapositions in the old town, where the grandiose is often foreshadowed by the ramshackle.

The three main architectural influences are: pre-baroque, emphasised by the use of masonry construction and tiled roofs; baroque, relying on sculptured and carved lines; and neoclassical Greco-Roman. Most of the structures which are still intact (it is estimated that at least half a dozen of these buildings simply collapse each year under the combined stress of the rainy season and decades of neglect) date back to the 18th and 19th centuries. Some are even older. With the development of new Havana beyond the old boundary walls and the construction of the Malecón in 1902 which facilitated this expansion, Habana Vieja became the town that time forgot until the post-revolutionary authorities and UNESCO woke up to the fact that its treasures were being allowed to crumble and disintegrate.

The narrow streets and crowded buildings of Habana Vieja can at times be quite claustrophobic. Designed with the horse and carriage in mind rather than the car, many of the roads were cobble-surfaced prior to some fool taking the decision to cover them over with tarmac. Thankfully this folly has been identified and as you wander around the streets you are likely to encounter workers busy excavating the roads, digging up the modern surface to reveal the delightful old cobblestoned highways of old. The street planning is orderly (basically conforming to a grid pattern, making it easy to find your way around) and the use of squares (*plazas*) to break up the monotony of the system means that there is always an opening where you can stop and take a rest as you wander around exploring the town.

The **Plaza de Armas** was the first public square built in the city. The square holds a deep religious significance for many of the citizens of Havana as not only was it said to be the venue of the first public mass, but it is also home to the hallowed *ceiba* tree, a tree that is regarded as sacred in the Afro-Cuban religion of Santería. Close by is perhaps the most beautiful square in the Caribbean, the Plaza de la Catedral, which is surrounded by examples of the finest baroque architecture in the country. The cathedral, partly built by the Jesuit order (who were actually prevented from finishing the construction when, in 1767, they were expelled from Cuba by royal decree), is open to the public although opening hours are infuriatingly erratic. The altar of the cathedral is made of Carrara marble and inlaid with onyx, silver and gold with intricately carved woods. The paintings are by the artist, Vermay, and the fine sculptures crafted by an Italian named Branchini. The uneven towers which sit uncomfortably on top of the cathedral contain two bells, one brought from Spain and the other from Matanzas. If you want to take a photograph that will capture the beauty of Cuba, the Plaza de la Catedral is the place to take it.

Not all of Havana lives up to the architectural splendour of Habana Vieja. As the city grew and prospered it was natural that it should extend beyond the old boundary walls. To the west of the old town the area of **Vedado** was developed. This part of the city is occupied primarily by office blocks and hotels, the most famous of which is the impressive Nacional Hotel overlooking the Malecón. The Malecón itself connects Vedado to Habana Vieja and as you walk along it from end to end, you are struck by the feeling of a city in waiting as people congregate to talk or simply gaze out to sea against a backdrop of fading pastel colours and crumbling buildings.

Prior to the Revolution money poured into Havana, some of it from the east-coat Mafia in the USA, and it became apparent that the commercial confines of Habana Vieja would need to be breached and a new area found to house the economic expansion. Vedado served this purpose and by the end of the 1950s, a multitude of high-rise developments mingled with and overshadowed the grandiose houses built by affluent Cubans in the early 1900s. Although many of these buildings have since been subdivided into apartments, the elegance of old Vedado can still be found simply by walking around the area. Today Vedado has eclipsed the old town as the engine room of the city. Much of Havana's commercial activity takes place on or around La Rampa (Calle 23), Vedado's most prominent artery. The area lacks the beauty and charm of Habana Vieja, but is nevertheless well worth a visit. Being laid out in a simplified grid pattern, it is relatively easy to explore.

Sandwiched between the old town and Vedado is the district aptly known as **Centro Habana**. This is an area where very few tourists venture as there are few facilities for them. Walking around this area, you quickly understand why Havana is sometimes referred to as a City of Columns; almost every building displays either one or a mixture of the Corinthian, Doric or Ionic types of this structure. The reasoning behind these columns was not simply aesthetic although obviously that was a prime consideration. The galleries formed by the colonnades made for excellent shelter from both the tropical sun and the rain. With the pre-eminence of fading pastel colours, again typically Cuban, Centro Habana could be described as one big tropical umbrella. Along with Habana Vieja, Centro Habana is the most populated and overcrowded part of the city. It is very much an area where life takes place on the streets as playing children, chatting neighbours and domino-playing elderlies vie for space. The affluence that once marked the area has long since disappeared and the crumbling neoclassical frontages bear a sad testimony to the decline of the city during the last few decades. Nevertheless, it is an interesting part of Havana and one worthy of exploration.

Further to the west is the area known as **Miramar** which is home to some of the most expensive hotels and restaurants in Havana. It also houses the majority of the country's foreign embassies.

The tree-lined avenues and stately mansions on and around Fifth Avenue (Calle 5) suggest that this is where Havana's elite reside. This was the case prior to the Revolution and the exclusivity of the area remains. The area contains a few interesting museums, most notably the Museo del Ministerio del Interior (on Fifth Avenue and Calle 14) which will be of interest to any one wanting to brush up on the antics of the cold war.

Havana also developed beyond the harbour to the east, an area now home to the districts of **Alamar** and **Habana del Este**. Built to a Bulgarian design, these areas are best described as functional and utilitarian. At worst they can be called vulgar and depressing. They were erected largely by volunteer mini-brigade workforces and, although they would not win any design-award prizes, they at least house people and are an improvement on the pre-revolutionary shanty towns. This is an area where most tourists don't go and there is little of any interest to recommend it.

To the south of Vedado is the area known as **Plaza de la Revolución** which is where you will find the offices of the Ministry of Interior (complete with huge mural of Che Guevara). The square has witnessed many a long-winded speech from El Commandante and, most recently, was the scene of a public show of support for Castro following the August 1994 disturbances.

GETTING THERE AND AWAY

Almost all people entering the country do so at Havana's José Martí International Airport. The airport has three terminals with Terminal One handling all Cubana domestic and international flights. Terminal Two accommodates all other international flights including those chartered from Miami, while Terminal Three is where you will find all Aerocaribbean charter flights bound for places such as Cayo Largo and Varadero.

The airport is situated 25km southwest of the city of Havana. It is possible to catch a bus or hitch a ride on the main road about 1km walk from the airport, but after a long flight you are more likely to opt for a taxi. The cost of a fare into any part of Havana should set you back no more than $12–14.

If you have brought your bicycle and intend to ride into town, the journey to Habana Vieja will take a little over an hour. The road and scenery on the way is flat and featureless and, although traffic isn't particularly heavy, the old Russian lorries with whom you will be sharing the road belch out enough fumes and pollution to make the journey a rather unpleasant and dirty one. Cycling at night (which you will have to do if you arrive on a Cubana or Viasa flight) is not recommended as the roads are potholed and your personal safety is much more at risk in the dark. Better to pay the extra cost and make your way into town in a taxi.

When leaving Cuba the same options of getting to the airport apply. It is possible to catch an airport bus (look out for the Aeropuerto sign) at the Parque Central. The buses are extremely irregular, however, and it is unlikely that you will want to take the chance unless you have plenty of time. Taxis are relatively easy to obtain, either by booking them from your hotel or hailing them on the street. Black-market taxis operate in Vedado and around the Hotel Inglaterra if you want to save an extra couple of dollars.

The facilities available at the international departure lounge are primitive by international standards and if you want to do some last-minute present buying you arc better off doing it in Havana (although you are unlikely to find a great deal there either). These facilities are, however, superior to those available in the domestic departure lounge, although there is now a bank in the forecourt where you can cash travellers cheques. Standing in the international departure lounge as you prepare to leave Cuba is a little like participating in a grand wake. Hundreds of Cubans with mournful stares and tear-filled eyes hug their departing relatives as they make their way to the departure gates for the return flights to Miami. Others simply look on, wishing they were getting on the plane with them. When Castro does finally introduce market reforms the person who owns the Kleenex franchise at the José Martí International Airport will be quick to make a fortune!

Airline offices

Almost all of the airline offices are conveniently situated in the same street, La Rampa (Calle 23) in Vedado (the end close to the Malecón). Office hours are 08.30 to 16.00 Monday to Friday and most offices are open from 08.00 to 13.00 on Saturday.

Aerocaribbean Calle 23 No 64, Vedado; tel: 7 797525; fax: 7 335016
Aeroflot Calle 23 No 64, Vedado; tel: 7 706292; fax: 7 333288
Aeromexico José Martí International Airport; tel: 7 707701–09; fax: 7 335169
Air Canada Calle 23 No 64, Vedado; tel: 7 333730; fax: 7 333729
Cubana Calle 23 No 64, Vedado; tel: 7 74911; fax: 7 333323
Iberia Calle 23 No 64, Vedado; tel: 7 335041; fax: 7 335061
KLM Calle 23 No 64, Vedado; tel: 7 333730; fax: 7 333739
LACSA Hotel Havana Libre, Calle L esq 23; tel: 7 333114; fax: 7 333728
LTU Calle 23 No 64, Vedado; tel: 7 333524; fax: 7 333590
Martinair Calle 23 No 64, Vedado; tel: 7 333730; fax: 7 333729
Mexicana Calle 23 No 64, Vedado; tel: 7 333511
Viasa Hotel Habana Libre, Calle L esq 23; tel: 7 333130; fax: 7 333611.

Departure tax
Unfortunately there is one and it is $12. You must pay this at a separate desk after checking in your baggage.

Representatives and embassies in Havana

The United Kingdom Embassy is at Calle 34 No 708, between Calles 7 and 17, Miramar; tel: 7 331717; fax: 7 338104. It is open between the hours of 08.30 and 12.30, Monday to Friday. The United States does not have an embassy in Cuba (yet). US interests are represented by the Swiss Embassy based at Calle Calzada between Calles L and M, Vedado; tel: 7 300551. Australian interests are looked after by the Mexican Embassy situated on Calle 12 No 518, between Avenidas 5 and 7; tel: 7 332498. Other embassies in Havana include:

Argentina Calle 36 No 511, entrance on Avenidas 5 and 7, Miramar; tel: 7 332549

Austria Calle 4 No 101, corner of Avenida 1, Miramar; tel: 7 225825

Brazil Calle 16 No 503, entrance on Avenidas 5 and 7, Miramar; tel: 7 332021

Canada Calle 30 No 518, on the corner of Avenida 7, Miramar; tel: 7 332516

France Calle 14 No 312, entrance on Avenidas 3 and 5, Miramar; tel: 7 332308

Germany Calle 28 No 313, entrance on Avenidas 3 and 5, Miramar; tel: 7 332460

Italy Avenida Paseo No 606, entrance on Calles 25 and 27, Vedado; tel: 7 333334

Netherlands Calle 8 No 308, entrance on Avenidas 3 and 5; Miramar; tel: 7 332511

Russia and the Commonwealth of Independent States (CIS) Avenida 5 No 6402, entrance on Calle 62; tel: 7 331085

Spain Calle Cárcel No 51, at corner of Calle Zuleta, Habana Vieja; tel: 7 338025

Venezuela Calle 36A No 704, entrance on Calle 7; tel: 7 332662

GETTING AROUND

By train

Havana has three railway stations, but the one that you are most likely to use is Central Station in the southwest corner of Habana Vieja on Calle Agido (tel: 7 621920). This is where you will catch the services to Santiago de Cuba, Matanzas, Camagüey and most stations east. If you are heading for Pinar del Río you will need to make your way to the Station of 19th November (Estación 19 de Noviembre). This station is also known as Tulipan. Less conveniently situated than Central Station, Tulipan is on the junction of Calle Tulipan and Calle Hidalgo to the southwest of the Plaza de la Revolución.

You can book tickets for all train services from Officina Ladis, the official organisation licensed to sell train tickets to foreigners. They are in Centro Habana behind the Central Station at Calles Arsenal and Cienfuegos, tel: 7 621770 (office hours 07.00–19.00 daily).

Havana's third railway station is in Casablanca, part of the city that lies across the bay and is of little interest to tourists. This station operates local line services and is little used by visitors to Cuba.

City transport
Buses
Havana's bus system is slowly grinding to a halt as petrol shortages and lack of spare parts means that vehicles can no longer be kept on the road. Those buses that do operate are invariably full to the rafters. Queues are long and patience is a prerequisite. It is possible to get hold of a bus route map but the services indicated on it are often subject to cancellation or are the work of a local route planner's vivid imagination. Buses are less crowded very early in the morning or late at night and, if you do decide to travel this way, you will at least guarantee yourself novelty status as you will probably be the only non-Cuban aboard. Getting around by bus is cheap (your fare can be paid for in Cuban centavos) but impractical. If you decide to give it a go, ask the locals for advice on which bus services are worth queuing for. And take a good book to read while you wait.

Taxis
Fortunately there is now a good supply of tourist taxis. There are two types: licensed and unlicensed and you should expect to pay around 30% less in an unlicensed taxi. Licensed taxis are operated by the state-owned Turistaxis and Cubanacán. Turistaxis can be found outside many of the larger hotels while Cubanacán taxis usually have to be ordered. Metered taxis are also now in operation. They are approximately 25% cheaper than the official tourist taxis.

Unlicensed taxis are operated by entrepreneurial freelancers who hang around the larger hotels, particularly in Vedado. There is no need to seek them out as they will approach you. This is one of the few opportunities for you to haggle during your stay in Cuba. If you are travelling alone then you should obviously be more cautious when using one of these cabs.

Licensed taxis can be ordered from the following organisations:

Cubanacán	tel: 7 331446/331349
Panataxi	tel: 7 810153/814142/811175
Turistaxi	tel: 7 791940/798820/795665
Veracuba	tel: 7 331890/220224
Transgaviota	tel: 7 237000/810357
Cubalse	tel: 7 336558/336452

Bicycle
Cycling is a great way to get around Havana. The vast majority of people using Havana's roads are cyclists and on the Malecón there are even special bicycle lanes. The roads are generally in good condition, although once you get out into the more remote areas of Havana they begin to

deteriorate. Cycling at night isn't a good idea as most other bicycles (and indeed most cars) do not have lights.

You can hire a bicycle from the Palacio del Turismo for around $10 a day or, alternatively, you can bring your own. If you are intending to do a reasonable amount of biking it is just as well to bring your own bike as the ones available for hire are of an inferior quality. If you do so, bring a good lock as bike theft is a problem in Havana.

ACCOMMODATION

One thing Havana isn't short of is high-standard hotel accommodation. It is always advisable to book somewhere in advance, especially during the high season, and in fact the immigration officials may insist that you have done so before allowing you into the country. If you do turn up on spec, however, you are more than likely to find an available room.

Hotels
Category 5
Habana Libre (572 rooms), Calles L and 23 (La Rampa), Vedado; tel: 7 305011; fax: 7 328722
This is one of Havana's premier hotels set in the Vedado district. It has international-standard facilities including a restaurant, bar, swimming pool, shopping arcade and tourist bureau. Prior to the Revolution, this hotel was the Havana Hilton and in the transformation seems to have lost whatever personal touch it used to have. It is handily situated and reasonably priced. It is also very popular with package tourists, although even in high season there are always rooms available, so vast is the hotel complex. There is a great view to be had from the top-floor roof-terrace, but you will need to cough up $3 to get in (you do get a cocktail thrown in with the price). If you are intent on taking home souvenirs the dollar shop in the hotel stocks the most extensive array of gifts in the city. A set of tacky maracas will cost you $6 while a wall-mounted crab is a pinch at $5.

Habana Riviera (360 rooms), Avenida Paseo and Malecón, Vedado; tel: 7 305051; fax: 7 304385
A four-star hotel offering air-conditioned accommodation with colour TV and mini bar in all rooms. Facilities include a restaurant, bar, hair salon, swimming pool and tourist bureau.

Hotel Inglaterra (83 rooms), Calles Prado (Paseo Martí) 416 and San Rafael, Centro Habana; tel: 7 338593; fax: 7 338254
Graham Greene buffs will recognise the name as this hotel was immortalised in his novel, *Our Man in Havana*. The Inglaterra is perhaps the most charming of Havana's hotels and is ideally situated overlooking Parque Central on the outskirts of the old town. It is the oldest hotel in the city and was completed in 1875. Its Spanish colonial elegance is typified by its delightful balconies and its lobby which has been decorated with tiles and iron grilles imported from Seville at the end of the 19th century. The Inglaterra was the most popular hotel with visiting correspondents covering the fall of the Batista regime and it remains

one of the most popular hotels for visitors to the country. The lobby makes for an excellent meeting point and the restaurants are generally first-class. You can buy a basic breakfast for around $3 although these days you are no longer allowed to keep replenishing your empty plate. The Italian restaurant, La Stella, serves a decent pizza and the roof-top bar, La Terraza, is a good place to sip a cocktail or two while enjoying the live cabaret. All rooms are air-conditioned and have their own private bath and many have their own individual safe. There is also a unisex beauty salon and a free solarium (not something you would generally need in a tropical country). The Inglaterra, sadly, does not have a swimming pool.

Hotel Melia Cohiba (462 rooms), Avenida Paseo, Vedado; tel: 7 333636; fax: 7 334555
Named after Cuba's premier cigar, this is Cuba's premier hotel. A towering modern blue smoked-glass development, it was opened by Fidel himself in 1994. It has most of the luxury facilities you would expect from a modern five-star hotel including a swimming pool, fitness centre and a shopping arcade. For such a prestigious establishment the location isn't great and there is a distinct lack of charm about the place which leaves me to conclude that the Nacional is a better bet for upmarket tourists on an extravagant budget.

Hotel Nacional (483 rooms), Calles O and 21, Vedado; tel: 7 333564; fax: 7 335054
Prior to the opening of the Melia Cohiba, this was Havana's leading hotel. Positioned on the brow of a hill overlooking the Malecón, the twin towers of the Nacional dominate the area and at night, when the hotel is illuminated, it is the most impressive sight in Vedado. It has been patronised by celebrities such as Winston Churchill, who most likely spent the warm nights puffing a Havana cigar whilst looking north across the Malecón and out to sea. The facilities, as you would expect, are of a high standard and include a swimming pool, several restaurants, cabaret entertainment and air-conditioned rooms with satellite TV. The room rates are of an international standard too.

Hotel Sevilla (188 rooms), Calle Trocadero 55, Habana Vieja; tel: 7 338560; fax: 7 338582
The most beautiful hotel in the old town and the one with the best facilities. Anyone who has read Graham Greene's *Our Man in Havana* will instantly recognise the name, as it is here (in room 501) that Wormold had his rendezvous with the spy-master Hawthorne, receiving his initial instructions on how to operate as a spy.

"'I'm leaving the key of my room in the basin. Fifth floor Seville-Biltmore. Just walk up. Ten tonight. Things to discuss. Money and so on. Sordid issues. Don't ask for me at the desk."

"Don't you need your key?"

"Got a pass key. I'll be seeing you."

Wormold stood up in time to see the door close behind the elegant figure and the appalling slang. The key was there in the washbasin – Room 501.'

The hotel was allowed to fall into a state of disrepair following the Revolution, but it has now been fully refurbished and restored to its former glory. The building is renowned for its beautiful Sevillian patio. It has all the first-class facilities one would expect of such an establishment including three restaurants, four bars, a games room and a swimming pool. It also has a splendid roof-garden restaurant with an excellent view over Havana. You don't have to eat there; you may simply look out over the city. It also has the advantage of being close to some of the most interesting things to do in Havana (eg the Gran Teatro de la Habana – home of the Cuban National Ballet, and the Museum of the Revolution).

Category 4

Hotel Ambos Mundos (54 rooms), Calle Obispo 153 esq Calle Mercaderes, Habana Vieja; tel: 7 669530; fax: 7 669532
Beautifully restored and reopened in 1996, this hotel is set on a prime spot close to the Plaza de Armas in the heart of the old town. It was Hemingway's first place of residence when he arrived in Cuba and an old meeting point for Cuban and international intellectuals. The facilities include air-conditioned rooms with satellite TV, a good restaurant on the sixth floor, and a café-bar on the first floor. A charming place to stay.

Hotel Capri (219 rooms), Calles 21 and N, Vedado; tel: 7 333747; fax: 7 333750
A four-star hotel with good facilities including air-conditioned rooms with colour satellite TV. Other facilities include a car-rental bureau, a barber and a swimming pool.

Hotel and Bungalows Comodoro (124 rooms), Calles 84 and 1ra, Miramar; tel: 7 225551–54; fax: 7 332028
High-class accommodation in the heart of one of Havana's most exclusive areas. Facilities include air-conditioned rooms with TV and mini bar, a selection of restaurants and bars and a swimming pool.

Hotel Plaza (188 rooms), Calle Ignacio Agramonte 267, Habana Vieja; tel: 7 622006–09; fax: 7 639620/12
Set close to the Parque Central, the Plaza is in the same price range as the nearby Hotel Inglaterra but lacks its history or ambience. The roof-terrace offers good views over the city and the food in the restaurant is generally quite tasty (by Cuban standards). It has good facilities including a medical service for residents and a bar and nightclub. It also has a solarium and a tourist shop.

Hotel Presidente (142 rooms), Calles Calzada and G, Vedado; tel: 7 327521–27; fax: 7 323577
This garishly coloured building is a popular place with visiting tourists even though it is set back from the heart of Vedado. It has a sense of style which is lacking from some of the newer hotels and its facilities are generally good. Rooms are air-conditioned and have satellite TV and there is a helpful tourist bureau in the lobby. The hotel also has its own restaurant and bar.

Category 3

Hotel Colina (79 rooms), Calles L and Jovellar, Vedado; tel: 7 323535–38
A characterless hotel set in Vedado with little to recommend it. The rooms are on the poky side and the service not always hospitable. The hotel restaurant/bar is a weekend rendezvous point for local prostitutes. If you want to stay relatively cheaply in Vedado then this will inevitably be one of your options. There is a tourist bureau in the lobby but it seldom gets used. Apart from that the hotel provides few services.

Hotel Deauville (141 rooms), Calle Galiano and Malecón, Centro Habana; tel: 7 628051–59
The Hotel Deauville is set in a prime position on the Malecón, midway between Habana Vieja and Vedado. Together with the Hotel Nacional it has some of the best views in the city. Unfortunately the Deauville has allowed itself to become slightly run down although it retains its popularity among visiting package tourists. It is renowned for two things: firstly, for Martha Gellhorn's observation that the building is 'a post-war pre-revolutionary blight on the Malecón' and, secondly, it was the one tourist hotel that was attacked and looted during the riots in Havana in August 1994. It has reasonably good facilities and boasts its own swimming pool.

Hotel Lincoln (135 rooms), Calle Galiano 164 at the corner of Calle Virtudes, Centro Habana; tel: 7 628061–69
This unassuming hotel is a popular place with lower-budget tourists. It has adequate facilities including a decent restaurant and a roof-top bar. The atmosphere is friendly and relaxed.

Hotel St Johns (94 rooms), Calle O between Calles 23 and Humboldt, Vedado; tel: 7 326501–03
A good mid-range hotel in Vedado with its own swimming pool.

Hostal Valencia (11 rooms), Calle Oficios between Calles A and Obrapia, Habana Vieja; tel: 7 623801
This beautiful building was formerly an old Spanish colonial house belonging to the Marquess of Sotolorgo. Built in the mid-18th century, it fell into a state of disrepair and was used, in more recent times, as a peso hotel for Cubans only. 1989 saw the completion of renovation work which enabled it to become a fully-fledged dollar hotel and it is certainly one of the most delightful examples of colonial architecture in the city. The rooms do not have numbers but are named after Spanish towns and cities. One drawback is that the hostel is situated in a narrow street and the early morning noise tends to reverberate throughout the entire building. Nevertheless, the setting more than makes up for any lack of sleep and the staff are charming and friendly. You will need to book in advance as there is limited space and rooms are deservedly sought after. Facilities include a good restaurant and bar and a tourist information service. Live music is a popular draw over the weekends.

Category 2
Hotel Caribbean (36 rooms), Prado 164 at the corner of Calle Colón, Centro Habana; tel: 7 622071
The most popular hotel with low-budget travellers and probably the cheapest legitimate accommodation in Havana. In its defence, it is clean and the staff are quite friendly. It is also nicely placed for a stroll down Obispo Street or along the Prado to the Malecón. Security isn't wonderful, however, and the rooms suffer from a shortage of natural light and can be unbearably hot. To say that the plumbing is erratic is an understatement and crawlies can be a problem, although the staff are always quick to fumigate affected rooms. Still, you pay for what you get and at the Caribbean you don't pay too much.

Hotel Morro (20 rooms) Calles 3 and D, Vedado; tel: 7 320530/323740
A small hotel with basic facilities, the Morro has its own restaurant and bar. Rooms are air-conditioned and have colour TVs. The hotel offers a reasonably priced laundry service.

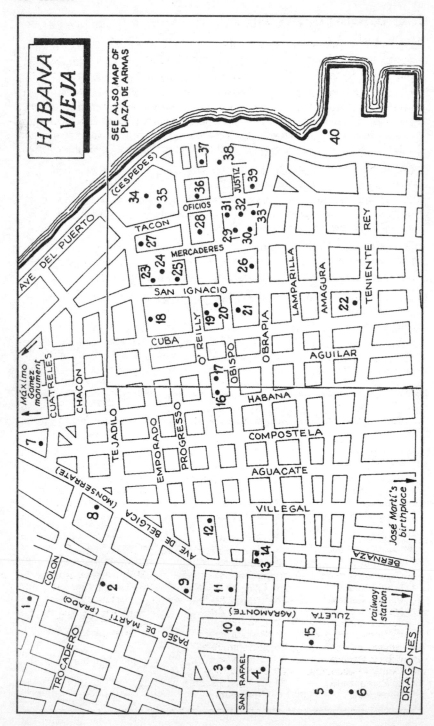

EATING AND DRINKING

There is an abundance of restaurants, cafés and bars throughout Havana, but even those catering for the highest spending tourists are not immune to the food shortages which are part of everyday life. Don't be fooled by the extensive range of dishes you see on most menus. The reality is that around half of those dishes will not be available. It is possible to eat fairly well for a reasonable price. Expect to pay around $8–12 for an evening meal in a restaurant. You can pay a lot more in some of the more exclusive restaurants, although this is no guarantee of quality and portion sizes are often a disappointment.

Almost every tourist hotel has at least one restaurant and some, like the Hotel Inglaterra or the Nacional, have three or more. While eating in your hotel might be convenient, you will miss out on some decent food and some excellent music if you don't venture out to the restaurants and cafés of Habana Vieja in particular.

The best meals to be had are in people's homes, *casa particulars* or in one of the ever burgeoning number of *paladares* in Havana.

Paladar Mi Bohio, Calle 22 No.711 e/7ma. Y 9na. Miramar; tel: 7 227332
Has the reputation of being one of the best *paladares* in Havana. $10 per head excluding drinks.

Paladar La Casa, Calle 30 between No 865 e/26 y 41, Nuevo Vedado; tel: 7 34869
An up-market *paladar* favoured by affluent Habaneros with the accent on Cordon Bleu. Still only $10 per head excluding drinks. They also have a wine list!

Paladar Sagitario, Virtudes No. 619, Gervasio y Escobar, Centro Habana; tel: 7 783205
Good seafood and pork dishes available. $8 per head. Drinks extra (beer $1).

Key to map

1 Hotel Caribbean	15 Cinema Payret	31 Perfumery Museum
2 Hotel Sevilla	16 La Lluvia de Oro	32 Casa de los Arabes
3 Hotel Inglaterra	Restaurant	33 Numismatic Museum
4 Gran Teatro	17 Palacio del Turismo	34 Castillo de la Real
5 National Museum of	18 La Bodeguita del Medio	Fuerza
Natural History	19 Café O'Reilly	35 National Museum of
6 Capitolio	20 Café Paris	the Castle of the
7 Museum of the	21 Hotel Ambos Mundos	Royal Forces
Revolution	22 Plaza Vieja	36 Plaza de Armas
8 Granma Memorial	23 El Patio Restaurant	37 Hotel Santa Isabel
9 Hotel Plaza	24 Plaza de la Catedral	38 El Patio Colonial
10 Parque Central	25 Colonial Art Museum	Restaurant
11 Moderna Poseia	26 Casa de Africa	39 Hostal Valencia
bookstore/Manzana	27 Don Giovanni	40 Los Marinos
de Gómez shopping	Restaurant	Restaurant
centre	28 Museum of the City	
12 Edificio Bacardi	of Havana	
13 Floridita Restaurant	29 La Mina Café	
14 La Zaragozana	30 La Torre de Marfil	
Restaurant	Restaurant	

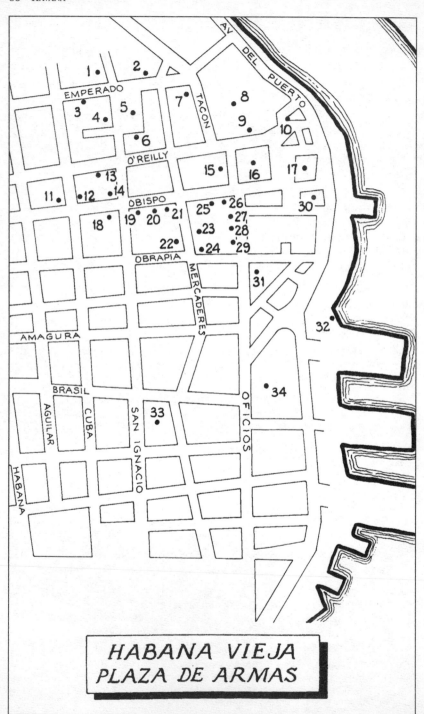

HABANA VIEJA
PLAZA DE ARMAS

Paladares Dona Rosario and **Arriba de la Bola**, 258 and 263 Calle San Lazaro, behind the Deauville hotel, Centro Habana.
Next door to each other, both of these *paladares* serve good food for around $8 per head including coffee. Other drinks are extra. Very popular.

Habana Vieja
Floridita, Calles Obispo and Avenida de Belgica, Habana Vieja; tel: 7 631111
Open: 12.00–01.00
This is the place where Hemingway used to come for his daiquiris (they were actually invented in the place). Hemingway developed his own recipe, the Papa's Special, which omitted the sugar; they still serve them here. Since being renovated the restaurant/bar has lost all of its old charm and is nowhere near as popular as that other Hemingway favourite, La Bodeguita del Medio. Food is generally reasonable although expensive and if Hemingway were alive and drinking today, he would probably need to re-negotiate the size of his royalty payments with his publisher as, at $5 per daiquiri, getting drunk does not come cheap.

La Bodeguita del Medio, Calle Empedrado No 207, Habana Vieja; tel: 7 624498
Open: 10.00–23.00
Loosely translated, this means the 'Little Store in the Middle of the Block'. Although this place is popular with tourists, it still retains that pre-revolutionary, bohemian feel and it is easy to understand why Hemingway used to come here to drink his *mojitos*. Almost every inch of the walls of the place bears the comments and signatures of those who have frequented it down the years. Hemingway's observation of 'My daiquiri in the Floridita, my *mojito* in the Bodeguita' is given pride of place. Other famous people who have been known to drink here include Graham Greene, Salvador Allende, Errol Flynn and even Fidel himself. The food is pricey but good and the *mojitos*, at $3 each, are probably not as strong as 'Ernesto' would have taken them. However, this place is an essential visit for anyone coming to Havana. Live music is a feature most nights. If you can find any space left on the walls, don't forget to tell the world you've been here.

Key to map
1 Wilfred Lam Center
2 Catedral de la Habana
3 La Bodeguita del Medio
4 El Patio Restaurant
5 Plaza de la Catedral
6 Galeria Arte Colonial
7 Don Giovanni Restaurant
8 Castillo de la Real Fuerza
9 National Museum of the Castle of the Royal Forces
10 Castillo de la Real Fuerza
11 Palacio del Turismo
12 La Lluvia de Oro Restaurant
13 Café O'Reilly
14 Café Paris
15 Museum of the City of Havana
16 Plaza de Armas
17 Hotel Santa Isabel
18 Hotel Ambos Mundos
19 Panderia San José (cake shop)
20 Farmacia Taqvechel (pharmacy)
21 La Luz Café
22 La Casa del Habana
23 Map shop
24 La Torre de Marfil Restaurant
25 Casa de Agua
26 La Mina Café
27 Numismatic Museum
28 Al Medina Restaurant
29 Casa de los Arabes
30 Café de Cuba
31 Hostal Valencia
32 Los Marinos Restaurant
33 Plaza Vieja
34 Iglesia de San Francisco

La Mina, Calle Obispo No 109, Habana Vieja; tel: 7 620216
Open: 10.00–02.00
Situated on the south side of the Plaza de Armas, this little café is one of the gems of the old town. The food is currently limited to chicken, omelettes or rice and beans but the cocktails are among the best anywhere and a *mojito* will set you back only $2.50. The setting, parallel to the Palacio de los Capitanos Generales is simply glorious and live music played by some of Havana's finest is a feature almost every evening. Many Latin American tourists come here to dance the night away, particularly at weekends. The facade of the building is deceptive, for once you walk into the courtyard you realise that the place is vast. It has recently been extensively refurbished resulting in a larger restaurant area as well as some small shopping facilities. Whether coming here for a night out or simply taking a well-earned rest after a morning of sightseeing, La Mina is a must for anyone in and around Habana Vieja.

El Patio, Calle San Ignacio and the corner of Empedrado, Plaza de la Catedral, Habana Vieja; tel: 7 618511
Open: 12.00–22.00
Its prime site overlooking the Plaza de la Catedral is the main reason why most people come here. It can't be because of the food, which is ordinary and over-priced. An average meal here costs over $25 per head and the downstairs café doesn't rate too highly in the value-for-money stakes either. Nevertheless, it is a good place to chill out over a cocktail while taking in the full glory of Cuba's finest baroque architecture that surrounds you. The building is an old converted Spanish house dating back to the 18th century. In the evenings there is usually live music or a cabaret.

Café O'Reilly, Calle O'Reilly between Calles San Ignacio and Cuba, Habana Vieja
Open: 12.00–23.00
Not a place you would come to for food as the menu deals only in snacks, but one of the friendliest and most pleasant bars in the old town and certainly one of the cheapest – *mojitos* for $2. Formerly a popular haunt of Havana's gay population (it is now equally popular with visiting tourists), this is a great place to meet the locals and make friends. It is also handy for most of the other interesting bars around the Plaza de Armas and Calle Obispo. In the daytime, a resident cigar maker will hand roll you a good smoke for a dollar.

El Patio Colonial, Calles Obispo and Baratillo, Habana Vieja; tel: 7 338146
Open: 12.00–24.00
Stuck away in the far southeast corner of the Plaza de Armas is where you'll find this place. Like La Mina the menu is restricted, although they do knock up a tasty pizza. Drink prices are around the same as La Mina (cocktails $2–3, beer $2) and the open-air setting is pleasant enough. The two caged cockerels kept in the corner are for display only. They don't fight, although they are liable to give you a nasty peck if you put your fingers through the cage. Music is played over a hi-fi system which, in a nation of sublime musicians, constitutes cheating in my book.

Café Paris, Calles Obispo and San Ignacio, Habana Vieja.
Open: 11.00–02.00
A popular haunt for both Cubans and tourists and a good place to eat and drink cheaply, this place is always busy and, although the advertised closing hours are 02.00, it is often open much later, especially at weekends.

La Zaragozana, Avenida de Belgica and Calle Obispo, Habana Vieja;
tel: 7 631062
Open: 12.00–22.00
A good place to come if you are hot, as the air-conditioning system in this restaurant is designed to give you hypothermia within an hour of arrival. The food here, as so often is the case in Cuba, is very over-priced (rice with seafood $20, lobster *enchilada* $25) and the decor and ambience is unimaginative and flat. The bar sells reasonably priced beer and cocktails (beer $2, cocktails $2.50–3.50) and it is possible to come here just for a drink without having to eat. Western pop dominates over Afro–Cuban and for that alone you should deduct points.

La Torre de Marfil, Calles Oficios and Obrapia, Habana Vieja; tel: 7 623466
Open: 12.00–21.00
The majority of people who visit Havana do not anticipate spending too much time indulging in Chinese cuisine. However, to fail to visit this restaurant is to spurn the opportunity of some of the best food in the capital. Cantonese food is the speciality and after a few days of rice and beans or omelettes, a Cantonese banquet for around $12 per head comes as something of a godsend. The staff are all Chinese and form part of a small but long-established Chinese community. The restaurant is close to the Plaza de Armas.

La Lluvia de Oro, Calle Obispo, Habana Vicja
Open: 10.00–02.00
More of a café than a restaurant, this is a good place to visit if you want to eat and drink cheaply. It is also open very late at weekends, often until four and five in the morning, and it is a good place to come to meet more affluent Cubans. Pizzas and sandwiches average around $2.50, ice-cream (*helados*) $1 and beer a mere $1.50. Not a particularly sophisticated place, but central and convenient.

Don Giovanni, Calles Tacon and Empedrado, Habana Vieja; tel: 7 614445
Open: 12.00–22.00
One of the most beautiful settings for a restaurant in Havana and one of the prettiest buildings, this restaurant has a pleasant view over the harbour while the courtyard has a small café selling snacks. It is worth coming here just to look around the building as it is a prime example of the Spanish architectural legacy. The food (mainly Italian cuisine) is good and the set meals at $12–15 per head are excellent value.

Los Marinos, Avenida del Puerto (Avenida Carlos Manuel de Cespedes),
Habana Vieja
Open: 16.00–01.00
This is actually a moored boat with a bar above and below deck. It's a pleasant place to take a drink as it is cooled by the sea breeze. It's inexpensive and popular with more affluent Cubans (and on the top deck, Cuban prostitutes). Though there is food served, the majority of people tend to visit this place to drink and socialise rather than eat.

Al Medina (Casa de los Arabes), Calle Oficios, Habana Vieja; tel: 7 630862
Open: 16.00–22.00 (closed Wednesday)
The food served here doesn't quite match the tourist brochure declaration that this is Havana's home of Arabic cuisine but it is worth coming here for the beauty of the setting alone.

Vedado

Most of the restaurants and bars in this area are actually in the tourist hotels, but if you are prepared to venture out you will come across some reasonable venues where you can eat, drink and be merry. Vedado pales in most aspects when compared to Habana Vieja and the restaurant and bar category is no exception.

La Torre, Edificio Focsa, Calle 17 at the corner of Calle M, Vedado; tel: 7 325650
Open: 11.30–24.00
This exclusive restaurant is set on the top (36th) floor of the FOCSA building, the tallest in Havana. The views over the city are stunning and it's worth coming here – if only for a cocktail – for that reason. When they are busy, you are required to eat as well as drink here. A meal will cost you over $40 per head. The food is good but at a price.

Las Bulerias, Calle L and 23, Vedado
Open: 11.00–02.00
Adjacent to the Habana Libre Hotel, this place is a bar/restaurant/disco rolled into one. Although the menu is limited (pizzas, pasta and sandwiches), the food is cheap and edible. You also get good sized portions for your money – a claim not always possible to make in Cuba. Pasta Napolitana costs $2 and a glass of imported beer $1.50. Fridays and Saturdays are disco nights, starting at around 22.00. This seems to be one of the current hot spots in Vedado and, if you are having soul and ragga withdrawal symptoms, you might want to check this place out. It is also a good place to meet young better-off Cubans with a penchant for first-world music and fashion.

Emperador, Calle 17 between Calles M and N, Vedado, Edificio Focsa;
tel: 7 324998
Open: 19.00–22.00
Another venue in the FOCSA building serving over-priced meals for people with dollars to burn. Long-established, this restaurant caters for visiting diplomats and the like. There is a fairly strict dress code and men are required to wear jackets. Reservations are usually required. Expect to pay $40 per head and upwards.

Polinesio (Habana Libre Hotel), Calle 23 and L, Vedado; tel: 7 334011
Open: 12.00–22.00
Another long-established restaurant in the Habana Libre Hotel. Both the decor and the menu are Polynesian as the name suggests and a meal averages around $12 without drinks. The food here has a deserved reputation for being very good. There is usually a Polynesian cabaret of dubious authenticity to entertain you while you dine.

Coppelia Ice Cream Park, between Calles L and K, Vedado
This place is popular with Cubans and tourists alike, although as a tourist you will have to pay in dollars. The ice-cream is actually quite good and, at around $1 for two scoops, reasonably priced. This is a good place to meet young Cubans who flock here during the daytime. In the evening it is less crowded and you are more likely to get in. The design of the park is like an adventure playground gone wrong – all concrete and rusting metal. If you're in Vedado this is a good place to check out.

Miramar

Miramar has several restaurants, both independent and as part of the tourist hotels. This is not the place to come to on a limited budget as it is the most exclusive part of Havana and that is reflected in the standards and prices of the food served.

Tocororo, Calle 18 at the corner of Calle 3a, Miramar; tel: 7 334530
Open: 12.00–01.00.
One of the most expensive restaurants in Havana, it is also one of the best. A meal for two will set you back around $100 minimum including drinks. If you want to impress your partner on the last night or if you have a book of travellers cheques to spare, this is the place to come. Dress to impress – jackets are a must for men.

Morambon, Avenida 5 at the corner of Calle 32, Miramar; tel: 7 23336
Open: 12.00–02.00
An international-class restaurant, this serves international-style cuisine at international prices. Dress smartly or you won't get in.

Others

There are a host of pizzerias dotted around Havana although, due to the chronic shortages, not all of them are fully operational. You can usually spot the ones that are by the huge queues outside and, if you want to try to get in, you will have to join the queue and wait. There is no guarantee that once you are in you will be served as the feeling is (and understandably so) that tourists are adequately catered for by the dollar hotels, restaurants and cafés and that you should be spending your dough on dollar pizzas rather than peso pizzas.

If you are feeling adventurous you may wish to make the trip west of Miramar to the Hemingway Marina where the pick of the restaurants is **Papa's,** a typical tourist trap with reasonable but over-priced food and generally not a great deal to commend it.

NIGHTLIFE

Prior to the Revolution, Havana was, together with Beirut, regarded as the hottest international nightspot in the world. With the dawn of the age of prohibition in the United States, people used to flock into the city from across the Florida Straits to engage in all manner of activities. Anything went – prostitution, gambling, dope. Havana had the reputation of a city where you could get anything – at a price. The Mafia ploughed a lot of money into the hotel and casino business and even famous film stars such as George Raft had a stake in the city. All this was swept aside when Castro came to power and, although there is plenty to do in the city these days, it is doubtful whether Havana will ever return to those days of debauchery and excess.

Today, nightlife for the tourist revolves around cabaret shows and Afro–Caribbean music and dance. If you simply want to while away the

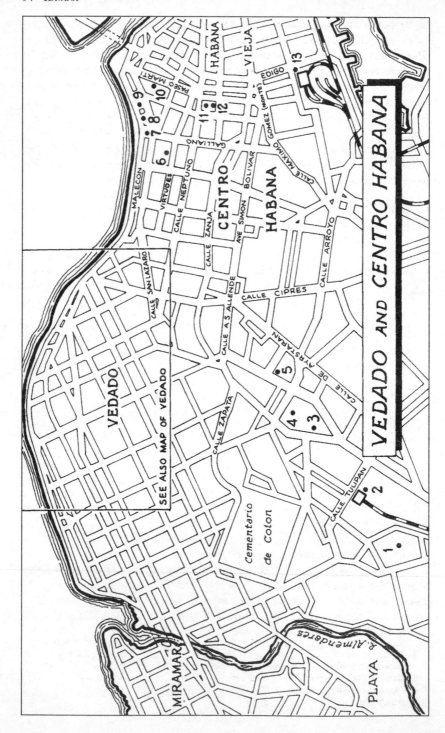

night becoming acquainted with the potency of Cuban cocktails in a quiet and friendly bar, there are plenty of places where you can go. There has also been a move towards discothèques and nightclubs catering for more European and North American tastes, many of these being found in the tourist hotels. Only the more affluent Cubans attend these as, being priced in dollars and aimed specifically at the growing tourist market, the vast majority could never afford to get in, let alone buy a drink. No doubt things will change and there will be a more general integration of tourists and Cubans in Havana nightlife but, whatever your tastes, you should find that after dark Havana will be able to satisfy most of them.

Cabaret

Tropicana, Calle 72 No 4,504, Marianao; tel: 7 205144/204215
Open: 21.00–03.00 (closed on Monday)

> 'It was not a night Wormold was ever likely to forget. He had chosen on Milly's seventeenth birthday to take her to the Tropicana. It was a more innocent establishment than the National in spite of the roulette-rooms, through which visitors passed before they reached the cabaret. Chorus-girls paraded twenty feet up among the great palm-trees, while pink and mauve searchlights swept the floor. A man in bright blue evening clothes sang in Anglo-American about Paree. Then the piano was wheeled away into the undergrowth, and the dancers stepped down like awkward birds from among the branches.'
>
> *Our Man in Havana* – Graham Greene

One of the most famous nightclub/cabaret shows in the world, the Tropicana is still the riot of colour and energy it was more than 50 years ago. Involving almost 300 singers, dancers and musicians, you wonder how such an ostentatious display can possibly be put on by a country in the midst of a grave economic crisis. The answer is that the show is strictly for the tourists and, such is its unique appeal, it remains extremely popular with visitors. A night out here can be expensive, especially if you choose to eat. The admission alone is $50. You can book nights out in advance usually through the tour operators at your hotel or else through the Palacio del Turismo. Few people make their own way here as it can be difficult finding transport back to the city.

Salon Rojo, Hotel Capri, Calles 21 and N, Vedado; tel: 7 320511
Open: 21.00–03.00 (closed on Monday)

Palacio de la Salsa, Kawama Caribbean, Hotel Habana Riviera, Paseo Malecón, Vedado; tel: 7 305051
Open: 22.00–04.00 (closed on Wednesday)

Key to map

1 Zoological park	6 Hotel Lincoln	10 Hotel Caribbean
2 Estacion de 19	7 Hotel Deauville	11 Hotel Inglaterra
Noviembre (Tulipan)	8 Paladar Dona	12 Gran Teatro
3 José Martí monument	Rosario	13 Central station
4 Plaza de la Revolución	9 Paladar Arriba de la	
5 Bus station	Bola	

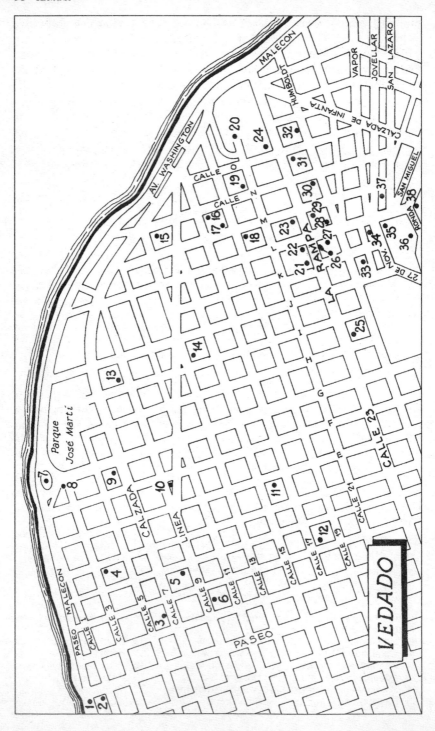

VEDADO

El Cortijo, Hotel Vedado, Calle O No 244, between Calles 25 and Humboldt, Vedado; tel: 7 326501
Open: 22.30–03.00 (closed on Monday)

El Parisien Hotel Nacional de Cuba, Calles O and 21, Vedado; tel: 7 333564
Open: 22.00–04.00 (closed on Wednesday).

Salsa Café, Hotel Habana Libre, Calle L between Calles 23 and 25, Vedado; tel: 7 305011
Open: 22.00–04.00

La Maison, Calle 16 No 701 and Calle 7a, Miramar; tel: 7 331543
Open: 20.00–02.00

Papa's, Hemingway Marina; tel: 7 331150
Open: 21.00–01.30

Ribera Azul, Hotel Deauville, Calle Galiana and Malecón, Centro Habana; tel: 7 628051
Open: 22.00–02.30

All of the above offer an entertaining and colourful night out. They all take their lead from the Tropicana although none of them are on such a grand scale. Nevertheless, if you fancy an evening of cabaret closer to home (especially if you are staying in Vedado where most of these clubs are situated) then any one of these clubs will do the trick.

Nightclubs/discos

Again, many of these can be found in the tourist hotels of Vedado, Habana Vieja and Miramar. It is always worth checking with the locals who will tell you which are the hottest clubs (although this will invariably be based on reputation as the vast majority of Cubans have never set foot in one) and, as with everywhere else, things change and clubs go in and out of fashion. The concept of the Western-style nightclub has begun to take off in Cuba and no doubt more will spring up in future, but for the moment at least the music retains, in general, a sense of its Afro–Cuban origins.

Key to map

1 Hotel Habana Riviera	14 Café Teatro Bretch	26 La Buleries Restaurant
2 Hotel Melia Cohiba	15 Amanecer Nightclub	27 La Taverna de Cuba
3 Teatro Hubert de Blanch	16 Emperador Restaurant	28 Hotel Habana Libre
4 Hotel Morro	17 La Torre Restaurant and Edificio FOCSA	29 Sofia
5 El Jardin Restaurant	18 Hotel Victoria	30 Hotel Vedado
6 Teatro Mella	19 Hotel Capri	31 La Rampa Cinema
7 Calixto Garcia	20 Hotel Nacional	32 Hotel St Johns
8 Ministry of Tourism	21 Coppelia Ice Cream Park	33 Casa del Estudeate Universitario
9 Hotel Presidente	22 Cine Yara	34 Teatro Sotano
10 Galeria de la Habana	23 El Mandarin	35 University
11 National Museum of Decorative Arts	24 Airline offices	36 Felipe Poey Museum of Natural History
12 Sayonara Bar	25 El Conchito Restaurant	37 Hotel Colina
13 Restaurante Da Rosina		38 Napoleonic Museum

El Galeón, Habana Vieja; tel: 7 338600–02; fax: 7 338536
The Galleon, as the name suggests, is a mock ship of war which has been fitted out as a restaurant/nightclub. It began operating late in 1993 and has on more than one occasion been the victim of an attempted hijack by Cubans whose idea of a good night out is stealing a ship and sailing it to Florida. It sets off for an 18km trip westbound at around 22.00 and by the time it returns at 16.00 you will have had the opportunity to sample some good food, some over-priced alcohol and the usual vibrant *salsa* music (pop music is also played). At $10 for the admission alone and $35 if you want a meal to go with it, it's hardly a cheap night out. It is, however, good fun and there is always that element of mystery and suspense hanging in the air generated by the possibility (albeit remote) that you might finish the evening off with a nightcap in Miami.

Disco Bar Caribe, Hotel Bio Caribe, Calle 158 between Calles 29 and 31, Vedado; tel: 7 217375
Open: 22.00–05.00 (closed on Wednesday)
Salsa, rumba and hip-hop and drinks at $3 a throw.

Salsateca Río Club, Calle 4 between Calle 3a and Avenida 5a, Miramar; tel: 7 293389
Open: 21.00–04.00
Frequented by affluent tourists and Cubans alike.

Amanecer, Calle 15 between Calles N and O, Vedado; tel: 7 329075
Open: 21.00–04.00 (closed on Tuesday)
One of the more popular nightspots in Vedado.

Cinemas

If you tire of sightseeing and want to relax and take in a movie, then you will be well catered for in Havana. Don't expect to see the latest Hollywood blockbuster; if it comes at all, it will be a few years out of date. Nevertheless, Cuba has a pretty active and impressive domestic film industry and, if your Spanish is up to scratch, it's well worth checking out a Cuban film. You can find out what films are showing where by looking in the daily paper *Granma* or asking at one of the tour desks. The most famous and up-to-date cinema is the Charles Chaplin Cinema at Calle 23 between 10 and 12, Vedado; tel: 7 311101. This is also the venue for the annual Latin American film festival, usually shown in Havana in December. Other cinemas are listed below.

Yara, Calle 23 and Calle L, Vedado; tel: 7 319430
La Rampa, Calle 23 between Calles O and D, Vedado; tel: 7 76146
Payret, opposite the Capitolio building, Habana Vieja; tel: 7 633163

Theatre

The most prestigious theatre in Havana is the **Gran Teatro**, next door to the Hotel Inglaterra opposite Parque Central. Recently refurbished, the theatre is now fully operational. Regular events held there include classical concerts, plays and comedy acts. It occasionally acts as host to the National Ballet of Cuba and the National Opera of Cuba, both of which have a deservedly high international reputation. If the opportunity arises for you to go and see either, take it. Guided tours of the theatre are available for $2.

Teatro Nacional de Cuba, Avenida Paseo and Calle 39, Vedado;
tel: 7 796011/793558
Often a venue for communist party extravaganzas and revolutionary celebrations.

Teatro Sotano, Calle K between Calles 25 and 27, Vedado; tel: 7 320630
Has a reputation for putting on more modern and occasionally radical plays.

Teatro Mella, Linea and Calle A, Vedado; tel: 7 38696/35651
Specialises in modern theatre and contemporary dance.

Teatro Guinol Nacional, Calles M and 19, Vedado; tel: 7 326262/38292
Havana's premier youth theatre.

Teatro Hubert de Blanch, Calle Calzada between Calles A and B, Vedado;
tel: 7 301011
A theatre presenting both classical and modern plays.

Teatro Karl Marx, Avenida 1 between Calles 8 and 10, Miramar;
tel: 7 38292/222248
With a name like this don't expect too much in the way of self-critical, anti-establishment theatre.

SHOPPING

If the truth be told, Havana is not one of the world's premier cities for shopaholics. Indeed, short of buying cigars or rum, there is very little to tempt most people to part with their dollars outside of eating, drinking, sleeping and sightseeing; but then, if you had wanted a shopping holiday, you would have gone to Singapore not Cuba anyway.

Almost all tourist hotels have dollar shops which, as well as cigars and rum, stock the usual tourist artefacts including books, ceramics, *diabolito* dolls and T-shirts with pictures of Che Guevara on the front. There are a few decent bookshops in Calles Obispo and San Rafael which stock pro-Revolutionary material and novels, as well as texts from Latin America and the former Soviet Union. Private enterprise markets aimed at tourists are now established features at the Plaza de Armas and the Plaza de la Catedral in Habana Vieja. These are much more interesting than the vast majority of state-owned shops and, as you are allowed to haggle, you stand a much better chance of securing a bargain. Musical instruments, such as maracas and bongo drums, are a popular buy and in places like Miramar it is now possible to lay your hands on a few designer-label clothes such as Boss and Armani (although they don't come any cheaper).

THINGS TO SEE AND DO
Habana Vieja
It is likely that you will spend most of your time sightseeing in the old town as this is where you will find most of the city's cultural and historical treasures. These apart, Habana Vieja is easily the most interesting and pleasant area to wander around and, if the heat and humidity become too taxing, there are numerous cafés and places to eat, drink and rest.

Museums
Habana Vieja is blessed with a multitude of interesting museums, most of which are open daily except Mondays. It is best to check opening times before visiting any of the museums as they vary, notoriously, from those times published by the tourist information centres. If you cannot contact them on the telephone, the Palacio del Turismo is generally a good guide as to when they are open and closed.

Museum of the City of Havana, Calle Tacon between Calles Obispo and O'Reilly, Habana Vieja
Open: Tuesday to Saturday 11.30–17.00; Sunday 09.00–12.00; closed on Monday
The City Museum is inside the Palace of the Captain's General, formerly the residence of Cuba's colonial governors for over 100 years. This impressive baroque building is one of the most beautiful in Havana and borders the Plaza de Armas, which it dominates. Built in 1791, the palace was the seat of colonial power right up until the formation of the Republic of Cuba in 1898. Officially the home of successive presidents of the Republic from 1902 to 1920, it became the headquarters of the municipal government of Havana from 1920 through to 1950.

The museum itself specialises in artefacts and memorabilia relating to the founding of the city and charts its progress to the present day. There is a special room devoted entirely to the Cuban wars for national independence. There is also the Hall of Flags which contains the flag flown by Carlos Manuel de Cespedes during the wars of independence in 1868. The original Cuban flag is represented alongside those used by the Spanish colonial administrations. There is an interesting art collection of porcelains, paintings and furniture as well as some fascinating exhibits pertaining to Cuban folklore and weaponry.

National Museum of Natural History, Paseo de Martí (Paseo del Prado), Habana Vieja
Open: Tuesday to Saturday 10.15–17.45; Sunday 09.15–12.45; closed on Monday
Housed in the Capitolio building which dominates the Prado, this museum exhibits fauna and flora from all over Cuba. There are

collections of insects, minerals and shells which some may find interesting, but the dominant exhibits are to be found in the anthropology room which houses a collection depicting the life of Cuba's indigenous Indian population which was wiped out shortly after the arrival of the Spanish. The room contains a life-size reproduction of the cave at Punta del Este on the Isle of Youth which, because of its wall paintings, has been declared a national monument. The museum is also home to a small planetarium.

Wilfredo Lam Center, San Ignacio 22, Habana Vieja
Open: Monday to Friday 08.30–16.30; alternate Saturdays 08.30–16.30; closed on Sunday
This centre is dedicated to the visual arts of the Third World and the paintings of the Cuban artist Wilfredo Lam. There is a gallery open to the public exhibiting the work not only of Lam himself but also of other Cuban and foreign artists. The centre also sponsors the Havana Biennial Exhibition which includes exhibits of work from up and coming artists, and various workshops and debates on the visual arts.

José Marti's Birthplace, Calle Leonor Perez No 314, Habana Vieja
Open: Tuesday to Saturday 10.00–18.00; Sunday 09.00–12.45; closed on Monday
This modest building can be found just a few metres from the main railway station in the old town. You would ordinarily expect something more grand and befitting for Cuba's national hero, but Martí was from a humble background and this small museum in a sense serves to underline his immense stature in Cuban history. Born on 28 January 1853, Martí became an important figure in Latin American literature and was an admired poet and journalist before he became a revolutionary inspiration. His life is fairly well documented here and the exhibits, including some of his personal belongings, cover his exile, his influence in forming the Cuban Revolutionary Party and then eventually his death in action on 18 May 1895 at Dos Ríos in Oriente. Other representations of his life include manuscripts, articles, books and paintings.

Casa de los Arabes (House of Arabs), Calle Oficios between Calles Obispo and Obrapia, Habana Vieja
Open: Tuesday to Saturday 14.30–18.30 and 19.00–21.45; Sunday 09.00–13.00; closed on Monday
Set in the heart of the old town, this beautiful building is a prime example of the influences of Moorish architecture in Habana Vieja. It is also a testimony to the presence of a small Arab community in Havana, a fact that comes as a surprise to many.

The hall of the building contains marquetry pieces and ivory and wooden inlays while the white walls are decorated with robes, rugs and

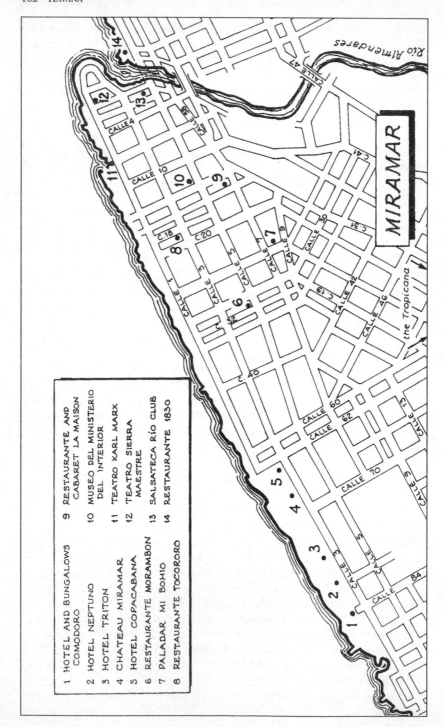

MIRAMAR

Río Almendares

the Tropicana

1 HOTEL AND BUNGALOWS COMODORO
2 HOTEL NEPTUNO
3 HOTEL TRITON
4 CHATEAU MIRAMAR
5 HOTEL COPACABANA
6 RESTAURANTE MORAMBON
7 PALADAR MI BOHIO
8 RESTAURANTE TOCORORO
9 RESTAURANTE AND CABARET LA MAISON
10 MUSEO DEL MINISTERIO DEL INTERIOR
11 TEATRO KARL MARX
12 TEATRO SIERRA MAESTRE
13 SALSATECA RÍO CLUB
14 RESTAURANTE 1830

tapestries, all typically Arabian. The house is home to a collection of 18th and 19th century weapons and ornaments. There is also an interesting collection of model dhows (a type of Arabian sailing boat which is still in use today).

The Casa de los Arabes has a small prayer room for practising Moslems. These days you are more likely to find it being used by visitors to the country rather than practising Cuban Moslems.

Colonial Art Museum, Calle San Ignacio No 61, Plaza de la Catedral, Habana Vieja
Open: Monday and Wednesday to Saturday 09.00–17.00; Sunday 09.00–13.00; closed on Tuesday
Situated on the Plaza de la Catedral – perhaps the most beautiful square in the Caribbean, let alone Havana – the Colonial Art Museum was formerly the home of Don Luis Chacon, the Military Governor of Cuba and the only Cuban who held the position, ordinarily the privilege of the Spanish colonists. Built in 1720 and reputedly the first building erected on what is now the baroque square, the museum houses a collection of exhibits taken from the great colonial mansions dotted around Havana during the 18th and 19th centuries.

Morro–Cabana Historical Military Park
Open: daily 09.00–20.00; Monday and Tuesday 21.00 for the cannon-firing ceremony
Designed by the engineer Antonelli, Morro Castle was built on the hill overlooking the bay to help protect the city from marauding invaders. Antonelli's own supposition was that 'whoever is the master of this hill will be master of Havana.' It didn't always work out that way and in 1762 the castle was stormed by the English who proceeded to take the city as a whole. When rule reverted to the Spanish they decided to reinforce the security of the castle by building the annexes of San Carlos and San Severino de la Cabana, thus developing the most extensive fortress complex in Latin America and the Caribbean.

Morro Castle itself houses a museum which deals with the history of navigation in the area and there are objects recovered from some of the shipwrecks in Havana harbour. The fortresses of San Carlos and San Severino de la Cabana house an extensive collection of antique weapons including a medieval catapult and battering ram.

Historically, at 21.00, the walled city of Havana would resound to the clap of cannon fire emanating from one of the cannons of San Severino de la Cabana, thus signifying the closing of the doors of the city. This tradition has been maintained to this day and every night a loud boom can be heard (most loudly in the old town). It is now possible on certain days to go to the fortress to witness the ceremony marking this tradition.

Museum of the Revolution and Granma Memorial

Refugio No 1 between Monserrate and Zulueta, Habana Vieja
Open: Tuesday to Saturday 13.30–18.00; Sunday 10.00–13.00; closed on Monday

The grand building which houses the museum was formerly the home of the various presidents of the Republic from 1920 to 1960. Today it is a popular draw and its exhibits, which are a collection of photographs, documents, paintings, sculptures, weaponry, personal belongings etc, are all impressive. There are also blood-stained items of clothing worn by luminaries of the Revolution, with Che Guevara's famous black beret given pride of place. The net effect is to give a lively and interesting account of the fight for independence and the success of the Revolution. If you are of the opinion that all museums of this type are a source of establishment propaganda then you won't be disappointed by the Museum of the Revolution. There is a special section, named the Corner of Cretins, which you may find amusing: it satirises the reigns and personalities of various political adversaries including President Reagan and the former dictator General Batista.

If you are wondering what that strange-looking boat is doing moored in a glass case opposite the museum then you obviously haven't been reading up on your Cuban history. It is the *Granma,* the boat that Fidel, Che, Raoul *et al* sailed in from Mexico, landing way off course on the southern coast of Oriente on 2 December 1957.

Cuba's involvement in the Angola war is also represented.

National Museum of the Castle of the Royal Forces

Calle Tacon between Calles Obispo and O'Reilly, Habana Vieja
Open: Tuesday to Saturday 11.30–17.30; Sunday 09.00–12.00; closed on Monday

Located in the Castillo de la Real Fuerza, the oldest fortress in the Americas (built in 1577), this place now houses, among other things, the works of Wilfredo Lam, Amelia Paláez and Rodríguez de la Cruz.

The building itself, until 1791 the residence of the Captain's General, is immensely impressive. It is made up of bulwarks and culverin and cannon turrets, and is surrounded by a protective moat. The belfry is crowned by the famous statue of 'la Giraldilla' – a figure which represents Dona Isabel de Bobadilla, the first female governor of Cuba. This figure has become the symbol of the city of Havana.

Perfumery Museum

Calle Oficios between Calles Obispo and Obrapia, Habana Vieja
Open: Tuesday to Saturday 14.30–21.45; Sunday 09.00–13.00; closed on Monday

Fascinating if a little off-beat, this museum is housed in a delightful 18th century cloister and has collections of perfumes of an international reputation as well as less well-known traditional Cuban fragrances.

Casa de Africa
Calle Obrapia No 157 between Calles Mercaderes and San Ignacio,
Habana Vieja
*Open: Tuesday to Saturday 14.30–18.30; Sunday 09.00–13.00; closed
on Monday*
It is less surprising to find a museum dedicated to the exposition and
promotion of African culture, given the profound influence Africa has had
in shaping Cuban culture and society. The museum was founded in 1986
and serves not only as a show-case for African art but also as a study
centre where researchers can present their work.

Needless to say, the museum building is another beautiful example of
Spanish colonial architecture and almost 30 African countries have
contributed to the collection of exhibits.

Numismatic Museum
Calle Oficios No 8 between Calles Obispo and Obrapia, Habana Vieja
*Open: Tuesday to Saturday 13.30–20.00; Sunday 09.00–13.00; closed
on Monday*
Even coin collectors are catered for in the old town. The extensive
collection in this building, which is situated close to the Plaza de Armas,
includes 'company store' currency issued by the sugar mills during the
early plantation years. There is also a small but interesting international
collection.

Walking around Habana Vieja
The main tourist thoroughfare running from east to west (from the
Plaza de Armas to Parque Central) is Calle Obispo. If you stay in either
the old town or Centro Habana you are likely to find yourself
wandering up and down this street, often for no particular reason other
than it's a pleasant walk. There are several things to see here, including
the famous Johnson's drugstore which is a quaintly preserved pharmacy
bedecked in mahogany and dating back to Spanish colonial times. The
Hotel Ambos Mundos, an old haunt of Hemingway's and where he
wrote *For Whom The Bell Tolls,* is here (at the Plaza de Armas end).
The hotel has recently undergone some restoration works and now
visitors may inspect and photograph Room 511, Hemingway's old pad.
On a more practical level Calle Obispo is also home to the Palacio del
Turismo and at the western end of the street you will find the Moderna
Poseia bookstore and the Manzana de Gómez shopping arcade (for
postcards, souvenirs etc). At the eastern end of the street is the wonderful
Café la Mina and next door the delightful Casa del Agua which, as the
name suggests, is simply a shop that sells water, filtered water from
earthen jars (25¢ a litre).

The Plaza de Armas is one of the liveliest areas of the old town and is a
central meeting place for tourists and Cubans alike. The rhythms of Cuba

are never far from earshot around the plaza, whether emanating from Café la Mina or from beneath the colonnades of the Palacio de los Capitanos Generales (Museum of the City of Havana). A few hundred yards north is the Plaza de la Catedral which is transformed during the daytime by a mini market selling trinkets and second-hand books which are often very good bargains. This cobblestoned square, together with the Plaza de Armas, has become a focal point for tourists visiting the old town.

Calle San Ignacio, along with Calles Oficios and Obrapia, is another of the old town's streets that has undergone an expensive facelift. Even in its present state it is already among the most interesting and beautiful parts of Habana Vieja. Another fascinating place is Calle Cuba, which intersects Plaza Vieja, an area slowly being restored in readiness for mass tourism. The area bordered by the Plaza de la Catedral, the Plaza Vieja, the Prado and San Pedro by the waterfront is a gold mine of architectural treasures and has the added benefit of being within a relatively confined area that can be comfortably walked in a day.

Vedado and Centro Habana
Museums
Napoleonic Museum, Calle San Miguel No 1,159 at the corner of Ronda, Vedado (next to the University of Havana)
Open: Monday to Friday 09.00–12.00 and 13.00–16.00; alternate Saturdays 09.00–12.00 and 13.00–16.00; closed on Sunday
The sort of museum you would hardly expect to find in Cuba, this collection of artefacts, including some of Napoleon's personal belongings, was assembled by a former wealthy Cuban politician, Orestes Ferrara, while he lived in Europe and America. It became part of the National Heritage after the Revolution. The collection was housed in the magnificent Ferrara mansion (designed and built in a style similar to Florentine Renaissance architecture) in 1961. The building forms part of the University of Havana.

Among the more prized exhibits are the pistols Napoleon used when he went into battle at Borodino and his death mask which was brought to Cuba by the doctor who attended him on his death bed – one Dr Francesco.

National Museum of Decorative Arts, Calle 17 No 502 between Calles D and E, Vedado
Open: Tuesday to Saturday 11.00–18.30; Sunday 09.00–13.00; closed on Monday
Formerly the home of the Countess of Revilla de Camargo, this palatial building now houses prized and expensive collections of porcelain and furnishings. The majority of the exhibits are permanent, although there are some temporary collections including recent examples of Wedgwood and Faillance china from Europe and collections of Oriental porcelain.

Perhaps the most important piece is the hand-woven rug crafted in 1772 by Francis Carolus Romanus. Well worth a visit.

Felipe Poey Museum of Natural History, Edificio 'Felipe Poey',
Planta Baja, Plaza Ignacio Agramonte, University de la Habana, Vedado
Open: Monday to Friday 09.00–16.00; closed on Saturday and Sunday
This museum can be found on the ground floor of the Felipe Poey building on the campus of the University of Havana. Poey was an eminent Cuban scientist during the 19th century and there are many interesting specimens of exotic animals, birds and fossils. Worth a visit.

Walking around Vedado and Centro Habana

Another pleasant stroll is the 3km walk along the Malecón from Vedado to Habana Vieja. The literal translation of *malecón* is 'pier' or 'jetty', but the Malecón is more of a sea wall which binds and protects the city from the crashing waves of the Atlantic. A leisurely walk along the Malecón from the Nacional to the old town takes about 25 minutes and gives you the opportunity to observe small pockets of Cuban life – people fishing off the rocks behind the sea wall and impromptu baseball games being played in the shadow of the monument to Antonio Maceo (the Malccón is also known as Avenida Antonio Maceo). As you approach the old town the old four- and five-storey buildings take on ever more adventurous colours of faded pastel green and pink. Most of these structures were erected in the early part of this century and will be worth a fortune if Havana ever discovers a prolonged and meaningful level of prosperity. The Malecón itself was designed by a Cuban engineer named Albear in 1857 but was not completed until 1902.

If you want to meet the Cuban people but don't know where to start, take a walk along the Prado. You are guaranteed to be accosted by children who will bombard you with questions – 'Where you from?' 'What's your name?' You are also likely to be pestered by people who want to sell you cigars or rum, but if you make your intentions known early enough you will generally be left alone to enjoy the walk. The Prado (also called the Paseo de Martí) was built towards the back end of the 18th century and is the central artery running through Centro Habana. The street is shrouded for almost its entire length with tall laurel trees and the pedestrian promenade running down its middle is distinctly reminiscent of Barcelona's Las Ramblas. The promenade is punctuated en route by statues of lions (some in need of repair) while some sections have been inlaid with a mosaic of coloured tiles. The Prado was one of Havana's prime shopping areas prior to the Revolution and one suspects that, as Cuba prospers, this delightful area will once again become a major focal point for life in Havana.

The area around the University of Havana is well worth a visit and you can walk around the grounds of the university itself at any hour. Situated on Calle 27 and L in Vedado, the campus is sited on a hill named Arostegui and comprises a series of neoclassical buildings set around a sequence of small parks. Founded in 1728, the university was first known as the 'Royal and Pontifical University of Havana'. Students were only granted admittance if they were of a sufficiently pure stock. Jews, negroes and mulattos were not eligible to study there. The university became secular in 1842 but it remained the schooling ground for students of the Cuban middle and upper class. There is a monument at the base of the steps of the university which contains the ashes of the student, Jolio Antonio Mella, an outspoken critic of the Machado regime, who was assassinated in Mexico in 1929.

Cristobal Colon, entrance near corner of Calle 23 (La Rampa) and 12, Vedado
This is Havana's most important cemetery and a place recognised for its historic and architectural value. The grand white stone entrance to the cemetery, dating back to 1870, was designed by the Spanish architect Calixto de Loira but is Roman in its influence. It is the gateway to a treasure trove of interesting monuments and mausoleums. Historical figures such as the Cespedes family, José Martí's parents and Máximo Gomez are entombed here along with many of those who fell during the struggle for liberation against the regimes of Machado and Batista. The cemetery is open from 6am to 6pm daily. There is an admission charge of $1.

Plaza de la Revolución

The Plaza de la Revolucíon is situated to the south of Vedado, west of Centro Habana. Within easy reach of the Vedado area on foot, you can also catch the number 84 bus from the junction of Calles O and Humboldt. Getting here from Habana Vieja is more difficult.

The Plaza is dominated by the monument to José Martí, a 140m Soviet-style concrete pillar. It is from the podium here that Castro makes the majority of his addresses to the public. Opposite the Martí monument is the Ministry of the Interior building, a modern and ugly construction with a huge and impressive mural of the face of Che Guevara on its front. The mural is a must for the photograph album.

Just south of the plaza at Calzada de Bejuca is the city's Zoological Park. This is a sad and miserable place, which is hardly surprising given that Cuba can barely feed her own human population yet alone cater to the needs of animals. There are innumerable more worthwhile things to do in Havana than visit this place.

DAYTRIPS FROM HAVANA

Parque Lenin (Lenin Park)

This recreation area (680 hectares) is situated around 16km south of the city. Opened in 1970, it comprises several fishing lakes, parkland, art galleries, cafeterias and more. There is a train service circling the park, making all the facilities accessible. There is also an amusement park and riding school which are both popular at weekends. At the southern end of the park you will find a large lake named Paso Sequito. It is possible to hire boats here for a couple of dollars an hour. If you are peckish you can get a good but expensive meal at **Las Ruinas** restaurant close by. Designed and built around the ruins of an old sugar mill just after the Revolution, the building alone is worth a visit as the mahogany interior and beautiful stained-glass windows, fashioned by the Cuban artist René Portocarrero, are extremely impressive. You will probably need to book in advance at weekends (tel: 7 324630).

Guanabacoa

That first appearances can be deceptive is a fact borne out by this town. It was formally established in 1743, although nobody really knows when this place was first founded. Nevertheless, Guanabacoa is undoubtedly one of the oldest European settlements in the whole of Cuba – something you would initially find hard to believe as the shell of the city is distinctly modern and grey. It developed as a pre-Columbian Indian village and grew during the slave-trade era before eventually being absorbed into the municipality of Havana. In the mid-16th century the Spanish governor Angulo decreed that all natives must settle in a territory close to the established cities, thereby making them easy to control. Thus, around 300 Indians moved into the area and their numbers were swollen by people retreating from Havana to avoid the frequent pirate raids aimed at the city. The town grew and prospered, largely as a result of the fertility of the surrounding land (the name Guanabacoa, when loosely translated, means 'land of many waters'). Because of the close proximity to Havana, the town was used as a base for slaves which, as well as ensuring the continued growth of the place, also meant that Guanabacoa absorbed the cultural and religious influences of the African slaves. There are several towns and cities in the Caribbean built on blood and this could be classed as one of them. The unsavoury history of the town is reflected in some of its street names, for example, Calle Amargura (meaning Bitterness Street); it was down this street that slaves and other prisoners were led on their way to being executed.

There is a very interesting museum here at Calle Martí No 108 between Calle Versalles and San Antonio which is open daily except Tuesday, 10.30–18.00. The exhibits include some fascinating objects relating to the Afro-Cuban religions which were practised here (Santería and Regla de Palo) as well as a collection detailing the town's distant Indian heritage.

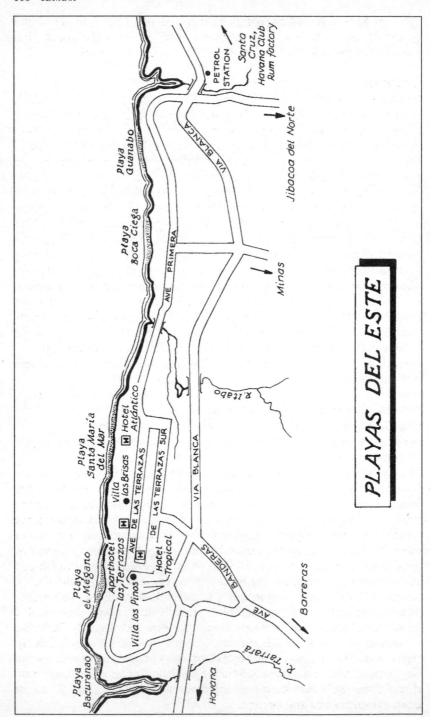

PLAYAS DEL ESTE

To get here you can catch the number 195 bus from Vedado or the number 5 from the Plaza de la Revolucíon. As it's only about 6km southeast of the city, you may wish to take a taxi to save time.

Cojímar

If you had visited this place in August 1994 you would have witnessed the heart-breaking sight of hundreds (possibly thousands) of Cubans fleeing Cuba on hastily put together rafts, trying to cross the Florida Straits to make it to Miami. Cojímar, a small and usually uneventful fishing village, held the spotlight of the world as satellite TV beamed pictures of the exodus around the world and photographers and journalists descended on it in their hordes to capture the moment. Thankfully, things have begun to return to normal and presently the only disturbance is created by the tourist buses which come here because it was the place on which Hemingway based his classic novel, *The Old Man and the Sea*. There are numerous reminders of Hemingway's influence on the village, including a statue of the author which keeps a watch over the port. Hemingway spent a good deal of his time fishing from this place and he is honoured and fondly remembered. There is a celebrated restaurant on the main street called **Restaurante la Terraza**. Built out overlooking the river, its speciality is obviously seafood and it was itself formerly home to the local fishing club before becoming a restaurant in 1972. You can catch a number 58 bus from Calle Monte near Capitolio in Habana Vieja. Cojímar is about 10km east of the city.

Ernest Hemingway Museum

Finca la Vigia, San Fransisco de Paula
Open: Wednesday to Saturday 09.00–16.00; Sunday 09.00–12.00; closed on Tuesday and rainy days
In a city which still has an abiding affection for the writer and which also recognises tourist potential when it sees it, Hemingway has been honoured by his own museum (although it's a bit out of the way on the outskirts of Havana). La Vigia was, in fact, Hemingway's house and the Cubans have been to great lengths in order to preserve it the way it was when 'Ernesto', as he is affectionately known, finally made his way to that great hunting lodge in the sky. Set in 22 acres of garden on a palm-fringed hill overlooking the city, the whole site was donated to the Cuban government following Hemingway's death in 1961. All the old hunting trophies (animals' heads and the like) are still stuck to the wall and his furniture and personal effects have been left untouched. Outside the house is moored the boat which carried him on many a famous fishing expedition. The museum constitutes only part of what is known as the Hemingway trail. This place is interesting, being popular not only with Hemingway buffs and those on organised tours, but also with school groups from Havana and beyond.

Playas del Este

About 15km east of Havana (only a 15-minute drive) are the beaches of
Playas del Este. To get there you have to go through the 1km-long tunnel
that crawls its way under the harbour in the old town across to the far side
of Morro and La Cabana fortresses. Taking the coastal road through the
village of Alamar, the first beach you come across is Bacuranao. A
popular weekend retreat for Habaneros, the area has also been developed
to accommodate the increasing number of foreign tourists who choose
this beach instead of Varadero as their prime area for rest and relaxation.
Further east are the remaining seven beaches which extend to almost
10km in length. The first five occupy a continuous strip from the villages
of Mégano to Rincon de Guanabo. Sandwiched between the two is the
beach area known as Santa María del Mar, the most developed and
touristy beach in Playas del Este. After Guanabo the beach disappears,
only to re-emerge to form the last two beaches known as Jibacoa and
Tropico. En route to the two you will pass through the village of Santa
Cruz del Norte, home of Cuba's largest rum factory, Havana Club.

Hotels

Playas del Este has been targeted by the Cuban government as an area of
great tourist potential and consequently a lot of money has been spent on
hotel development. There is an abundance of hotel accommodation across
the price spectrum.

Category 4

Hotel Atlántico (20 rooms), Avenida de las Terrazas and Calle 16,
Santa María del Mar; tel: 0687 2561
Popular and reasonably priced. Facilities include disco, swimming pool and air-
conditioned rooms with TVs.

Tropicoco Beach Club/Hotel Tropicoco (180 rooms), Avenida Sur and
Avenida de las Terrazas, Santa María del Mar; tel: 0687 2531
A modern hotel surrounded by pretty gardens very close to the sea. There are a
few good restaurants and nightclubs within easy walking distance.

Category 3

Villas las Brisas (85 rooms), Calle 11 between Calles 1ra and 3ra,
Santa María Loma; tel: 0687 2469
A quiet collection of apartments set in pleasant tropical gardens with good views
over the sea-front. Has a decent on-site restaurant and bar.

Villa los Pinos (70 rooms), Avenida de las Terrazas Sur and Avenida 5a,
Santa María del Mar; tel: 0687 2591
Pleasant and affordable rooms in a quiet setting close to the beach. Restaurant, bar
and nightclub form part of the complex.

Aparthotel las Terrazas (143 rooms), Avenida de las Terrazas Sur and
Avenida de las Banderas, Santa María del Mar; tel: 0687 4910
A five-storey modern building less than 50m from the beach. Its facilities include
a tourist bureau, swimming pool and games room.

Chapter Five

Pinar del Río Province

The province of Pinar del Río has the deserved reputation of being the most beautiful in Cuba. It is also the region where the country's, and arguably the world's, finest tobacco is grown. The north of the province is marked by a  multitude of caves and keys formed as a result of natural erosion (the Archipelago de Colorados), while the south is primarily a combination of sandy groves and swamp. Just under one third of the province is still forested with pine trees. Upon leaving Havana, the main highway crosses over rolling plains, where sugar cane and citrus fruits are grown, before giving way to a more mountainous stretch of land crowned by dense vegetation. It is here that you are most likely to see the *bohío* – the traditional thatch-roofed cottages used by rural workers. These are primitive but functional structures based on a design used by Cuba's Indian population in the 16th century.

The geological difference between Pinar del Río and the rest of Cuba is profound. One of the defining characteristics of the province is the preponderance of small but fertile valleys, called *hoyos,* in which much of the area's tobacco is grown. Another prime feature is the *mogotes* which are essentially flat-topped buttes made of limestone and peppered by caverns and subterranean rivers. They date back to the Jurassic period, around 160 million years ago. Stretches of these underground rivers are becoming a popular tourist draw.

The first inhabitants of the area were the Guanahatabey, the oldest of the Indian tribes which were scattered among more than 160 sites in the province. It wasn't until the start of the 18th century that the area began to attract a larger population. Predominantly white tobacco farmers moved into the area away from Havana to take advantage of the excellent soil quality, prime for the growth of the tobacco leaf. The area was well-positioned and remote enough to make smuggling a popular industry and there is no doubt that this was crucial to the growing prosperity of the

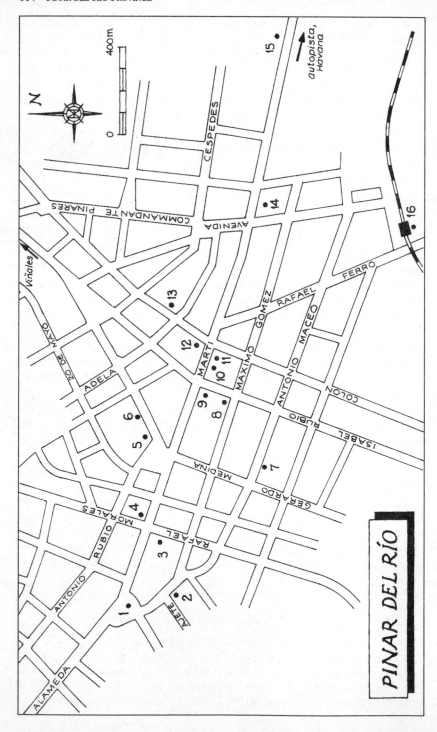

PINAR DEL RÍO

region. Nevertheless, in comparison with most of Cuba, which was beginning to experience more rapid development as a result of the success of sugar harvesting, Pinar del Río remained a backwater and its people were (and still are) fiercely independent and reluctant to take orders from the administration of Havana. Since 1959, however, efforts have been made to better the lot of the average Cuban in the province and the introduction of sugar, citrus fruits and state-owned dairy farms into the region has seen its dependency on tobacco farming reduced, although tobacco is still the area's number one crop.

Cigars and Pinar del Río

Cubans will tell you, and many experts will agree with them, that the best tobacco in the world comes from Pinar del Río. To be more specific, the best tobacco in the world comes from Vuelta Abajo in the province of Pinar del Río and, to be even more specific than that, the best tobacco in the world comes from the area of San Juan y Martinez in Vuelta Abajo in the province of Pinar del Río.

Every November the farmers of the area scatter fresh seeds into well-irrigated and fertilized channels in the soil. The seeds are planted in stages to enable the farmer to be able to harvest different parts of his crop at different times. This is important, as the methods of farming are still labour intensive and the crop needs to be harvested at the right time if it is to go into the production of premium cigars. The main harvest is picked in March and April and the tobacco is cured immediately, being exposed to direct sunlight for four days. The leaves are then hung in drying houses for a further 40 days where both light and moisture levels are carefully monitored. Every plant contains around 16 leaves and, dependent on the position of the leaf on the stem, each leaf varies in strength (the higher leaves are generally the strongest). Each plant produces a minimum of five strengths of tobacco and the farmer or *veguero* must ensure that each batch of leaves is dried separately according to its strength. The best leaf, the *corona,* comes from the top of the plant. These give the cigar strength. The middle leaf, the *centro fino*, is left longest on the plant and also adds strength to the cigar. The larger middle leaf, the *centro gordo* (capa leaf), is used to wrap up the other two leaves. The *volado*, which is the leaf near the base of the plant, is used as an inner skin to help the cigar burn consistently.

Key to map

1 Plaza de la Independencia	7 Catedral de San Rosendo	11 Milanes Theatre
2 Tobacco Museum	8 Cabaret La Cueva	12 La Casona Restaurant
3 Casa de la Trova	9 Hotel el Globo	13 Bus station
4 Café Parqueo	10 Provincial Museum of the History of Pinar del Río	14 Museum of Natural Sciences
5 Pizzeria Terrazzina		15 Hotel Pinar del Río
6 Coppelia		16 Railway station

The tobacco leaves are taken to the factory after they have been left to mellow for up to two years. They are are bundled and bound together and moistened. The central stem of the leaf is then stripped by *despalilladores* and the leaves are then passed on to the *rezagado* whose job it is to sort them out according to their strength. This is a particularly skilled occupation and a good *rezagado* will be able to differentiate between a wide range of tobacco leaves simply by judging their colour. In the case of cigars of exceptional quality, such as the Cohiba, the leaves are left to ferment for a further two years before the next stage in the intricate process. Once the *rezagado* has finished, the leaves are then passed on to the *tabaqueros,* the person responsible for rolling the finished article. A skilled *tabaqueros* can roll well over 100 cigars in a day. They are also allowed to smoke them while they work. After they have been rolled and trimmed, the cigars are graded by the placing of an *anillo* around their perimeter. They are then boxed before undergoing a final quality-control inspection. In all, there are around 80 different stages in the cigar-making process and so, when you go into the dollar shop to buy a box of Cohibas only to be told they cost $200, you may wish to dwell upon the love, care and attention that has gone into producing what are, after all, the world's finest cigars.

It's possible to visit some of the tobacco factories in the province. The tourist bureau at the Hotel Pinar del Río will be happy to provide you with tour information.

PINAR DEL RÍO CITY
History and orientation
The city of Pinar del Río, 180km from Havana, was founded in 1774, much later than many other Cuban cities. It derives its name from the area of pine forest that used to line the banks of the River Guamá. Although there is a fair amount of traffic and activity on the streets, the city gives the impression of being geographically isolated as well as a little behind the times. As you enter the city by road, passing through a corridor of shady carob trees, you are struck by the prettiness and the once vibrant, but now fading, colours of the surrounding buildings. Much of its architecture is neoclassical and, purely from an aesthetic point of view, the city is well worth a visit. Most visitors tend not to linger, preferring to travel into the surrounding countryside and, more particularly, to Viñales. However, if you are in the area, you should dedicate at least a day to seeing the city and, despite what the people of Havana will tell you (they see the inhabitants of Pinar del Río as being dull and unsophisticated country bumpkins), you are guaranteed a warm and hospitable welcome.

Getting there and away
Your alternatives in this respect are limited to two. Cubana Airlines have yet to bother including Pinar del Río on their flight path, so to get to the city or the province you have to travel either by road or by rail.

By rail

Trains depart daily at 08.00 from Tulipan station in Havana. The journey, on the uncomfortable cattletruck type *segunda* service, is scheduled to take five hours but you should build in a couple of hours' tolerance just in case. The fare is $7 one way. The line is an ageing one and is due for repair. Cancellations of services at the last minute are not unknown. Although not the most comfortable way of getting around, the train will get you there in the end although, if you have been lucky enough to get one of the hard wooden seats, your backside will most likely require 24 hours to recover from the rigours of the journey.

Pinar del Río's rail station is on Calle Ferrocarril between Calles Rafael Ferro and Commandante Pinares, a few minutes southeast of the centre.

By bus

The usual problem of getting a ticket applies. Services from Havana to Pinar del Río are usually booked up weeks in advance. Buses from Havana usually arrive at the Terminal de Omnibus Interprovincial on Calle Adela, slightly east of the city centre. There are regular daily services from Havana, almost all taking the fast route along the *autopista*. The journey takes 2½–3 hours.

By car

If you come by car or private taxi then there are two routes you can choose. The simplest option, and easily the quickest, is to take the six-lane *autopista* that extends west from Havana to Pinar del Río. The Sierra del Rosario looms en route to your right as you pass through the towns of San Cristobal and Consolación del Sur (close by here is an outcrop which, at 648m, is the highest point of the province). The *autopista*, as a result of the shortage of petrol and the crumbling national economy, is almost empty. The coastal route is much more interesting and scenic although it will take you considerably longer to get to the city. This route takes you through Mariel (scene of the 1980 boat lift), Cabanas, Bahía Honda and La Palma before sweeping south through the beautiful Viñales and then Pinar del Río.

Accommodation

The province is reasonably well served by decent tourist hotels including four in Viñales. Once you begin to travel west of the city, finding accommodation becomes more problematic.

Category 4

Villa Cayo Levisa (20 rooms), Cayo Levisa
Situated on a small islet off the northern coast of the province, this secluded little villa is on the edge of a small white sand beach fringed by palm trees. This is an ideal place to come for a quiet and tranquil holiday, although for the more energetic there are some good scuba-diving sites close by and the area is also home to one of the largest coral reefs in the world. Part of the reef is black coral.

Hotel Moka (26 rooms), Las Terrazas Tourist Complex, Pinar del Río;
tel: 085 2996; fax: 3355/6
A very pleasant place to stay set in the heart of the Sierra del Rosario, an
environmental area granted UNESCO status in 1985.

Category 3
Hotel Pinar del Río (136 rooms), Calle José Martí (at the eastern edge of the city
by the *autopista*); tel: 59 5070
The most popular tourist hotel in town particularly with package tourists, the city
is a 15 minute walk away if you want to escape from the hotel's tacky cabaret. The
building is a featureless 1970s-style establishment. The facilities are three-star and
include a swimming pool and a nightclub.

Hotel el Globo, Calle José Martí (close to the junction with Calle Isabel Rubio)
This is the most pleasant hotel in the city and the most central. The interior is
elegantly decorated and there is more of an air of style and sophistication about
the place than in the Hotel Pinar del Río. The facilities are not as good, but it's
worth staying here if only to be closer to the city.

Eating and drinking
Your hotel is the only place where you are guaranteed a meal, although
there are several peso restaurants in the city centre if you want to try to get
in. Try **La Casona** on Calle Colón at the junction of Calle José Martí or
Café Parqueo on Calle Rafael Morales also at the junction of Calle José
Martí.
   If you fancy a pizza you could try **Pizzeria Terrazzina** on Calle I de
Mayo. Ice-creams (*helados*) can be bought from the **Coppelia** on Calle
Gerrado Medina if you can stomach the queuing.

Nightlife
The **Hotel Pinar del Río** has its own nightclub and all the tourist hotels
have their own bar which tends to stay open provided you're prepared to
keep buying drinks. In the city itself, the **Casa de la Trova** on Calle José
Martí and the **La Cueva** on Calle Máximo Gómez between Calles Gerrado
Medina and Isabel Rubio are quite lively and entertaining. La Cueva
usually has a cabaret at weekends.
   The **Milanes Theatre** on Calle José Martí was restored during the
1960s. This theatre was allowed to fall into a state of disrepair following
its construction at the end of the 19th century. Check locally for details of
performance.

Shopping
The area has a good reputation for the production of high-quality ceramics
and woven work. There are a few workshops which sell to visitors and
these goods make a better buy than the usual tourist tat on sale in the dollar
shops of the tourist hotels. Calle Antonio Maceo to the south of the city
centre is a good place to buy from local workshops.

Things to see and do

Most people come to Pinar del Río to sample the delightful countryside or the excellent beaches. Viñales is the big attraction but the city of Pinar del Río is both interesting and attractive and you should try to fit it into your itinerary. There are four churches in the city, the most interesting being the Santa Iglesia Catedral de San Rosendo on Calle Antonio Maceo.

Provincial Museum of the History of Pinar del Río

Calle José Martí No 58 between Calles Isabel Rubio and Colón
Open: Tuesday to Saturday 14.00–18.00; Sunday 09.00–13.00; closed on Monday
The museum deals with the province's history dating back to the aboriginal settlements. There have been some interesting archaeological discoveries made around these settlements and the lifestyle of the Indians is remembered by a mock cave dwelling. Other exhibits include crystal and furniture dating back to the 19th century as well as examples of some of the weaponry used during the wars of independence. The local musician, Enrique Jorrin, creator of the cha-cha-cha, is also remembered.

Museum of Natural Sciences (Tranquilino Sandalio de Noda)

Calle José Martí No 202 (at the junction of Avenida Commandante Pinares)
Open: Tuesday to Saturday 14.00–18.00; Sunday 09.00–13.00; closed on Monday
Situated in an old colonial mansion house, Guach Palace, this museum houses examples of natural wildlife indigenous to the province. The building, an eclectic structure incorporating Gothic gargoyles and Athenian columns, was completed between 1909 and 1914 for one of Pinar del Río's more wealthy citizens (a doctor) and was donated to the people after the Revolution. Among the more interesting displays are the fossilised remains of a plesiosaurus, a gigantic marine animal that survived in the seas that once covered the province millions of years earlier.

Tobacco Museum (Fabrica de Tobacos)

Calle Máximo Gómez, at the junction of Calles Antigua Carcel and Ajete
An interesting museum which details the history of tobacco production in the province as well as offering a more contemporary insight into local cigar making.

Calle José Martí

This street is the busiest and most vibrant in the city and cuts through its heart from east to west. If you continue east on Calle José Martí you will end up in Havana. Many of the city's places of interest are either on or just off this street.

EAST OF PINAR DEL RÍO CITY

Viñales

Viñales Valley, regarded by many as Cuba's premier beauty spot, lies 27km from the city of Pinar del Río. The valley is famed for its *mogotes*, large limestone formations which date back to the Jurassic period. With the exception of similar formations in Malaysia, they are unique. They were formed when the roof of the valley collapsed leaving these *mogotes*, which acted as supporting columns for the roof, as a testimony to the change in the physical environment. The *mogotes* are honeycombed by caverns (some containing subterranean rivers and springs). The pick of the caves is the Cueva del Indio which was formerly used by the Guanahatabey Indians. It was also used as a hiding place by slaves who had fled from captivity. For $2 you can travel over 1km down the river that flows through the cave (it's 8km long) past stalagmites and stalactites. This journey isn't recommended for those people who suffer from claustrophobia.

Cuevas de Viñales close by doubles as a bar/disco.

Accommodation
Category 3
Hotel la Ermita (64 rooms), Carretera a la Ermita, Viñales; tel: 8 93208; fax: 93294
A modern two-storey hotel which, thankfully, has been constructed to blend sympathetically with the surroundings. Although it is 2km from the Viñales valley there are, nevertheless, excellent views around here and the staff of the hotel are warm and courteous. The three-star facilities include a swimming pool and all rooms are air-conditioned.

Hotel los Jasmines (90 rooms), Carretera de Viñales, Viñales; tel: 8 93205
Situated high up on a cliff overlooking Viñales valley, the views from this place are breathtaking. The building itself is a strange cross between modern and neoclassical design. Its facilities are excellent and include air-conditioned rooms, a swimming pool and a decent restaurant. There is a disco, mainly at weekends, but in the low season it's not the liveliest of affairs.

Pre-historic mural
In the small valley of Dos Hermanas (Two Sisters) on the sides of a large *mogote* is this strange and gigantic mural. It measures 120m in height and 180m in width. It is supposed to depict the evolutionary process of the area and the man responsible for painting it, on the behest of Castro, was the artist Leovigildo Gonzalez. This place is heavily pushed by the Cuban tourist authorities as a must to see, but many people come away from it with a sense of disappointment. In truth, it's not all it's cracked up to be.

San Vicente Valley
Five kilometres from Viñales valley is San Vicente. The area is renowned for its spa waters which have, reputedly, amazing restorative powers. You can stay over as there is a good tourist hotel nearby:

Category 2
Hotel Rancho San Vicente, Carretera a Puerto Esperanza, Pinar del Rio; tel: 8 93200
A quiet hotel set in the hills near Viñales.

The Caverns of Santo Tomás
These caverns are part of what is one of the largest systems of subterranean corridors in Latin America. So far only around 30 of them (formed over a period of millions of years) have been charted. Many more wait to be explored.

La Guira National Park and Los Portales Caverns
Sandwiched between the villages of La Guira and San Diego de los Banos is this pleasing national park which is home to a rich variety of bird life. On the outskirts of the park are the caves of Los Portales. These caves have been created by the erosive qualities of the Caiguanabo river, a process of natural erosion that has taken thousands of years. The caves were discovered in 1800 by a Spaniard named Los Portales. Che Guevara used them as his staff headquarters during the Cuban Missile Crisis.

Soroa
The town of Soroa, 80km west of Havana, is not what draws people to the area as it is relatively modern, drab and uneventful. Rather, the big attractions are the nearby botanical gardens which contain an excellent orchidarium, home to more than 700 different types of orchid (250 are indigenous). There are guided tours of the orchid garden daily (except Friday) at hourly intervals beginning at 10.00 and ending at 17.30. The surrounding countryside is lush, hilly and very pleasant to wander around. For those into birdwatching, there are several viewing stations dotted around. For photographers, the area affords a good opportunity for fauna and flora shots. The Cuban tourist brochures claim that the waterfall at Soroa is one of the country's finest natural wonders but in reality it is small and, although pretty, hardly breathtaking.

The park was formerly owned by a Spaniard, Don Ignacio Soroa, who cultivated coffee in the region. The town, as you might have guessed, is named after him.

Accommodation
Villa Soroa (70 rooms), Carretera Soroa, Soroa; tel: 2122
Predominantly bungalow accommodation, this is about the only place to stay if you do decide to stop over for a night to check out Soroa. The facilities are OK but Viñales is a much more inviting prospect.

Maspotón
If you are feeling tough and want to take advantage of the opportunity to blow a few unarmed, defenceless ducks away, then visit the Villa Club de Casa Maspotón on the southern coast (30km from Pinar del Río city). At

around $80–100 per day for the privilege, you would need an Uzi sub-machine gun to get your money's worth. For an account of the hunting experience at Maspotón read *Driving Through Cuba* by Carlo Gébler (published by Abacus Books). You can also fish here.

WEST OF PINAR DEL RÍO CITY

Previously uncharted territory as far as tourists are concerned, the area west of Pinar del Río is still relatively unspoiled, but the adventurous few who make the effort to travel this far will be well rewarded. The road as far west as La Fe is adequate, but from there to the beach resort of María la Gorda, the journey can be a little bumpy and uncomfortable.

María la Gorda

Playa María La Gorda is an up and coming resort on the western end of the province (and the island). It is approximately 145km from the city of Pinar del Río. Home to an international scuba-diving centre, this is the place to come to if you really want to get away from it all. On the edge of the Bahía de Corrientes, the surrounding waters are reputedly littered with shipwrecked galleons laden with treasure. The area was a popular sheltering point for pirates and corsairs of old. To get here you have to make the journey by road via San Juan y Martinez and La Fe.

The name María La Gorda when translated means 'Fat Maria.' Behind the name is a curious but interesting legend. Seemingly, a few centuries ago, a gang of pirates looted a tavern in Venezuela and, as part of their haul, kidnapped the barmaid, a young, pretty and plump maiden named Maria. Rough seas forced them to take haven in the Bahía de Corrientes where they built Maria a house on the beach. One day the pirates embarked on another voyage of plunder but failed to return. Maria was left alone and destitute. In order to survive she turned to a life of prostitution, plying her business under the auspices of a small bath house. Locals who used her services referred to the venue as the Casa de las Tetas de María La Gorda (House of Fat Mary's Breasts). Maria apparently continued to put on weight before dying of natural causes. Nobody knows where she was buried.

You can stay at the Villa María Gorda (Category 3 hotel).

Guanahacabibes Peninsula National Park

Situated on the westernmost tip of the province, this area was recently declared a 'Reserve of the Biosphere' by UNESCO. What is essentially a large forest is also a natural environment for a variety of indigenous animals and plants. There is a strict preservation order on all that lives here and any form of hunting or tampering with the natural environment is expressly forbidden. The area was also home to the last of Cuba's aboriginal population who fled here to escape the savagery of the Spanish following colonisation. Archaeological digs have uncovered many remnants of old Indian settlements including a very important site at nearby Cayo Redondo.

Chapter Six

Matanzas Province

East of Havana is the province of Matanzas, the second largest in Cuba. The north of the province is marked by rolling hills and the beach resort of Varadero, Cuba's premier tourist spot for beach holidays. The south of the province is  home to a large area of swamp land and the beach of Girón, better known as the Bay of Pigs. Central Matanzas is a long stretch of rolling plains whose red and fertile soils produce the highest yield of sugar crop in the country. Other crops such as tobacco, citrus fruits and vegetables are also produced in abundance, and much is exported in return for desperately needed hard currency. The province is one of the most popular areas for visiting tourists, largely because of its varied topography and natural beauty.

MATANZAS CITY
History and orientation
The city of Matanzas, 100km east of Havana, is situated between two rivers, the Yumuri and the San Juan on the northwest coast of the province. Its sheltered position on the edge of the Bahía de Matanzas, close to the centre of the province's sugar-producing industry, has largely been responsible for its growth although there are other contributing factors.

The name *matanzas* means 'slaughter', a seemingly ill-fitting title for what is a fairly calm and laid-back city. There are differing theories as to why the city adopted this name, the most widely touted being that sometime during the 16th century a group of Indians, having convinced a boatload of Spanish colonists to come ashore for provisions, killed them. Another theory, which runs along the same lines, claims that the colonists were guilty of the habitual slaughter of the local Indian population (historians agree that the Indians were often the victims of such actions

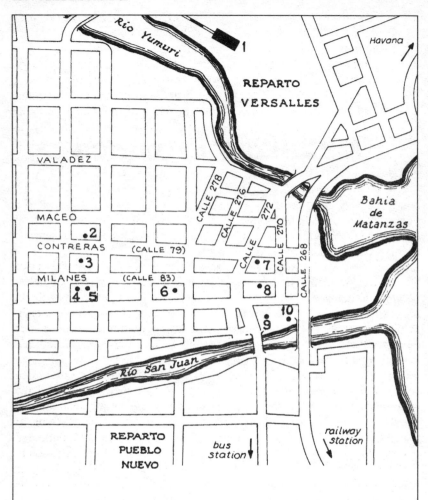

1 HERSHEY RAILWAY
   STATION
2 CINEMA VALAZCO
3 PARQUE LIBERTAD
4 PHARMACEUTICAL
   MUSEUM
5 HOTEL LOUVRE

6 CATHEDRAL OF
   SAN CARLOS
7 MUSEO HISTÓRICO
   PROVINCIAL
8 TEATRO SAUTO
9 PLAZA DE LA VIGIA
10 CASA DE LA TROVA

MATANZAS

rather than perpetrators). The final plausible theory is that the city's role as a cattle market and slaughter house (salt meat production once played a key role in the local economy) gave rise to the name.

Apart from its role as the sugar capital of Cuba, Matanzas was also a prime exporter of both tobacco and coffee, especially during the 17th and 18th centuries. With Cuba's sugar plantations in dire need of labour and with Matanzas being the prime exporter of much of the country's sugar produce, the city also developed into an important slave depot and there is no doubt that the slave trade played a major part in its growth and prosperity. Much of the wealth generated by these associated industries was spent on increasing the architectural and cultural profile of the city, so much so that it became known as the 'Athens of Cuba'. Many artists and poets, the most famous being Jacinto Milanes (who gave his name to the city's cathedral park), José Maria Heredia, Bonifacio Byrne and Miguele Failde, either lived or were born in Matanzas, and the place in general experienced something of a renaissance.

Matanzas has also had its fair share of insurrections. The treatment of black slaves in the port was particularly brutal and gave rise to a number of violent, though unsuccessful, revolts. Following Castro's assault on Moncada in 1953, the barracks at Goycuria also came under attack, equally unsuccessfully. The barracks was later turned into a school after the Revolution (Castro's assertion after his victory was that all Batista's barracks should be turned into schools).

The two rivers flowing into the bay naturally divide the city into three sections – Versalles to the north, Pueblo Nuevo to the south and the downtown area, sandwiched between the two. Whoever decided upon the street numbering system in Matanzas didn't study town planning at university. All streets are both named and numbered, with odd-numbered streets running east–west and even-numbered streets from north–south. Some streets have two names and a general sense of confusion takes over when studying a map of the city. Being a taxi driver in Matanzas must be a frustrating occupation.

Getting there and away
There are no flights to Matanzas city although road and rail links are good. Flights to the area arrive at Varadero, although these are almost exclusively charter flights bringing in package tourists from other countries.

By rail
You have two alternatives when travelling by train from Havana to Matanzas: the conventional train service or the Hershey train – an electric railway developed by the American chocolate company prior to the Revolution. These days the carriages are rusting and in a state of advanced decay, but the journey, which lasts around three and a half hours is a pleasant one. Services depart from the Casablanca railway station in

Havana and arrive at Matanzas' small second railway terminus to the north of the city. Normal rail services operate daily to and from Havana and beyond.

By bus
Bus services from Havana take around three hours and are usually booked weeks in advance. The main bus terminal is on the junction of Calle 298 and 127 to the south of the city centre. Bus services to Varadero and on as far as Santiago de Cuba are scheduled to run daily but often don't. Again, trying to obtain a ticket is a major problem.

By car
If you are feeling flush then you can hire a taxi from Havana which will cost you $60 one way or $109 return. The coastal road from Havana to Matanzas is both scenic and interesting, the beauty of the blue Caribbean sea being marred intermittently by the preponderance of oil plantations and factories, especially on the section closest to Havana. There is another road which branches off the *autopista* northeastwards, taking you through the centre of the western section of the province through the villages of Madruga and Ceiba Mocha. It adds a few hours to the journey and there is little in terms of scenery and interest to recommend it. Hitching is an option, although you may have to be patient as there are many people trying to make the same trip.

Accommodation
The vast majority of tourist accommodation in the province is to be found in Varadero (see page 131). Matanzas city itself has relatively little by way of hotels of any description. Perhaps because of this, the idea of black-market accommodation (people renting out their homes) seems to have caught on. You may be approached directly, although a trustworthy waiter should be able to point you in the right direction if you are interested in seeking out accommodation for yourself.

Category 2
Hotel Louvre, Calle Milanes on Parque Libertad (next to the Pharmaceutical Museum); tel: 52 4074
A good, clean and comparatively cheap hotel which has some excellent *vitrales* and a very pleasant courtyard.

Hotel el Valle (40 rooms), Carretera Chirino (6km from the city centre); tel: 52 4584
A small and recently-established hotel with good facilities including a restaurant and swimming pool. A 30-minute walk into the centre.

Eating and drinking
Both the **Hotel Louvre** and the **El Valle** have decent restaurants and these are your best bets when it comes to getting a meal. There are some good

paladares in the area around the Plaza de la Vigia. Locals will be happy to direct you. The cafés on the main square are all prone to food shortages and queues tend to be prohibitively long. There is no guarantee that after queuing you will be served anyway (they are peso cafés designed to feed hungry Cubans not hungry tourists). If you are lucky you will find some local produce on sale in stalls along the pedestrianised Calle 85. On a good day you may be able to put together enough items for a picnic.

Nightlife

There are two Casa de la Trovas in Matanzas, the secondary one being situated on Calles 83 and 304. The main one, by the Plaza de la Vigia, is legendary as it was here that the group, Munequitos de Matanzas, perfected their brand of rumba which was exported throughout the musical world. You won't often find the band playing in Matanzas any more, but the **Casa de la Trova** is still the best place to go for a good Cuban night out. The **Teatro Sauto** is worth checking out – there are usually performances of some sort taking place, especially at weekends. For most Matanzanians the area around the Plaza de la Vigia by the waterfront is the place to congregate. People tend to make their own entertainment in Matanzas and for many that means an evening of swapping stories over a game of draughts. The plaza is a good place to meet and talk to local people. The **Cinema Valazco** on Calle 79 shows mainly Cuban movies.

Things to see and do

There are plenty of interesting buildings, monuments and museums to keep you occupied, although much of the city can be covered in little more than a day. The area around the Parque Libertad holds most of the architectural treasures, although it is worth exploring a little further into the back streets which, although quiet, have a certain charm.

Pharmaceutical Museum

Open: Monday to Saturday 10.00–18.00; Sunday 09.00–13.00
Situated on Parque Libertad (formerly the Plaza de Armas – the old parade grounds), this used to be a thriving pharmacy, established by a Frenchman named Triolet in 1882, before being turned into a museum in 1964. The instruments used to process and manufacture medicines and other pharmaceutical products have been preserved and are on display. Also on display is an extensive collection of porcelain jars containing all manner of ointments, potions and medicines. At the back of the museum is the old laboratory, which contains a brick oven that was once fuelled only by firewood. The copper and bronze utensils used in the distilling process have been preserved in immaculate condition.

The *vitrales* were originally the colour of the French tricolour, but, on the insistence of the Spanish authorities, the colours were changed to represent the Spanish flag.

This museum is worth a visit even if you have no particular interest in pharmacology.

Museo Histórico Provincial (formerly the Palacio Junco)
Open: Tuesday to Sunday 10.00–18.00; closed on Monday
This museum is housed in an old colonial house built during the 19th century. Formerly the home of a rich plantation owner, it has undergone extensive restoration and among the exhibits is a section dealing with the role of slavery in the development of the city.

Teatro Sauto
Situated on Plaza de la Vigia, the theatre was built in 1863 with money raised from public subscription. Like its sister, the Tomás Terry Theatre in Cienfuegos, it was restored following the Revolution. Its three-tiered balconies are part of a design that is typically neoclassical and the theatre still hosts both local and national drama and dance troops. It is also possible to wander around the stylish interior on Wednesdays to Sundays. There is a small dollar admission fee.

Cathedral of San Carlos
The original cathedral occupied this site, at the junction of Calles Milanes and Jovellanos, in 1693 but was destroyed by fire and replaced, in 1878, by the present structure. It was allowed to fall into a state of disrepair, a situation which is being remedied largely thanks to a donation from a visiting German who fell in love with the building. Noted for its frescoed ceilings and walls, the cathedral is well worth a visit.

Bellamar Caverns
About 4km west of the city centre, these caves were accidentally discovered by local workers in about 1850. They are one of the longest established and most popular tourist attractions in the area. The 3,000m cave system contains many stalagmites and stalactites and there is also a network of underground streams. Some of the streams flow into small subterranean lakes. Visitors are not allowed into the caves unaccompanied. A guided tour costs $2. There is a restaurant close to the cave entrance which serves pretty miserable food for dollars.

VARADERO
History and orientation
Varadero is Cuba's principal beach resort, lying 34km northeast of Matanzas and 140km east of Havana. Situated on the narrow Hicacos peninsula, the white sands of Varadero extend like a tentacle for over

20km into the Atlantic. Bathed by the calm and warm waters of the Gulf Stream, the setting is ideal for commercial exploitation and Cuba hasn't been slow in seizing the opportunity.

Prior to the arrival of Columbus, the peninsula was home to a small Indian population who knew it as Punta Hicacos. With the extinction of the Indian population nationwide, the area remained unoccupied for hundreds of years, the only people making use of it being mariners who would, when needs determined, call in to make repairs to their ailing vessels. It wasn't until the beginning of the 20th century that people began to realise its potential as a tourist resort. Wealthy families from Matanzas and Cardenas started to erect holiday homes and retreats and, in 1910, the first hotel, the Hotel Varadero, was built. In 1930, an American industrialist by the name of Irene du Pont bought almost all of the peninsula for a pittance and immediately began to turn the place into a recreational haven, selling off tracts of land to other American businessmen who built hotels and holiday getaways for themselves. Du Pont also built his own huge private mansion with landscaped gardens and a golf course thrown in. After the Revolution the fortunes of Varadero began to wane as tourists, especially those from the USA, ceased coming. The beaches of the peninsula were declared open to the public, and locals, who had previously been barred from walking along the sands of the coastline, were now free to do so.

Now that Varadero is once more the jewel in Cuba's tourist crown things seem to be reverting to the old days. There has been a great deal of hotel development in recent years and the tourist infrastructure has grown out of all recognition. Stretches of beach are now the preserve of foreign holiday-makers staying in dollar hotels overlooking the beach. Prostitution and pimping has, as in many other third-world holiday resorts, begun to take root and the area is fast losing its Cuban characteristics. Nevertheless, if you want to eat and drink (reasonably) well, sunbathe under a clear blue sky, swim in warm, turquoise tranquil waters that caress endless stretches of pure white sand, then Varadero is for you.

The street pattern operates at right angles to the beach, numbered 1 to 69, beginning in the suburb of Kawama in the west of the peninsula and ending at the suburb of La Torre in the east. Avenida Primera runs along the north and centre of the peninsula from the bridge crossing Puente Bascular in the west, while the *autopista* hugs the southern coastline from west to east.

Getting there and away
By air
With Varadero now an international tourist resort, it is possible to fly there direct from both Europe and Canada. There are also direct flights from Holland, but you may need to travel as part of an organised tour when you

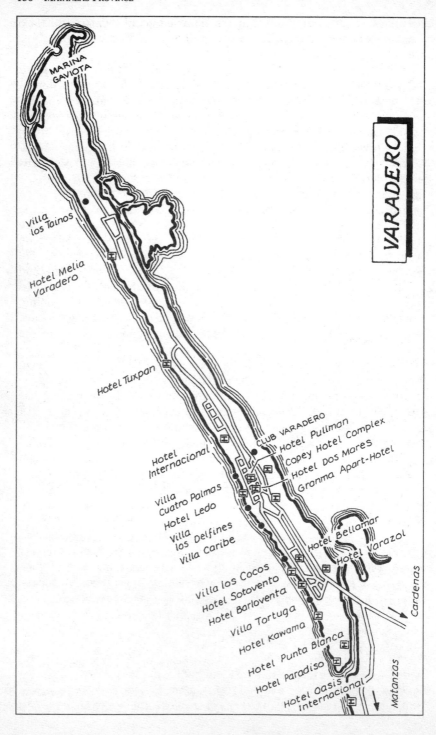

MARINA
GAVIOTA

Villa
los Taínos

Hotel Melia
Varadero

VARADERO

Hotel Tuxpan

Hotel
Internacional

CLUB VARADERO
Hotel Pullman
Copey Hotel Complex
Hotel Dos Mares
Granma Apart-Hotel

Villa
Cuatro Palmas
Hotel Ledo
Villa
los Delfines
Villa Caribe

Hotel Bellamar
Hotel Varazol

Villa los Cocos
Hotel Sotovento
Hotel Barloventa
Villa Tortuga
Hotel Kawama

Cardenas

Hotel Punta Blanca
Hotel Paradiso
Hotel Oasis
Internacional

Matanzas

book to fly. The airport, Aeropuerto Internacional de Varadero, is 16km inland from the peninsula; tel: 5 63016 or 5 62010.

By bus
The bus service from Havana to Varadero is poor. This can largely be explained by the fact that most Cubans do not visit Varadero, as it's far too expensive a holiday resort for them. It is assumed that most people who arrive in Havana will already have pre-booked some form of transfer transportation. Your best bet of catching a bus is to make your way to Matanzas (by train) and take one of the direct services that regularly link Matanzas and Varadero. Direct bus routes from Havana to Varadero (and vice versa) do operate, but are infrequent and over-booked.

By car
The coastal road from Matanzas to Varadero is an enjoyable ride once past the oil plantations. Heading slightly north through a road lined with casuarina trees, the clear blue waters of the Atlantic are never long out of sight. The temptation is simply to pull over, park the vehicle and dive headlong into the sea. Car hire is available in Havana and there are several agencies who rent out cars in Varadero.

Hitchhiking
Hitching is relatively easy from Matanzas to Varadero as the road is heavy with tour buses and coaches. The stretch from Havana to Matanzas is more problematic as you will be in direct competition with a multitude of others. It may be worth attempting to cajole your way on to one of the tour buses that leave from one of the bigger hotels in Havana rather than leave everything to chance.

By train
There is no direct rail link to the resort; you will need to alight at Matanzas and continue the journey by road.

Accommodation
There is no shortage of choice when it comes to picking somewhere to stay in Varadero; the resort has more than 70 tourist hotels and new ones are opening constantly. Many of them are on the pricey side as the Cuban authorities have been making great efforts to attract the type of holiday-maker (ie: the affluent type) who frequents many of the other Caribbean islands. If you come as part of a package tour, however, the cost of staying in Varadero can be quite reasonable.

Category 5
Hotel Melia Varadero (490 rooms), Autopista Sur, Playa de las Américas; tel: 5 66221; fax: 5 337011
A large modern five-star hotel complex situated close to the golf course overlooking the beach, the Melia has excellent facilities including a vast

swimming pool (probably not something you would want to use too often given that the hotel is only a stone's throw from the beach). The tacky mock waterfall in the hotel lobby is designed to bring a touch of class – but it doesn't work.

Hotel Tuxpan (233 rooms), Carretera las Morlas, Playa de las Américas; tel: 5 66200; fax: 5 335242
Perhaps the most luxurious hotel in Varadero, the Tuxpan is a recently-built five-star hotel with top-class facilities. It's also just about the most expensive place to stay on the peninsula.

Category 4

Hotel Cuatro Palmas, Avenida Primera between Calles 60 and 62; tel: 5 63912; fax: 5 337004
A four-star hotel which is set within a stone's throw of the beach. Good facilities.

Hotel Internacional (163 rooms), Avenida las Américas; tel: 5 63011; fax: 5 337004
One of the most luxurious and important hotels in the resort, the Internacional has recently undergone extensive refurbishment. It has all the facilities you would expect in a good four-star hotel and the cabaret venue – The Continental – has the reputation of being the best in the resort. The discothèque and nightclub are both lively and restaurant facilities here are also good.

Hotel Kawama (207 rooms), Calle O and Camino del Mar; tel: 5 63015
The original structure was built in traditional Spanish hacienda style in 1934. It was then, and still is, one of Varadero's more elegant hotels, although it has now been extensively refurbished to include bungalow accommodation, turning it into a tourist complex rather than a simple hotel. It is still, however, a peaceful place to stay and relatively inexpensive given that it's classed as a four-star hotel.

Hotel Oasis Internacional (147 rooms), Vía Blanca; tel: 5 63911
Situated at the gateway to the resort, the Oasis comprises hotel and bungalow accommodation. Most rooms have good views to the sea. Facilities include restaurant, bar and disco. The Oasis has a more relaxed atmosphere than many of the other hotels in the area.

Hotel Paradiso-Puntarena (510 rooms), Final de Kawama; tel: 5 63917
Situated at the western end of the peninsula, the Puntarena is another of the modern multi-storey hotels that have sprung up in Varadero during the last five years. Consisting of two ugly, seven-storey buildings, the Puntarena is classed as a five-star establishment although it's not as pleasant a place to stay as the Internacional or the Melia.

Hotel Punta Blanca (320 rooms), Kawama Final; tel: 5 63916
Situated at the beginning of the peninsula, the hotel is set out in a series of low-rise apartments which back on to the beach. There are several bars, a good restaurant, a cafeteria and a swimming pool.

Club Varadero (160 rooms), Carretera las Américas; tel: 5 66180
Close to the centre of Varadero, Club Varadero is a four-star self-contained holiday resort a short walk from the beach. Noted for its good sports facilities including pool, gym and tennis courts, the hotel also has a couple of decent restaurants and three bars.

Category 3

Hotel Bellamar (290 rooms), Calle 17 and Avenida Primera; tel: 5 63014
A modern multi-storey hotel set in central Varadero. The three-star facilities include a swimming pool, good restaurant and a discothèque. The hotel staff are warm and accommodating, making this a pleasant place to stay.

Copey Hotel Complex (272 rooms), Calle C between Avenidas 62 and 63; tel: 5 63012; fax: 5 337004
Incorporating both the Hotel Siboney and the Hotel Atabey, this is a huge tourist complex built close to the Autopista Sur. A package holiday favourite.

Granma Apart-Hotel (634 rooms), Calle 30 and Avenida Tercera; tel: 5 62246
Another huge tourist complex comprising several two-, three- and four-storey buildings. Good sports and recreational facilities and a big swimming pool.

Hotel Dos Mares (32 rooms), Calle 53 and Avenida Primera; tel: 5 62702
A recently-built hacienda-type house close to the Hotel Pullman towards the northeastern end of the peninsula. A good setting close to the older part of Varadero and a friendly place to stay.

Villa Tortuga (279 rooms), Calle 9 between Camino del Mar and Calle Bulevar; tel: 5 62243
A three-star hotel popular with tour groups. Facilities include two restaurants, two bars, a currency exchange desk, vehicle hire and a recreation room.

Hotel Varazul, Avenida Primera between Calles 14 and 15; tel: 5 63918
A three-star hotel and one of the most popular in the resort. Good facilities.

Category 2

Villa Caribe (124 rooms), Avenida de la Playa and Calle 30; tel: 5 63310
Big, modern, clean, featureless and popular with package tourists because of its size and price. Decent facilities including pool.

Hotel Pullman (15 rooms), Avenida Primera between Calles 49 and 50; tel: 5 62575
One of the longest established hotels in the resort, the Pullman is also one of the smallest. If you want to stay here you should book in advance. Clean, cheap and friendly.

Category 1

Hotel Ledo (20 rooms), Calle 43 and Avenida de la Playa; tel: 5 63206
One of the few hotels on the island that ranks as a one-star establishment, this place is nevertheless clean, although basic. The rooms do have air-conditioning which is almost essential in a tropical climate.

Eating and drinking

Like Havana, Varadero offers a big range of restaurants and cafés from which to choose. All the hotels have their own restaurants, most of which are quite adequate although uniformly expensive. On average, a meal out in Varadero will cost you a minimum of $20 per head and often a lot more. Even breakfasts can set you back over $5. The standard of food is generally a lot higher than on other parts of the island, but you would expect this as Varadero is competing for the Caribbean tourist market against places like Antigua and Barbados. There are plenty of restaurants outside of the hotels, although they too can be expensive. The majority are situated in the more developed western end of the peninsula. Don't expect that by venturing away from the confines of your hotel you will discover the true Cuban-Varadero experience. The only Cubans on the peninsula are those employed in the service industries looking after foreigners and that includes prostitution which has flourished since Cubans were allowed to possess dollars.

There is also a wide choice of bars to frequent both in and away from your hotel.

Mi Casita, Camino del Mar between Calles 11 and 12; tel: 5 63787
Open: 18.00–23.00
Used to be noted for its quality seafood and steak dishes. Still one of the most popular restaurants on the peninsula.

La Barbacoa, Calle 64 and Avenida Playa; tel: 5 63435
Open: 19.00–23.00
As the name suggests, barbecued and grilled dishes (predominantly red meat) are a speciality.

La Cabanita, Camino del Mar and Calle 9; tel: 5 62215
Open: 19.00–01.00
Serves similar food to Mi Casita but the atmosphere isn't as friendly.

Barlovento, Calle 11 and Avenida Playa; tel: 5 63721
Open: 10.00–22.00
Serves international cuisine at international prices.

Retiro Josone, Calle 1a between Calles 56 and 59; tel: 5 62740
Open: 12.00–23.00
Plush restaurant, international dishes, big bill.

La Casa de Antiguedades, Avenida Primera between Calles 56 and 59, Retiro Josone; tel: 5 62004
Open: 16.00–23.00
Pleasant restaurant with helpful staff. International cuisine.

Casa del Habano, Avenida Primera between Calles 63 and 64
Open: 12.00–24.00
Opens for lunch as well as dinner. International cuisine.

Pizzeria Capri, Avenida Playa and Calle 43; tel: 5 62117
Open: 11.30–22.45
The best place in Varadero to get a pizza. In reality they are nothing special, but they are reasonably priced and filling and the staff help to make the place warm and friendly. They serve pasta dishes too.

Castel Nuovo, Avenida Primera and Calle 11; tel: 5 62428
Open: 12.00–23.45
Italian cuisine. Steep prices.

Taberina Dortmunder Kneipe, Camino del Mar between Calles 13 and 14
Open: 12.00–22.00
Get your lederhosen on, practise your Bavarian beer songs and get on down to the
only German restaurant in Varadero (and in Cuba as far as I know). German food,
German beer and a sort of German ambience. If you like this sort of thing, then
you should be in Munich rather than Cuba.

Taco Taco, Camino del Mar and Calle 11; tel: 5 63721
Open: 12.00–22.00
Mexican cuisine, although the spices required for successful attempts at this sort
of cooking seem to be in consistently short supply on the island. You are more
likely to burn your mouth if you fall asleep with it open on the beach than with
the dishes sold in this restaurant!

Lai-Lai, Avenida Primera and Calle 18; tel: 5 63927
Open: 19.00–01.00
Fairly good quality Chinese food although the prices tend to be on the high side
for what you get.

Halong, Camino del Mar and Calle 12; tel: 5 63787
Open: 19.00–23.00
Newly established rival to Lai-Lai in the Chinese food market and there is little to
choose in terms of quality and price.

El Criollo, Avenida Primera and Calle 18; tel: 5 63297
Open: 19.00–22.45
Native Creole cuisine.

Mediterraneo, Avenida Primera and Calle 54; tel: 5 62460
Open: 11.30–22.45
Another Creole restaurant serving good, reasonably priced Cuban food.

Arrecife, Camino del Mar and Calle 13; tel: 5 63918
Open: 17.00–23.00.
Specialises in seafood. Good but expensive.

Cafeterias
Varadero is also home to several decent cafeterias which provide a more
affordable alternative to dining out in expensive restaurants.

Caracol, Camino del Mar and Calle 9; tel: 5 62555
Open: 10.00–22.00

Heladeria Coppelia, Avenida Primera between Calles 44 and 46; tel: 5 62866
Open: 10.00–22.45
Essentially an ice-cream parlour but snacks and drinks are on the menu.

Mi Rinconcito, Camino del Mar between Calles 11 and 12

Bars
The majority of decent bars are in the tourist hotels; nearly all hotels have
at least one bar and often two or three. If you fancy checking out the action
away from your hotel then the following places are worth a look. Many
are open throughout the night.

Caleta Club, Calle 19 and Avenida Primera; tel: 5 63513
Reasonably priced drinks and a friendly, bustling atmosphere.

La Cancha, (Club Tropical) Avenida Primera and Calle 22; tel: 5 63915
If you wake up at four in the morning dying for a drink, then this is one of the places you'll find one. Open 24 hours a day.

El Vampiro, Carretera a Du Pont; tel: 5 62217
There are no vampires here but again the bar remains open day and night. One of the liveliest places to go at night and if you prefer pop to *salsa* then you'll feel at home here.

Ranchon Bar, Avenida Playa between Calles 52 and 53
Open: 12.00–24.00

Nightlife

Nearly all hotels provide evening entertainment of some sort, usually in the form of a cabaret. The standard of show available in Varadero falls some way short of those set by the famous Tropicana in Havana and some of the cabaret acts are downright tacky. Scantily clad women in garish and revealing costumes trying desperately hard to appear as if they are enjoying themselves is generally what passes as entertainment. The pick of the bunch is the **Cabaret Continental** at the Hotel Internacional, although you will catch similar sorts of shows most nights of the week almost everywhere on the peninsula. Among the better ones are:

Cabaret Varadero, Vía Blanca and Carretera de Cardenes; tel: 5 62169
Open: 21.00–03.00; closed on Monday

Cabaret Kawama, Hotel Kawama, Avenida Kawama and Calle 0; tel: 5 63015.
Open: 21.00–03.00; closed on Monday

Cabaret Cueva del Pirata, Autopista Sur (11km from Varadero); tel: 5 66160
Open: 21.30–03.30; closed on Monday

El Eclipse, Hotel Bellamar, Calle 17 and Avenida Primera; tel: 5 63014
Open: 21.00–03.00; closed on Monday

Cinema

The only cinema in Varadero is centrally located on Avenida Playa and Calle 42. As is the case all over Cuba, the films shown have generally done the rounds on the international circuit for a number of years before ending up here. You will probably have already seen the sequel to the sequel of whatever movie is currently showing.

Shopping

The shopping facilities are of the sort that you would expect in a foreign beach resort. Most sell tacky souvenirs (bizarre ceramics, multi-coloured maracas and assorted knick-knacks) but the best buys remain cigars and rum. Most hotels have dollar shops and there are now two commercial centres which stock a wider range of goods including CDs and cassettes, leather goods, sports equipment and Latin American arts and crafts. The best is the Centro Comercial Copey at Calle 63 and Avenida Tercera, Copey Resort. The other, Centro Comercial Caiman, is on Avenida Primera between Calles 61 and 62. If you are intent on buying cigars then the Casa del Habano on Calle 63 and Avenida Primera offers the best selection. Sports equipment can be bought from Kawama Sport on Avenida Primera and Calle 63. If you run out of camera film or can't wait until you get home to have your film developed, then try Photo Service on Calle 63 and Avenida Segunda. Alternatively, most decent hotels offer a photo-developing service.

Useful addresses

Policlínico Internacional Varadero, Avenida Primera and Calle 61; tel: 5 62122 Open 24 hours. This hospital is for foreigners only. Facilities are adequate although basic. Treatment is expensive.

Pharmacies
Avenida Playa and Calle 44; tel: 5 62636. Open 24 hours.
Avenida Primera and Calle 28; tel: 5 62772. Open 24 hours.

Post offices
Calle 64 and Avenida Primera (main post office)
Avenida Playa between Calles 39 and 40

Police station, Avenida Primera between Calles 38 and 39

Taxis
Cubanacán, Calle 32 No 108 between Calles 1 and 3; tel: 5 63259
CubaTaxi, Calle 28 between Avenida Primera and Avenida Segunda

Petrol stations
Avenida Primera between Calle 15 and 16
Autopista Sur and Calle 17

Things to see and do

People do not go to Varadero to visit interesting museums and admire traditional and colonial architecture. The principal attractions in Varadero are the beach and the sea and the majority of entertainment to be had inevitably revolves around them. If you tire of simply sunbathing or swimming, Varadero affords you the opportunity to go scuba diving, water skiing, deep-sea fishing, horse riding and yachting. Car and moped hire is available at many hotels and you can even take a helicopter ride around the resort. For the less energetic there are a few sights worth checking out.

Retiro Josone

Situated off Avenida Primera and Calle 59, this small recreational park is a pleasant enough place to while away a few hours if you fancy a change from the beach. In the centre of the park there is a small lake containing a miniature picture postcard island. There are several cafés in and around the park.

Varadero National Park

Situated on the eastern tip of the peninsula, the park is made up of more than 450 hectares of woodland. There are remnants of old colonial buildings and what's left of the original salt flats is not one of Cuba's premier tourist draws. There are a few small caves dotted around but, these aside, there's little of interest. In the northern section of the park there is a nice stretch of beach which is soon to be developed for tourists.

Ambrosio Cavern

Situated in a small cliff on the southern coast of the peninsula, the caves contain the most important aboriginal pictographs ever to have been discovered on mainland Cuba. There are six drawings with concentric circles, groups of dotted lines and various geometric displays. Some of the drawings have been added to at a later date and the theory is that these additions were done by African slaves who had escaped captivity and used the caves for shelter. It is believed that both aboriginals and Africans used the caves for religious ceremonies. It is possible to make your own way to the caves although most hotels run organised trips with a guide.

Marinas

There are three marinas in Varadero which give access to the peninsula (Varadero is a recognised port of entry for Cuba). On arrival you can obtain tourist cards from the customs bureau.

Marina Acua

Situated on the Paso Malo Lagoon, this marina has moorage facilities for more than 100 boats. There are facilities for light repairs, but if your boat requires more extensive works to be carried out then the repair office will make arrangements with the larger shipyards in nearby Cardenas.

Marina Gaviota

Situated on the Vizcaino Channel on the tip of the peninsula in what is the most under-developed part of Varadero, this marina has sailboats and pleasure crafts for hire and offers comfortable but limited facilities for mooring. It is possible to hire a boat and a crew from here.

Marina Chapelin

Located in the Chapelin Canal, this marina has the most difficult access. There are facilities for minor repairs and it is possible to arrange for the provision of necessary supplies before setting off on the next leg of your trip. Crewed vessels may be hired for one or more days if you fancy touring the island.

Sports

Sports enthusiasts will find more than enough to do to satisfy their competitive instincts. Snorkelling and scuba-diving equipment is available for hire from almost all hotels. Windsurfing is becoming increasingly popular off the peninsula and many hotels have their own tennis courts and gymnasiums. Even golfers are catered for (no need to bring your own clubs unless you want to – they are available for hire). Varadero's one and only golf course is the Las Américas Golf Club at Mansion Du Pont, Carretera Las Américas, at the eastern end of the peninsula. Cycles and mopeds are also widely available for hire.

CARDENAS

History and orientation

Eighteen kilometres southeast of Varadero (52km east of Matanzas) is the city of Cardenas. Founded on 8 March 1828, the city prospered on the back of the sugar industry, its development given additional impetus by the natural harbour and port. Cardenas was the venue for the first flying of the Cuban flag following the invasion of the forces led by Narciso López, a Venezuelan who used Cardenas as his port of entry during his attempted invasion of Cuba in 1850. His aim of freeing the country from colonial rule failed, largely due to the apathy of the local people who failed to rally around him. After raising the flag in a gesture of defiance, López and his band of revolutionaries got back aboard their ship and sailed off into the annals of minor history. Today, the city is in dire need of a coat of paint. Many of its buildings, particularly the fortifications overlooking the harbour, are in need of renovation, but, with Havana and Trinidad eating up most of the regeneration budget, it seems that Cardenas will have to bite its lip and bide its time. It is none the less a charming little city worth a look. Bicycles and horses and carts vastly outnumber motorised vehicles on the streets, although there is still a sense of industriousness and purpose about the place.

The city is laid out in a typical grid pattern with the most important street, Avenida Cespedes, intersecting Parque Colón, the focal point for city life. The Calles run from northwest to southeast and cross the Avenidas which run from northeast to southwest. Most streets have both a name and, confusingly, a number.

Getting there and away

Road is the best option although Cardenas is linked to the rest of the country by a provincial rail line. There is an erratic bus service from Varadero which charges in pesos. Alternatively, a taxi ride from Varadero will take little more than 15 minutes and shouldn't cost more than $12–15, one way. Bus services operate to Havana and Santa Clara, but they are oversubscribed and unreliable. Your best chance of travelling onwards to

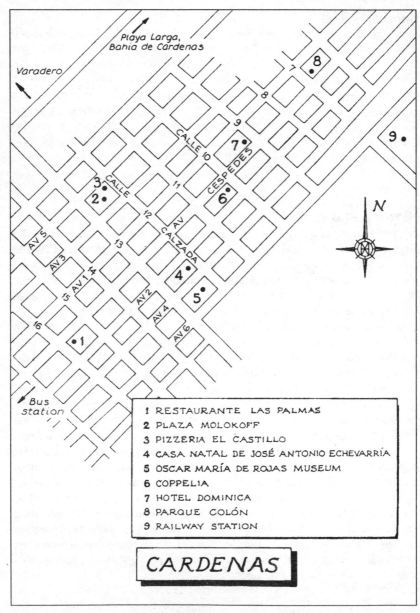

Playa Larga,
Bahía de Cárdenas

Varadero

CALLE 10

CALLE

AV 5

AV 3

AV 1

CESPEDES

AV CALZADA

AV 2

AV 4

AV 6

Bus
station

N

1 RESTAURANTE LAS PALMAS
2 PLAZA MOLOKOFF
3 PIZZERIA EL CASTILLO
4 CASA NATAL DE JOSÉ ANTONIO ECHEVARRÍA
5 OSCAR MARÍA DE ROJAS MUSEUM
6 COPPELIA
7 HOTEL DOMINICA
8 PARQUE COLÓN
9 RAILWAY STATION

CARDENAS

all destinations (including hitching) is to make it back to Varadero, if you intend to continue your journey by road, or to Matanzas, if you are travelling by rail.

The bus station in Cardenas is at Avenida Cespedes and Calle 32; the railway station, a delightful colonial-style building, is on Avenida 8 and Calle 5.

Accommodation

Cardenas isn't yet established on the Cuban tourist trail, a fact emphasised by the almost complete absence of tourist hotels and facilities. Only one hotel accepts foreigners at the moment, the **Hotel Dominica** on Parque Colón. At $18 for a double room, this is an interesting place to stay, primarily because of its colourful history (don't expect too much in the way of comfort). The area was formerly a loading point for the sugar industry and, in order to meet the needs of the workers, overnight accommodation was built. In 1919 the workers' accommodation was enlarged to turn the building into a hotel. The building was also occupied by the hapless Narciso López and his men, and their thwarted efforts at insurrection are commemorated by a plaque in the hotel. The Hotel Dominica was declared a national monument some years ago.

Eating and drinking

The choice is limited to either of the two hotels or the **Pizzeria el Castillo** on the Plaza Molokoff or the **Restaurante las Palmas** on Avenida Cespedes and Calle 16. The pizzas from El Castillo are edible although often, due to food shortages, the place is closed. When it is open, queues tend to be lengthy and prohibitive. El Castillo is a peso restaurant and there is no guarantee you will be served.

Things to see and do
Oscar María de Rojas Museum
Calle Calzada (Calle 12) No 4, Cardenas
Open: Tuesday to Saturday 13.00–18.00; Sunday 09.00–13.00; closed on Monday
Founded in 1900, this is one of the oldest museums in Cuba. It contains a strange mixture of exhibits ranging from photographs and documents depicting the city's role in the War of Independence to a substantial collection of butterflies, shells and insects. There is also a fountain pen/pistol which was the possession of a Nazi spy named Lunin who was captured in Havana in 1942. He was tried and found guilty of providing the Germans with information relating to the whereabouts of American submarines and executed at the Castillo del Principe. A curious museum well worth a visit.

Catedral de la Immaculada Concepción
Situated on Parque Colón, this is the main place of worship in Cardenas. An interesting place to visit although its opening hours are erratic.

Parque Colón
A central gathering point for the folk of Cardenas, the most surprising aspect of the park is the statue of Christopher Columbus which was erected in 1858 by the mayor of the time. The sculptor, Piquier, was the

man responsible for fulfilling the commission and the finance for the statue came partly from the donations of local people.

Plaza Molokoff
This building, a cross-shaped structure made primarily from iron, is currently closed awaiting renovation. Following the foundation of the city, it became apparent that a market venue was required to house the buying and selling activity of the city's traders. A leading citizen, named Parodi, was allowed to build the market plaza on the undertaking that it be handed over to the city's public administration within 25 years of being completed. The cross shape is augmented by an impressive 15m dome (built in the USA) and a series of intricate wrought-iron balustrades.

Casa Natal de José Antonio Echevarría
Avenida 4 and Calle 12; tel: 4919
José Antonio Echevarría was a student leader at the forefront of the anti-Batista movement during the 1950s. Born in this house in 1932, Echevarría was killed in 1957 during his anti-establishment activities and the house has been turned into a museum in recognition of the importance of his contribution towards the Revolution. The building itself is neoclassical in style and would benefit from some remedial work which, apparently, is scheduled for sometime in the near future.

ZAPATA PENINSULA
History and orientation
To the south of Matanzas province is the Zapata peninsula or Zapata marshes as it is sometimes known. The peninsula is a huge natural reserve for all manner of wildlife including local and migratory birds, lizards, crocodiles and rock crabs. It juts out south from the main body of the island with the southwestern section, primarily because of its ecological importance, designated a National Park. The area is also home to one of the largest underground cave and lake systems in Latin America. To the east of the peninsula lie a number of good and relatively secluded beaches, the most popular of which are Playa Larga and Playa Girón. These two beaches and the Treasure Lagoon at Guamá are among its principal tourist attractions, but the province's genuine claim to international fame is that it is home to the Bay of Pigs (at Playa Girón), site of the failed CIA-backed attempt at sparking a counter-revolution against Castro in 1961.

Getting there and away
Zapata peninsula can only be reached by road and then, in the case of Guamá, by boat. From Guamá to the resorts of Playa Larga and Playa Girón the road cuts south through the swamp of Zapata. Encounters with

local wildlife can make the journey an eventful one, as this extract from
Carlo Gébler's book *Driving Through Cuba* describes:

'A long way further south, we entered Ciénaga de Zapata, a forsaken area of
swamp and forest, now a national park. A huge billboard showing the Bay of
Pigs invaders bore the legend mercenarios. We were getting close to the
invasion site. Crabs in small, and then greater and greater numbers came out
from the dense, semi-tropical vegetation and scuttled across our path. I got
out of the car with India to photograph one. Our subject had lost one of its
claws. It was a big crab with a dark red body patched with black, about five
inches across; from leg-tip to leg-tip it must have measured about twelve
inches.

We each returned to the car and drove on. Still green ponds lay to the side.
Then we drove around a corner and suddenly the road ahead as far as we
could see was strewn with the remains of crabs crushed flat onto the tarmac,
thousands of them, a carpet of them, with hundreds of live ones crawling on
top of the dead. It was disgusting and our interest in wildlife turned to
revulsion.

We crawled forward at five miles an hour. I steered carefully from side to side
to try to avoid the crabs. Through the open windows we heard the clacking of
their claws on the tarmac as they ran across our path. Then came a noise like a
Big Mac styrofoam container exploding, and with horror we realised this was
our first casualty. I drove even more slowly, but the numbers of crabs running
about increased until it was impossible to avoid them. They covered the road,
and from under the tyres came an almost continuous sound of their bodies
exploding. I put my foot down. Swollen-bodied turkey vultures, feeding from
the road, waited until the last moment before heaving their swollen bodies out
of the way of our bumper, and flapped away with pieces of crab meat dribbling
from their beaks. The smell grew more palpable. It could be tasted in the mouth.
We wound up the windows but the smell persisted. Dragonflies streamed
towards us, crashed into our windscreen, and dissolved into what looked like
pools of discoloured phlegm. The sky above was blue and cloudless and the sea
glimmered turquoise beyond the trees.'

Facilities

The choices are limited to either the Indian Village of Villa Guamá or
hotels on Playa Girón and Playa Larga situated on the beach area south of
Zapata marshes. The hotel restaurants and cafeterias are the only places a
tourist can get a meal.

Guamá

Situated 186km southeast of Havana, Guamá was Castro's first project when
attempting to build up a tourist infrastructure. Sometimes called the Venice
of Cuba, the resort consists of a series of artificial islands (12 in total) in the
middle of what is the country's largest lagoon. All the islands are interlinked
by a network of wooden bridges. The accommodation on the island consists
of wooden huts which are supposedly built in a replica style of the one of the
Taino Indian villages that existed in the area prior to the arrival of Columbus.
The lagoon, known as Treasure Lake, is situated in the middle of Zapata

National Park and is a haven for mosquitoes. Insect repellent is essential here if you value your skin. Legend has it that the Indians threw their treasures and most-valued possessions into the lagoon rather than allow them to fall into the hands of Spanish *conquistadores*. If you want to check this legend out the lake is relatively shallow (maximum 5m).

Accommodation
Category 3
Villa Guamá (50 rooms), Laguna del Tesoro (Treasure Lagoon), Ciénaga de Zapata; tel: 59 2979
The accommodation comes in bungalow form. Facilities are classed as three-star although they are a bit on the primitive side. The peace and tranquillity of the setting is disturbed, needlessly, by piped music over the resort tannoy. There is a restaurant and bar on site as well as a swimming pool. The restaurant is a large thatched premises which serves below-average food at above-average prices ($5 for a very small continental breakfast.) Perhaps the crocodiles of Guamá have hidden access to the Villa Guamá foodstores!

Crocodile breeding farm
Following the Revolution, a campaign was set up to protect the indigenous crocodile from extinction caused by indiscriminate hunting. Hundreds of the species were rounded up and brought to the breeding farm situated in Boca de Guamá, which is close to the channel that leads into the lagoon. It is possible to visit the breeding farm through pre-arranged tours bookable from the resort. Enquire at the reception desk for details.

Playa Larga
A smaller and less popular resort than Playa Girón, the area is noted for its birdwatching as well as its sun, sea and sand. It is possible to arrange treks from here into the marshes to catch a look at the varied bird life of the area. Species include hummingbirds, parrots, owls and the national bird, the *tocororo*. Enquire at Villa Playa Larga for details.

Accommodation
Category 3
Villa Playa Larga (56 rooms), Playa Larga, Ciénaga de Zapata; tel: 59 7219 or 7225
Smaller and less popular than Playa Girón, the area is, however, popular with divers and those interested in recent Cuban history (the area saw some heavy fighting during the Bay of Pigs invasion – there is a small monument in remembrance of the struggle). Facilities are basic but the rooms are clean and the staff friendly. The restaurant is better and cheaper than at Villa Guamá.

Playa Girón
Situated on the eastern coast of the bay, Playa Girón is a sweeping stretch of beach popular with tour groups. The area was a popular haunt of the French pirate, Gilbert Girón, during the early 17th century. For his efforts,

the fortunate Frenchman was honoured by the decision to name the beach and the area after him. There are two distinct stretches of beach: one, small and more frequented, the other, known as Enamorados (Lover's) beach, larger and more secluded. In the vicinity is the Caleta Buena, a seascape of coral and sponges which is popular with scuba divers.

Accommodation
Category 3
Villa Playa Girón (245 rooms), Playa Girón, Ciénaga de Zapata; tel: 59 4110
Nothing pseudo-authentic about the style of accommodation here – just straightforward, no-nonsense modern and featureless chalets with air-conditioning thrown in. The facilities include a restaurant and bar (with a nightclub of sorts for those keen to boogie). The food is better and cheaper than at Villa Guamá. The sports facilities are good with both an on-site swimming pool and tennis court. The diving sites in the area are among the best in the province. Villa Playa Girón is a popular place for package tourists so it's best to try to book in advance.

Playa Girón Museum
Open: Tuesday to Sunday 09.00–17.00; closed on Monday
Situated around 100m from the scene of the landings, the museum documents the events surrounding the attempted counter-revolution in April 1961. Photographs, documents and weaponry (including one of the fighter planes used in defence of the Cuban forces) make it an interesting side-trip for those prepared to venture away from the beach or the confines of their mock Indian village.

Chapter Seven

Cienfuegos Province

Once a predominantly agricultural province, Cienfuegos has undergone substantial development since the Revolution and is now one of the most industrialised of all the provinces. Its location on the southern coast of central  Cuba has made it vulnerable to attack from pirates and corsairs through the ages. As the Cuban authorities look towards promoting tourism on their island, so Cienfuegos has begun to gear up to accommodate a more welcome type of visitor. Although much of the province is relatively flat, the foothills of the Escambray mountains in the east are a pleasant and scenic attraction and there are several good, unspoiled beaches stretching along the coast towards the province of Sancti Spiritus. Sugar is the area's main crop, with much of it being exported from the port of Cienfuegos, the capital of the province.

CIENFUEGOS CITY
History and orientation
Situated on the southern coast of central Cuba, 337km east of Havana, the city of Cienfuegos lacks the glamour of Havana and the splendour of Trinidad. Most tourists seem to pass it by or use it as a stopping-off point en route to Trinidad. To do so would be a mistake, as Cienfuegos is a delightful and interesting town with a history largely different to that of the rest of the country.

> 'The light here is wonderful just before the sun goes down: a long trickle of gold and the seabirds are dark patches on the pewter swell. The big white statue in the Paseo which looks in daylight like Queen Victoria is a lump of ectoplasm now. The bootblacks have all packed up their boxes under the arm-chairs in the pink colonnade: you sit high above the pavement as though on library-steps and rest your feet on the back of two little sea horses in bronze that might have been brought here by a Phoenician!'
>
> *Our Man in Havana* – Graham Greene

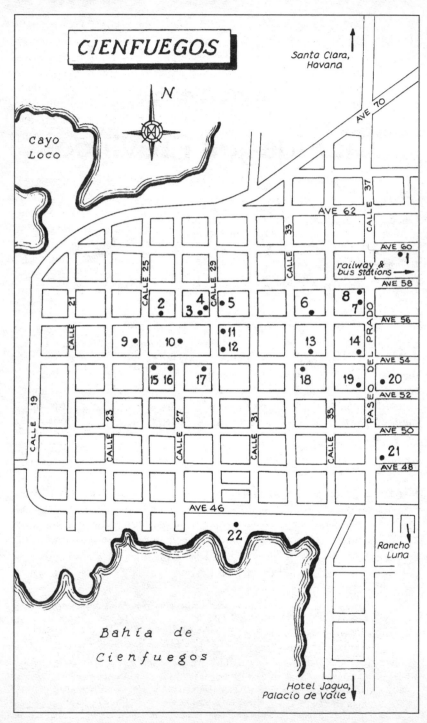

Known as 'The Pearl of the South' (an exaggerated description), Cienfuegos is a pleasant city which, because of its role as an important port, both domestically and internationally, has a slightly more cosmopolitan feel about it than most other areas in the south. Located on the southern coast of the country, it borders a very picturesque bay which was guarded, in olden times, by the Castillo de Jagua. Unusually, the castle was a precursor to the city. The Spanish, who finished building the castle in 1745, saw it as a necessity in order to protect the area from marauding pirates and corsairs for whom the bay was a popular stopping-off point.

The streets are straight and wide, like French boulevards, with the Paseo del Prado (Calle 37), which dissects the city and extends out to the peninsula's end, being the most important street. Like the Prado in Havana, this tree-lined boulevard is the focal point for city life especially in the evenings. The street extends south through the Punta Gorda area and north along the bay. There are some excellent views to be had from here, especially at sunset when the bay takes on a quiet and brooding appearance. In common with the layout in many other towns and cities in Cuba, the streets of Cienfuegos run at right angles to each other with odd-numbered streets crossing over even-numbered ones.

Prior to the arrival of the French settlers, the city (only a small village at the time) was known as Fernandina de Jagua. The site was also home to an Indian settlement which, like all Indian settlements, quickly disappeared after the arrival of the Spanish.

In 1817, Don Juan Luis Lorenzo de Clouet, a French emigrant living in the USA, formulated a settlement plan which would encourage white colonists to invest and develop the area. To entice settlers, he suggested that each should receive 33 acres of free land and their travelling expenses to Cuba would be paid for. The governor, Don José Cienfuegos, agreed to the plan and within two years nearly 150 settlers, predominantly from France, had occupied the area. The town was effectively born. Cienfuegos proceeded to develop largely as a result of successful trading in sugar and tobacco, its subsequent growth as a major port mirrored by the simultaneous decline in importance and stature of nearby Trinidad.

Key to map

1 Café Guamá	10 Parque José Martí	17 Central Government
2 Galeria del Arte	11 Catedral de la	Office
3 Teatro Tomás Terry	Purisíma Concepcíon	18 La Verja Restaurant
4 Colegia San Lorenzo	12 Restaurante Polinesio	19 Coppelia
5 Hotel Ciervo de Oro	13 Restaurante Dragon	20 Restaurante El
6 Hotel San Carlos	Dorado	Colonial
7 El Pollito Restaurant	14 Ciné Prado	21 Tropizul
8 Pizzeria Gioventu	15 Bodegon el Palatino	22 Ferry Terminal
9 Casa de la Cultura	16 Museo Histórico	Castillo Jagua

Today, evidence of the city's former importance is reflected in the grandeur of parts of its downtown area which bear the hallmarks of a distinctly French neoclassical influence. The area also has its eyesores, foremost among them being the part-built and abandoned nuclear power station, thankfully out of view of the town itself.

Getting there and away
There is no air link to the city so road and rail are your only options.

By train
The rail link between Havana and Cienfuegos is not the best in the country, although you can travel direct in both directions three times a week. The journey takes between eight and ten hours and will set you back $14. It is easier to catch the daily *especial* service to Santa Clara and then the morning train to Cienfuegos which takes around two hours. The problem in doing this is that you arrive in Santa Clara at 20.25 which means an overnight stop, but one night in Santa Clara hardly constitutes hardship and it's an interesting enough place to spend a night or two anyway. If you feel able to dispense with comfort and reliability then the ordinary (cattle truck) service is the one for you.

The railway station in Cienfuegos is six blocks east of the Prado on Calle 51 and Avenida 60.

By bus
The road link from Havana to Cienfuegos is excellent. Most of the journey can be done on the *autopista* – as far as Aguada de Pasajeros – before you complete the remaining 60km by B road. The problem remains the same in that trying to obtain a long-distance bus ticket either into or out of Cienfuegos can develop into a full-time career (and there's no guarantee of job satisfaction). Buses depart to and from Havana daily (there are usually four services a day from Cienfuegos). There is a daily service to Santa Clara (local buses operate around eight services a day), Trinidad and Camagüey and buses run three times a week to Santiago de Cuba.

The bus terminal is opposite the train station on Calle 51. Both local and interprovincial services operate into and out of this station.

By car
Cienfuegos is one of those cities which becomes instantly accessible once you have hired a car. Close to the main *autopista*, the surrounding countryside, especially en route to Trinidad through the Sierra del Escambray, is best explored by car. Hiring one in Santa Clara for a few days enables you to take in Cienfuegos, Trinidad and the surrounding area with a lot less discomfort than you would otherwise experience.

Hitching to Cienfuegos is possible, although you will more than likely have to change lifts on the way, usually at Santa Clara.

Getting around

Walking is the best way to get around and become acquainted with the city. If you're feeling footsore then the most widely used form of transport is the horse-drawn cab. Like the local bus service (which isn't reliable), you can pay in pesos. There are peso taxis in operation although they are few and far between. If you need to take a taxi then the best place to hail one is at your hotel.

Accommodation

The city isn't overflowing with tourist accommodation with only one designated tourist hotel in town. There are a few peso hotels in Cienfuegos, for example **Hotel Ciervo de Oro** on Avenida 58 and Calle 29 or **Hotel San Carlos** on Avenida 56 and Calle 35. There are others on or around the Prado.

Category 4

Hotel Jagua (144 rooms), Calle 37 No 1, Punta Gorda; tel: 432 6362; fax: 335056

Situated in the suburb of Punta Gorda to the south of the centre, this six-storey hotel was formerly a deluxe gambling joint frequented by high rollers from Havana and Miami. It was owned, prior to the Revolution, by the brother of General Batista. These days it is a four-star establishment with its rooms and balconies offering good views over the bay and across the city. It's a big hotel with modern facilities including a nightclub, swimming pool and regular cabaret acts.

Eating and drinking

Cienfuegos is well stocked with decent restaurants. *Paladares* are to be found on and around Paseo del Prado. The peso restaurant **El Colonial** on Calle 37 No. 5208 (tel: 432 7974) will also serve you an excellent meal if you pay in dollars (around $8 per head). The town's tourist hotels all have reasonable, if overpriced, restaurants. In addition, there are several other peso restaurants which may be worth a try, for example, **Café Guamá** on Calle 39, **Pizzeria Gioventu** on Avenida 58 and **Restaurante Polinesio** and **Restaurante Dragon Dorado**, the latter selling Chinese food, on Avenida 54.

La Verja, Avenida 54
A beautiful but faded colonial-style establishment built in 1831, La Verja boasts an extensive menu (although not as extensive as they would have you believe). Seafood is something of a speciality with lobster selling at between $25–30. You can eat quite well here for under $15 per head. There is often live music or a cabaret to entertain you while you dine.

El Pollito, Calle 37 at the junction of Avenida 56
Chicken is the speciality, although they do cook other dishes and the pasta is tasty and good value at $3–4 a plate.

Covadonga, opposite the Hotel Jagua
Specialises in Spanish cuisine particularly paella.

Palacio del Valle, Punta Gorda
You can't beat this place for setting and the food is above-average. It is expensive (bargain on around $25–35 per head), but, if you want to splash out for one night and add a touch of romance to the proceedings, then this is the place to dine. The view over the bay from the terrace, especially at sunset, is delightful.

Bodegon el Palatino, Parque José Martí (south side)
Has a reputation as being the place to go for wines and cheeses which are not always available and, when they are, are not particularly good value. They do sell other dishes (mainly snacks) and there is the added advantage of its pleasant setting opposite the park. A good place to go for a drink rather than a meal.

Nightlife

There is enough going on in the city to keep you occupied and at the weekend there are usually one or two late-night discos (for Cubans, but tourists are normally allowed in if accompanied by a local). The **Teatro Tomás Terry** is worth checking out as there is often live music and it can be a boisterous venue at weekends. The open air **Tropizul** on the Paseo del Prado (Calle 37) at the junction of Avenida 48 is the liveliest place to go if you fancy a spot of *salsa* with some young Cienfuegans. Back at the **Hotel Jagua** there is a nightclub which can sometimes be quite fun depending on the season and whether the hotel is full or half empty. If you fancy taking in a ten-year-old former blockbuster, there are also a couple of local cinemas, the most noteworthy being the **Ciné Prado** on Calle 37 and Avenida 54.

Things to see and do

The city isn't blessed with a host of designated museums, but you should find a stroll around the central section of the city on and around the Paseo del Prado a rewarding experience. There is plenty to look at and the people of the city are friendly and forever curious about who you are and where you're from.

Parque José Martí

Named after the Cuban national hero, the park is situated at the junction of Calles 54 and 29. Together with the surrounding buildings, it is the showpiece of the city's historical centre. Martí is remembered by a large white marble statue guarded by two watchful marble lions. The entrance to the park is protected by a *majagua* tree which was the marking point when the founders of Cienfuegos first began to lay out the city's streets. The tree shades a triumphal arch which was unveiled on the day that Cuba was declared a republic.

On the eastern side of the park is the impressive Catedral de la Purísima Concepción, which was built in 1870. The stained-glass windows depicting the twelve apostles are regarded as the finest in all of Cuba's

Above: *Palacio del Valle, Cienfuegos* (SF)

Below: *Traditional thatched house, Pinar del Río* (SF)

Above: *Tobacco drying house, Viñales, Pinar del Río* (CM)

Below: *Cigar rolling* (SF)

US classic cars, Havana (SF)

COMMUNISM AND CHRISTIANITY
Above left: *Che Guevara mural, Plaza de la Revolución* (SF)
Above right: *Colon Cemetery, Havana* (SF)
Below: *Choir in rehearsal, Havana Cathedral* (CO)

churches. Also overlooking the park is the Provincial Government Palace, a grand building with great columns and marble floors. Due west of the park stands the Casa del Cultura, originally the home of the sugar millionaire Don José Ferrer. It has an attractive blue-tiled tower. The old Spanish casino and the San Lorenzo school have been fully restored and are well worth a visit.

Teatro Tomás Terry

Situated on the north side of the Parque José Martí, this theatre was built in 1890 and has been recently restored. It is a beautiful and impressive structure whose facade is topped by three multi-coloured mosaic murals (purported to represent different expressions of the arts). The auditorium is open during the day and guided tours are on offer for $2. In the middle of the lobby is a statue of Tomás Terry made out of white marble. It was actually crafted in Italy and shipped here. The theatre seats over 900 people and the interior is fashioned from dark Cuban hardwoods.

Home for all manner of local cultural and political events, its inaugural performance was Verdi's *Aida*. The ceiling above the orchestra pit is adorned by a large fresco comprising 23 figures, mainly women floating romantically between clouds. If you want to catch a performance at the theatre you should ask the attendant staff who will be able to tell you about any forthcoming events.

Museo Histórico

Located on the south side of the Parque José Martí, this isn't one of Cuba's more interesting museums, containing little more than local military memorabilia that once belonged to those who took part in the various struggles for independence and freedom. The building itself is, however, quite splendid.

Tomás Acea Cemetery

Open: 07.00–18.00
Situated on a hill overlooking the bay off the main highway to Rancho Luna, the cemetery contains a huge marble portico similar to the Greek Parthenon, supported by 64 columns. Those buried here include local revolutionaries who died during the anti-Batista uprisings.

Palacio del Valle

On the Punta Gorda, diagonally opposite the Hotel Jagua, this Moorish-style country house was bought by Alejandro Suero Balbin and given to his daughter as a wedding present upon her marriage to Valle. Its fading pink colours fail to diminish the overall grandeur of the building which contains some excellent furnishings and porcelains. Close by the palace (behind Hotel Jagua) is a small fort which was once part of a site owned by the first Spanish settler in the area, José Diaz. He is believed to have wed a Siboney

Indian named Anagueia. Legend has it that, because Diaz was homesick, he and his wife, using the powers of Indian magic, spirited a Moorish-style house to appear on the site now occupied by the palace. One of his sons, who was concerned that his parents' dabbling in the occult would affect their chances of eternal salvation (they were Catholics), severed the spell and the house vanished, leaving only the foundations which Valle then used to construct the genuine article that stands there today. This story is much easier to believe after a few glasses of Cuban rum.

There is also a good restaurant here, see *Eating and drinking*, page 151.

Sport

The Estadio Municipal, the city's main sporting venue, is situated in the Punta Gorda district to the south of the city. This is the place to come if you want to see a baseball game. The standard is high – Cuba has some of the world's best amateur baseball players. Check locally for details of fixtures. The stadium is also home to other sports including athletics, something else at which the Cubans excel.

OUTSIDE CIENFUEGOS

The botanical gardens

This 90-acre site is in Soledad, 30km east of Cienfuegos. It is perhaps the most famed botanical garden in the country, housing over 2,000 tropical and sub-tropical plants. Initially owned and established by the Atkins family, local sugar-plantation owners, the concern was then handed over to Harvard University in 1901 and then to the Cuban Institute of Botany following the Revolution. Among the impressive collection of plant species are more than 200 types of cactus and nearly 300 types of *araceae*. There is also a collection of different types of palm trees indigenous to Cuba. The gardens are usually open daily between 09.00 and 17.00 but you should check locally for up-to-date information.

Playa Rancho Luna

Situated 20km east of the city, this arc of white sand beach is now home to a handful of tourist hotels. However, it is still very quiet and secluded. If you walk west of the tourist hotels for a few minutes, you can catch a few rays before cooling off in the waters of the Caribbean – without a soul to bother you.

Accommodation
Category 3
Hotel Faro de Luna (38 rooms), Carretera Rancho Luna (16km from the city); tel: 048120
Close by the Hotel Rancho Luna, this is another modern hotel although on a much smaller scale than the others. Being smaller it is a more friendly and intimate place and from the terraces there are good views across the Caribbean.

Hotel Pascaballo (188 rooms), Carretera Rancho Luna (22km from the city); tel: 096280
Situated at the mouth of the bay, this modern five-storey hotel has good views overlooking the entrance to Cienfuegos Bay across from the Castillo de Jagua. The ugliness of its eastern European design is in part compensated by its beautiful setting.

Hotel Rancho Luna (225 rooms), Carretera Rancho Luna (16km from the city); tel: 048120; fax: 335057
Situated on Playa Rancho Luna, this hotel which has cabin/bungalow accommodation is popular with package tourists from Germany and Canada. It's clean and pleasant enough and if you are into scuba diving there are some good sites nearby. Although just a stone's throw from the Caribbean, the hotel does have its own pool and the facilities in general are good.

The Castle of Our Lady of the Angels of Jagua
Open: Tuesday to Sunday 09.00–17.00; closed on Monday
The castle, situated 22km from the city, opposite the Hotel Pasacaballo, was originally used by the Spanish as a small fort to keep out smugglers (primarily from England) who used to enter Jagua Bay to obtain fresh water and food from the locals. It is now a much more substantial structure following the Spaniards' decision to develop it to defend the city from the more forceful threat offered by the English navy during the war between Spain and England. The present construction was built between 1732 and 1745. Its first commander was a man by the name of Juan Castilla Cabeza de Vaca.

Local legend has it that every night a black bird would fly around the castle before turning into the 'Lady in Blue' who stalked the fortress frightening the poor soldiers out of their wits. One night a brave soldier decided to stand guard and the following morning was found clutching his sword surrounded by segments of the lady's blue garb. The poor soldier, sent mad by the events of that night, spent the rest of his life in a lunatic asylum. He was too far gone to explain to anybody exactly what took place. The legend may well have its roots in the life and times of the beautiful wife of the commander, Cabeza de Vaca, who lived in the castle and rests beneath the floor of the chapel.

Chapter Eight

Villa Clara Province

Historically, Villa Clara, one of the country's central provinces, has been regarded as one of the most strategically important areas of Cuba. During both the wars for independence and the Castro Revolution, the province played venue for
a host of vital and ferocious battles. Although the area has yet to be recognised as one of Cuba's premier tourist destinations, there are some good beaches in the north and the capital of the province, Santa Clara, home to one of the country's four universities, is interesting enough to warrant a visit. The province is the second largest producer of sugar in Cuba, with other crops, particularly tobacco, playing an important part in the local economy. In the south, the mountain resort of Hanabanilla in the Escambray Mountains is being primed for tourism. It is this area's natural beauty which holds most appeal to the visitor.

SANTA CLARA

History and orientation

In 1698, tired of constantly being preyed on by the host of pirates and corsairs who operated in the waters around Remedios, a group of families decided to opt for the relative peace and tranquillity of the inland. What was then a small settlement grew and prospered, largely due to the fertile and arable lands surrounding it. Its position in the centre of the country also contributed to its rise and growth. In 1878 Santa Clara adopted its current role as capital of the province of Villa Clara. Having escaped from the unsavoury clutches of both pirates and corsairs, the old Remedios families might have hoped that their descendants would settle into a more idyllic lifestyle, free of violence and upheaval. However, the city of Santa Clara has historically been of immense strategic importance and in 1896, in a particularly brutal battle during the struggle for independence, Leoncio Vidal, a Cuban hero,

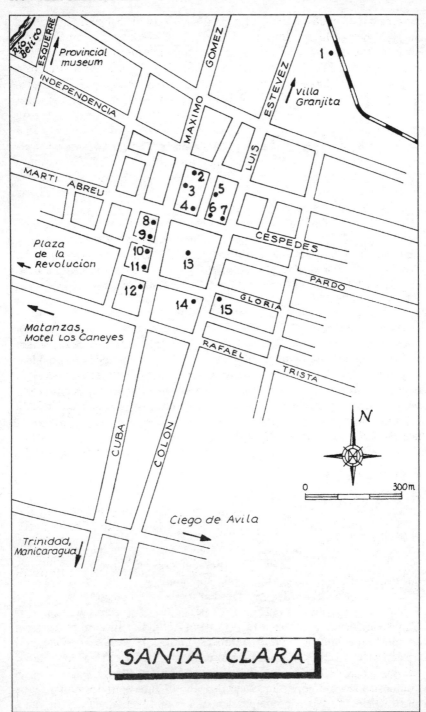

SANTA CLARA

launched an unsuccessful attack on the local Spanish garrison, sacrificing his life in the process. Over 60 years later during the anti-Batista struggles, none other than Che Guevara himself stormed the city along with his revolutionary troops, capturing the city from Batista's forces. The city has been referred to as *El último reducto de la tirania Batistiana* – the last fortress of Batista's tyranny. As part of the battle for the city, Guevara managed to derail a troop train carrying reinforcements east to the Sierra Maestra. Once Batista found out that the city of Santa Clara had fallen, it is said that he knew his reign was over and prepared himself for his flight into exile. Some of the carriages of the train have been preserved as monuments to the battle and can be found close to the station. The bullet holes scarring the walls of the Hotel Santa Clara Libre have been left intact.

Those days of trial, tribulation and excitement are, for the moment, over. These days the city and the province are pictures of serenity, with only tourists threatening to disrupt the local way of life. Santa Clara can be thoroughly explored in a day, although you may wish to spend a little longer to get to know the locals, a fair proportion of whom are students at the city's university.

Layout
The centre of the city and focal point for city life is Parque Vidal. In the centre of the park is a monument which marks the spot where Leoncio Vidal is said to have met his violent end. The main street is Calle Independencia, the middle section of which is pedestrianised. The Plaza de la Revolucíon, to the west of the city centre, is where most rallies and festivals are held.

Getting there and away
There are no flights to or from Santa Clara but both road and rail links make the city easily accessible.

By train
Trains run daily from Havana with the best service being provided by the *especial* that is scheduled to chug into Santa Clara station at 21.31 every night. There are two other services scheduled to ply the route daily but they are both uncomfortable and unreliable. The *especial* train continues on to Santiago de Cuba, stopping off at most cities en route. The railway station is 1km north of the city centre.

Key to map

1 Railway station	6 Coppelia	11 Hotel Santa Clara
2 Restaurante Pullman	7 Museum of	Libre
3 El Colonial	Decorative Arts	12 Bureau de change
Restaurant	8 Hotel Central	13 Parque Vidal
4 Caridad Theatre	9 Cultural Centre	14 Post office
5 El Rapido Restaurant	10 Cinema	15 Coppelia

CHE GUEVARA

Born in Rosario, Argentina on 14 June 1928, Ernesto 'Che' Guevara developed a chronic asthma condition in his childhood years which was to afflict him for all of his life. Despite this, the young Che flourished intellectually and excelled at sports whilst at school. Qualifying as a doctor, he travelled widely across Argentina and Latin America where his travels brought him into contact with people whose backgrounds differed widely from his own middle-class roots.

In his formative years Che read expansively, devouring the works of, amongst others, Marx, Engels and Freud.

While living and working in Mexico City, Guevara met with Fidel and Raoul Castro who had been exiled there following their release from the model prison on the Isle of Youth. In Fidel, Guevara finally found the leader he had been looking for. Che was amongst those who sailed with Fidel and Raoul on board the *Granma* in 1956, intent on fomenting revolution to overthrow the Batista dictatorship. His primary role was as doctor to the crew and then as commandant of the Revolutionary Army. Guevara was regarded as an excellent military tactician and allied to the fact that he was both politically shrewd and militarily ruthless (he had no compunction in shooting defectors from the revolutionary cause nor indeed supporters of the Batista regime), by the time Batista was overthrown Che was of sufficient status to adopt the position of Castro's right-hand man.

In 1959 he married Aledia March. In 1960, as Minister for Industry, he signed a trade deal with the Soviet Union and in the process helped push Cuba away from its historic links with the USA. Later (in 1965) he was to denounce the Soviet Union, asserting that they were 'a tacit accomplice of imperialism' while addressing the Organisation for Afro-Asian Solidarity at Algiers.

In 1965 Che, disillusioned with Cuba's growing dependency upon the Soviet Union, resigned from his ministerial position and set off for Africa where he helped rebel factions fighting in Zaire (then the Belgian Congo). He later returned to Cuba to prepare for a guerrilla campaign in Bolivia in the hope of recreating a Cuban-style revolution to bring down the Bolivian establishment. He was captured by the Bolivian army on 8 October 1967 and the next day, on the orders of Bolivia's president, General Rene Barrientos, he was executed. His body was put on public display in a hospital laundry house in Vallegrande before disappearing shortly after. Agents from his home country, Argentina, cut off his hands to check his finger prints against those they kept in files back home while Bolivian soldiers took his body to a secret burial place. The Bolivian government, conscious of the fact that any burial site could become a place of international homage decided that the body should vanish. Che had been a legend in his own life time. Upon his death, he became a martyr and international folk hero.

In late 1995 one of the officers of the Bolivian army present at the secret burial reported that Guevara's body was buried in a mass grave under the airstrip in Vallegrande. Vargas, who had met with Che's executioner, told the world that Che's last words uttered to the soldier as he trained his rifle on him were, 'Shoot coward! You are going to kill a man.'

On 28 June 1997, the skeleton of Che was unearthed, his skull shrouded by an olive green combat jacket. Both Cuban and Argentinian geophysicists who conducted the search were overcome with emotion upon the realisation that the legendary revolutionary's grave had finally been discovered. Guevara's remains were flown to Havana where his relatives and Fidel Castro received them in a private ceremony. They remained in Havana until 9 October 1997 when, on the thirtieth anniversary of his death, they were transferred to a mausoleum in Santa Clara.

By bus
There are two bus stations in Santa Clara, both situated north of Parque Vidal. The interprovincial station occupies a particularly inconvenient location about 1½km away from the centre. There are regular services to and from Havana but they are heavily booked up in advance. The journey, if you do manage to get a ticket, takes only four hours as the cities are linked by the country's main *autopista*. Services also operate to Camagüey, Trinidad, Sancti Spiritus and Santiago de Cuba. Check locally for the current timetable as all services are subject to alteration due to problems with bus stock and fuel shortages.

By car
The easiest way to get to the city from Havana is by car. The *autopista* which links the two cities is largely unused and the 300km journey can be completed in about three hours. Hitching to Santa Clara is also a possibility worth considering, although you will be in competition with many Cubans attempting the same trip.

Accommodation
The only hotel central to the city in which you are likely to be able to find shelter is the **Hotel Santa Clara Libre**. There are a few other hotels in the city but they are peso hotels and you are unlikely to be accepted. The **Hotel Central** is currently being restored and should be ready some time in 1998.

Category 3
Hotel Santa Clara Libre (159 rooms), Parque Vidal; tel: 422 27548
This multi-storey monstrosity looms over the square, casting an unwelcome shadow across what is otherwise a fairly pleasant little area. It is slap bang in the middle of the city, which is a plus, and the facilities in the hotel are generally quite good. You will be surprised to note that there is, however, no swimming pool, something of a rarity in Cuban tourist hotels, especially those inland. The cafeteria and the restaurant serve reasonably-priced food. All rooms are air-conditioned.

Motel los Caneyes (90 rooms), Carretera de los Caneyes between
Avenidas Eucaliptos and Circunvalacíon; tel: 422 4512
Five kilometres from the city centre, this establishment is a collection of thatched bungalows which are purportedly designed in the fashion of a traditional Indian village. It is a pleasant enough setting with nicely landscaped gardens and there is a large well-tended pool. The main drawback is its isolated location, although it is possible to catch the local number 11 bus which connects the motel to the Parque Vidal. It's most definitely a quiet and humble retreat recommended for those who like peace, quiet and their own company.

Villa la Granjita (24 rooms), Carretera de Maleza; tel: 422 26051
A relatively new hotel just 2km outside the city, this has good facilities which include a restaurant, two bars, a swimming pool and a nightclub.

Eating and drinking

You are more likely to eat in your hotel than anywhere else as tourist restaurants are thin on the ground in Santa Clara. The best restaurant is in the **Hotel Santa Clara Libre**, although there are some adequate peso restaurants close to Parque Vidal if you fancy trying to pass yourself off as Cuban (**El Colonial, Restaurante Pullman** and **El Rapido**, all north of the park are the pick of the bunch). The local **Coppelia** ice-cream store tends to have less of a queue than in other cities so you may wish to try a Cuban *helado*. It is situated just south of Parque Vidal. There is a peso pizza parlour a few doors down on the same street. It is difficult to miss as the queues seem to stretch all the way back to Havana.

Things to see and do

Santa Clara isn't one of Cuba's architectural gems, but there are some interesting museums worth taking in and the small brick red-tiled houses lend themselves to an atmosphere of calm and discretion. This rural drowsiness contrasts with the other side of Santa Clara, a city that is also home to the huge INPUD factory employing more than 1,500 workers. There are other big manufacturing plants close to the city along with over 100 educational establishments. It is possible to visit these institutions if you travel as part of an organised study tour. For most people, the area around Parque Vidal seems to hold most interest.

Villa Clara Provincial Museum

Ciudad Escolar Abel Santamaría, Reparto Osvaldo Herrera, Santa María
Open: Tuesday to Saturday 13.00–18.00; Sunday 09.00–13.00; closed on Monday
Situated in the Abel Santamaría school, which was a military installation prior to the Revolution, the exhibits here cover the development of the province of Villa Clara in general and the city of Santa Clara in particular. There is also a hall dealing with the struggles for independence during the 19th and 20th centuries. The battle for Santa Clara in 1958, when Che Guevara toppled the Batista forces holding the city, was one of the last and one of the most crucial battles of the Revolution. The museum's most prestigious exhibits deal with this battle as well as covering the fight against Batista in other areas of Cuba.

Museum of Decorative Arts

Open: Monday and Wednesday to Saturday 13.00–18.00; Sunday 09.00–13.00; closed on Tuesday
Situated on Calle Marta Abreu on the north side of Parque Vidal, this museum is housed in one of the most attractive buildings in the city. It used to be the colonial home of the Carta family. It exhibits a collection of furniture and furnishings, detailing the different tastes and styles found in the city's former colonial mansions.

Tren Blidado

Situated east along Independencia, across the bridge over the railway track, this exhibition is housed in some of the armoured cars which Che Guevara managed to derail in 1958 while they were en route to the Sierra Maestra region, taking troops and supplies to Batista's beleaguered forces. Defeat at Santa Clara heralded the end of the Batista regime – he left for sanctuary in America shortly after. The display inside the carriages gives an account of what happened that day. Check locally for opening times.

Museum of the Revolution

By now you may well be tired of visiting museums of the Revolution, but if you're not then this one is west of Parque Vidal, a five-minute walk from the centre, and it relates pretty much the same story. It would be better to visit the one in Havana.

Recreation

Parque Vidal is the most eventful place in a city in which not a lot happens. As well as being the geographical heart of the city, it is also its social centre and there is usually some sort of entertainment going on at weekends. There are two local **Casa de la Trovas** – on Calle Colón (opposite Coppelia) and on the west side of Parque Vidal close to the Hotel Santa Clara Libre. Cuban troubadour music is played live most evenings, although you should check with the local Intur office to find out the current listings. The **Caridad Theatre** on the north side of Parque Vidal is also worth a visit. Again, details of performances can be obtained from the Intur office situated on the west side of the park.

AROUND SANTA CLARA

Lake Hanabanilla

Travelling south along the road from Santa Clara to Trinidad the countryside becomes progressively more mountainous as you begin the ascent up the Sierra Escambray, the second highest mountain range in Cuba after the Sierra Maestra. The main form of transport up here is the horse and the area around the mountains is known as cattle-raising country. Passing through small villages, you will come across some examples of the *bohío*-style house, a design directly descendant from the Indian population. Lake Hanabanilla is 52km south of Santa Clara. It is an attractive stretch of water which is, in fact, a man-made reservoir, supplying both Santa Clara and Cienfuegos with fresh water. There is also a large hydroelectric power plant situated by the lake which generates energy to supply the surrounding area.

It is a place worth an overnight stop, especially if you want to take advantage of its good fishing. The nearby **Hotel Hanabanilla** (124 rooms; tel: 49125) charges $20–23 for a single room and $26–31 for a double, depending on the season. There is a good restaurant, **El Río Negro,** by the lakeside with delightful views across the lake.

Remedios

The town of Remedios, 50km northeast of Santa Clara, was founded in 1514 when a grant of land was given to a man named Vasco Porcallo de Figueroa. By rights it should have become one of the first of the seven cities, but Senor de Figueroa refused permission for either a city hall or a municipality to be instituted and so Remedios never made the record books. Initially the town was known as Santa Cruz de la Sabana and was moved twice, in 1544 and 1578, because of persistent attacks from pirates. Upon moving the second time, it adopted the name San Juan de los Remedios del Cayo. In 1690 it divided, some moving to the site which is now Santa Clara while those who remained opted for the name Remedios for their small town.

The town is a typical, but beautiful, example of Spanish colonial architecture. The intrusion of the sugar and cattle industries have not detracted from its laid-back atmosphere. The centre is marked by the Plaza Martí and, as with all Spanish cities, the streets span out from the Plaza with well thought out symmetry. The Plaza Martí is similar in style to the Plaza Mayor in Trinidad.

Most people visit Remedios as a day trip, mainly because there is no hotel accommodation in the town.

Things to see
Museum of the Remedio Parrandas, Calle Máximo Gómez No 71
Open: Tuesday to Saturday 13.00–18.00; Sunday 09.00–13.00; closed on Monday
The museum celebrates the history of the festivals of Remedios which have been ongoing events since 1822. They used to take place on Christmas Eve when the people of the town celebrated and generally made a lot of noise, ostensibly to motivate the townspeople to head for midnight mass. The two sections of the town, El Carmen (portrayed by a hawk) and San Salvador (represented by a rooster), competed against each other in the various games that formed part of the festivities. The victors were the sector that made the loudest din. Following the Revolution, this festival was moved to 24 July, two days before the anniversary of Moncada. These days it is usually held on the last Saturday of the month of July and the celebrations last all night until dawn. If you're in the vicinity late in July, Remedios is a fun place to be.

The Church of San Juan Batista de Remedios
Situated in the Plaza Martí, this church dates back to the mid to late 16th century (although the construction process wasn't actually completed until 1692). The highlight is the ceiling which has recently been restored after it was crudely covered over with plaster.

Chapter Nine

Sancti Spiritus Province

This is the most central province of Cuba and its northern and southern coastlines are washed by the waters of the Atlantic and the Caribbean respectively. Tourism seems set to replace sugar and tobacco as the prime source of wealth creation in the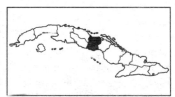
Sancti Spiritus economy. The beaches in the north of the province are excellent and the city of Sancti Spiritus itself is worth a visit. The jewel in the provincial crown is, however, the beautiful and historic city of Trinidad, a UNESCO-protected national monument, recognised as one of the most charming cities in the whole of the Caribbean and Latin America.

SANCTI SPIRITUS CITY
History and orientation
Founded in 1514 by Diego Velázquez, the site of the city was moved in 1522 away from the banks of the Tuinicu river to the banks of the Yayabo river, where irrigation of the surrounding land was better. Capital of the province of the same name, Sancti Spiritus city was the temporary home of Fernández de Córdoba, the man who led the Spanish expedition to the Yucatán, a journey which is said to have been the inspiration behind Hernán Cortés' conquest of the Aztec empire. During the 16th and 17th centuries, Sancti Spiritus was prey to constant attack from pirates and on two occasions was almost razed to the ground. The wealth of the area, which developed on the back of the province's arable farm land, proved a continuous attraction to pirates and corsairs up until the mid-18th century.

The city is 380km east of Havana and today is generally only visited by tourists calling in en route to Trinidad. However, as one of Cuba's oldest cities, there is sufficient of interest here to warrant more attention and a day's exploring is justified.

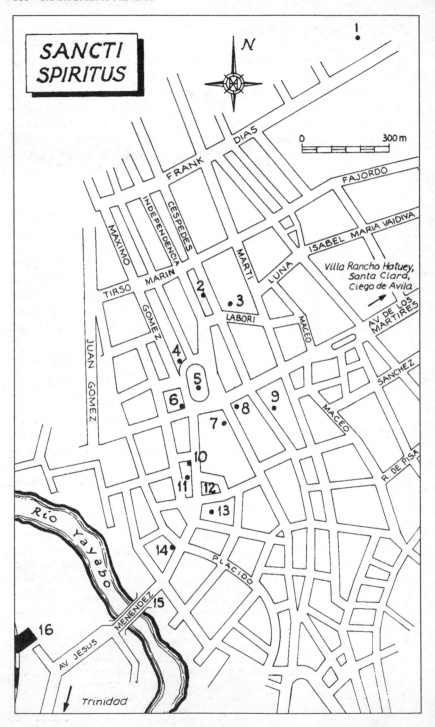

Getting there and away
By road
The *autopista* which takes you as far as Santa Clara is the easiest stretch
of the journey. After Santa Clara, the road drops southwards passing
through the towns of Placetas and Cabaiguan with the Sierra del
Escambray to your right. If you're coming by car then the journey is easily
completed within an hour. Trying to catch a bus from Santa Clara is more
problematic as they rarely run when they're supposed to and are usually
full when they do. Hitching can also be difficult, even though the road is
the main communications artery through Cuba.

By train
Train services to the city are poor. A *segunda* class train is scheduled to
leave daily to and from Havana, but the journey is long (allow 15 hours)
and you can't always depend on it running. The *especial* service
operating between Havana and Santiago calls in at Guayos station
which is only 15km from Santa Clara. There is usually a local bus
service that links the two and, if you must travel by rail, this is your best
bet. One problem you will have to overcome is the fact that the train
from Havana arrives at Guayos at 23.06 (or at least it's scheduled to).
If the local bus has conked out or has run out of petrol, then you are
going to be left 15km from your destination with only your wits and a
prayer to help you.

Accommodation
There isn't a great deal of choice for the tourist when deciding on where
to stay in Sancti Spiritus, but the three main hotels are pleasant enough.
Hotel Perla de la Cuba on Parque Serafín Sánchez is currently being
restored and will be ready for occupancy in 1998. In addition there are a
couple of peso hotels which may let you in, **Hotel las Villas** and **Hotel
Colonial**.

Category 3
Villa Rancho Hatuey (22 rooms), Carretera Central, Sancti Spiritus;
tel: 41 26015 or 26406
Situated at the entrance to the city, off the main drag in a green and hilly spot, the
accommodation is three-star and, given the location, relatively expensive.
Facilities include a restaurant, bar and a swimming pool. It's a quiet location so

Key to map

1 Plaza de la Revolution de Serafín Sánchez	6 Library	12 Plaza Honorato
2 Museo Archeologico	7 Post office	13 Parroquial Mayor Church
3 Restaurante 1514	8 Gran Café	14 Museo Arte Colonial
4 Hotel Perla de la Cuba	9 Museo Histórico Provincial	15 Yayabo bridge
5 Parque Serafín Sánchez	10 Casa de la Trova	16 Railway station
	11 Mesin de la Plaza	

don't expect much in the way of thrills and entertainment. It is, however, accessible for the city and tours to the surrounding countryside (and to Trinidad) can be booked from here.

Hotel Zaza (128 rooms), Finca San José, Zaza; tel: 41 26012
Situated 5km south of the city on the banks of Lake Zaza, this large three-star establishment isn't ideal for access to the city but it's a nice place to stay with fine scenic views over the lake. The facilities here include a swimming pool and tennis courts and it's also possible to hire fishing tackle and charter small boats if you want to pit your wits against the local perch in the lake.

Category 2
Hotel Plaza, Calle Independencia (by Parque Serafín Sánchez)
Its biggest advantage is its central location. Formerly a peso hotel it now charges in dollars.

Eating and drinking
Most people tend to dine in their hotels, but if you are prepared to venture out of an evening you will find (or rather, be led) to one of the *paladares* around Parque Central. **Restaurante 1514** on the junction of Calles Lavorri and Cespedes (close to Parque Serafín Sánchez) is still going, although the food hasn't improved. **Restaurante Mesón de la Plaza** on Plaza Honorato is the most popular with tourists. **Gran Café** by Parque Serafín Sánchez is worth a visit. If you're after some local nightlife, try the **Casa de la Trova** on Plaza Honorato.

Things to see and do
The Colonial Art Museum
Calle Placido 64 (at the junction of Avenida Jesús Menéndez)
Open: Tuesday to Saturday 15.00–20.00; Sunday 13.00–18.00; closed on Monday
Formerly the Palace of the Valle–Iznaga family, the 19th century colonial structure has been beautifully preserved. Its wrought-iron balconies and bars are some of the finest examples in the province. The museum houses an elegant collection of furniture and ceramics dating back to Spanish colonial times.

Parroquial Mayor Church
Avenida Jesús Menéndez
Work on the original building started in 1536 with money donated by local merchants and landowners. It was constructed almost entirely of wood and was destroyed by pirates in 1620. A more sturdy structure, made out of stone, was erected between 1671 and 1680 with work on the tower finally being completed in 1764. The cupola was a late addition to the building (mid-19th century). The church actually functions as such; it is not simply a museum piece, and services are held almost daily.

Yayabo bridge

Work on the bridge, one of only a handful of stone bridges remaining in Cuba, was begun in 1817 and completed in 1825. The arched structure, part of Avenida Jesús Menéndez, spans the Yayabo river and connects the two different parts of the city.

TRINIDAD
History and orientation

The best-preserved colonial city in the country, Trinidad is 460km southeast of Havana and 78km southeast of Cienfuegos. It has a population of approximately 35,000. Declared a national monument by the Cuban government, the city is very much as it was four centuries ago, the beauty of its baroque architecture and cobblestoned squares harking back to a bygone era when Trinidad was a key player in the Caribbean slave trade. Many of the aged red-tiled buildings have been restored to their former glory. Trinidad is a must on anyone's itinerary.

Founded in 1514 by Diego de Velázquez, Trinidad (or Villa de la Santísima Trinidad, to give it its full title) was one of the first established settlements in the colony. Before the arrival of the Spanish it was populated by Taino Indians who used to pan the surrounding rivers for gold. It was this which initially attracted Velázquez, although the amount of gold ultimately retrieved was paltry compared to the riches the Spanish were busily plucking from Mexico and other Latin American countries.

In the 16th and 17th centuries the town prospered primarily on the back of the lucrative slave trade, although there was also money to be made from cattle ranching. Like Havana and especially Santiago de Cuba, Trinidad was vulnerable to attack from pirates and, in response to this, established its own local militia to defend itself. Geographically and politically isolated, much of its trade was done with England and other Caribbean countries and it wasn't until the mid-18th century that the town began fully to integrate itself with the rest of Cuba.

Trinidad's growth was checked following the development of the port at Cienfuegos, which was superior in terms of location. Trinidad's own port, Casilda, fell into disuse and that, coupled with the demise of the slave trade, marked the end of Trinidad's economic golden days. Ironically, it is from about this time that the town began to develop its reputation as a cultural centre, founding its own language school teaching English, French and Italian. In 1820 it launched its own newspaper and in 1827 established an academy of music, dance and theatre.

This golden era of cultural development collapsed following the Ten-Year War of Independence, during which Trinidad sent over 1,000 troops into battle. With the establishment of a republic and the growth of vast sugar estates elsewhere on the island (the *centrales* system of

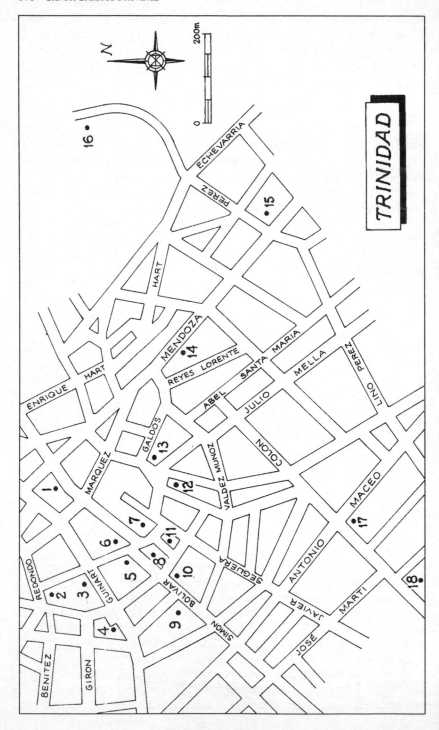

production didn't take root in Trinidad), Trinidad's economy began a downward spiral that was to last until the Revolution. Its geographical position, effectively cut off by the encircling Escambray mountains, was also a contributing factor in its decline. By the time of the Revolution, Trinidad had the worst health and education statistics in the whole of the province.

Ironically, it is probably due to the collapse of the local economy then that the city is the architectural wonder it is today. With no money and therefore no development of the city, it remained an architectural throwback to bygone centuries and the unique character and beauty of its architecture has not only been preserved but also restored following investment by both the Cuban government and UNESCO (it was declared a Heritage of Mankind site by UNESCO in 1988).

In its position a few kilometres inland from the Caribbean Sea, crouched in the southwest corner of the province of Sancti Spiritus and surrounded by the Sierra del Escambray to the north and west, Trinidad lies on what is the plain of the River Manati which is some 20km to the east. The city does not conform to the usual grid system in terms of its layout. Rather, it's a mish-mash of streets and squares which seem to have grown spontaneously rather than been planned. Calles Bolivar, Antonio Maceo and José Martí are the city's main streets.

Getting there and away

Until recently the only way to get to Trinidad was via the Carretera Sur, the highway that links the cities of Sancti Spiritus and Cienfuegos. Thankfully, Cubana Airlines, in their infinite wisdom, saw fit to begin operating flights from Havana, which means that it is now more accessible than before. At present there are only two flights a week but there may soon be an increase in this number as demand to see the city (it is a linchpin in Cuba's drive to attract more tourists) means the route will become a profitable one.

If you are coming by road then don't despair, for although the journey will obviously take a lot longer, the scenery in the Escambray mountains will more than make up for the additional time and discomfort experienced.

Key to map

1 Paladar Estela Comidas Caseras	6 Romantic Museum	13 La Ruina Café/Bar
2 La Canchanchara Restaurant	7 Church of Santísima Trinidad	14 Paladar La Rosa
3 Museum of the Struggle against Bandit Bands	8 Plaza Mayor	15 Church of Santa Ana
4 Restaurante el Jigue	9 Municipal Museum	16 Motel las Cuevas
5 Guamuhaya Archaeological Museum	10 Art gallery	17 Restaurante Trinidad
	11 Museum of the Architecture of Trinidad	18 Parque Cespedes
	12 Casa de la Trova	

By train

Unfortunately, Trinidad's railway station has closed down and been left to go to seed. If you take the train from Havana you will have to alight at Santa Clara and complete the trip by road.

By bus

You can catch buses from Havana, Santa Clara, Sancti Spiritus and Cienfuegos, although the services are booked weeks, and sometimes months, in advance. The bus journey from Havana, if you do manage to get on one, takes around six hours. The most regular bus service, and the one you have more chance of getting a ticket for, is from Sancti Spiritus. There are usually around six buses a day plying this route. Both Cienfuegos and Santa Clara operate a daily bus service to the city. Travelling by local bus can be extremely cheap if you manage to overcome the obstacle of getting a ticket. Although some drivers insist on payment in dollars you can usually get away with paying in pesos. The bus terminal in Trinidad is on the intersection of Calles Gustavo Izquierda and Piro Guinart.

Hitchhiking

Your best chance of hitching a lift is from Santa Clara, as the route is popular with tour buses which stop off to visit Lake Hanabanilla, midway between the two cities. If possible you should try to arrange a lift before setting off from the city as, tourist buses aside, traffic to Trinidad is generally sparse and it can be a long wait before someone finally stops to pick you up.

Accommodation

For what is undoubtedly one of the principal tourist attractions in the country, Trinidad is surprisingly short of tourist hotels. This can largely be explained by the fact that, as a monument city, the construction of modern hotels in what is, in effect, a historical site is, thankfully, unlikely to happen. No doubt, as tourism grows and demand needs to be met, the Cubans will get around to developing some more much-needed accommodation on the outskirts of the city. If you intend to spend a couple of days here you are advised to book your accommodation well in advance.

Category 2

Motel Las Cuevas (124 rooms), Finca Santa Ana, Trinidad; tel: 419 2324
The closest tourist accommodation to the city, this modern motel is stationed high on a hill with good views over the city. The facilities are good and there is both live entertainment as well as a disco in the evenings. Other facilities include air-conditioned rooms with TVs and, you've guessed it, a swimming pool.

Eating and drinking

Whilst not blessed with a surplus of restaurants, Trinidad is at least capable of satisfying the needs of a hungry sightseer, albeit at typically inflated prices. There is, however, a good supply of *paladares* around

Parque Martí. You will be approached and led to the one of your choice if you hang around there for a few minutes. Two of note are **La Rosa** on Calle Mendoza and **Estela Comidas Caseras** on Calle Simon Bolivar.

Restaurante el Jigue, Calle Guinart
Situated just north of the Plaza Mayor, this newish restaurant has an extensive menu ranging from lobster to a cheese sandwich. The lobster will set you back a wallet-emptying $25 while a sandwich (they have a greater selection than just cheese) costs between $2–4.

Restaurante Trinidad, Calle Colón (at the junction of Calle Antonio Maceo)
Set in an old colonial building with a delightful courtyard, this restaurant is popular with those visiting the city on organised tours (no doubt because it is owned by Cubatur). It actually stocks most of what is on the menu and if you fancy treating yourself to a good blow-out (at a price), this is probably the best place to come.

La Canchanchara, Calle Martinez Villena
La Canchanchara is a drink consisting of *aguardiente* (brandy liquor), lime juice, honey and ice and one too many of these will make life very difficult when you trundle across the cobbled streets on the way back to your hotel or tour bus. The speciality here is cocktails, although they do have a reasonably good food menu as well.

Nightlife
In what is essentially a museum city, you would hardly expect to come across the type of nightlife that would have the authorities looking to twin the town with Ibiza. Except at weekends things close down early in Trinidad as the city attempts to preserve its dignity in the face of an increasing number of visitors. With the exception of the **Casa de la Trova**, **La Ruina Café/Bar** (owned by the Rumbas group) on Calle Jesús Menéndez is about the only place open in the evening in downtown Trinidad.

Casa de la Trova, Calle Echerri
One block east of the Plaza Mayor, this is the best place to go for a good dance and a good sing, and the booze isn't too bad either. Popular with both tourists and locals alike, the liveliest night is Saturday although it is open daily except Mondays. The Casa de la Trova was due to be refurbished in mid-1997 with works scheduled to be completed by the end of the year.

Shopping
There are a few shops and stalls in and around the Plaza Mayor selling the usual stuff: T-shirts, trinkets and souvenirs. There is also a dollar shop on Calle Antonio Maceo.

Things to see and do
There are many interesting things to see but the greatest pleasure is simply strolling around the city's charming streets. There are very few cars on the roads and only masochists bother attempting to cycle on the

cobbled streets. As the city is compact and most of the things worth seeing are close to its centre, exploring Trinidad isn't too tiring although you should not try to cram too much into one day as there are plenty of things to grab your attention. The kids here are no exception and, as usual, Chiclets, chocolate, soap and dollars are the most popular requests. Be prepared to be followed.

Trinidad Municipal Museum
Calle Simon Bolivar No 423
Open: Monday to Friday 10.00–18.00; Sunday 09.00–13.00; closed on Saturday
Housed in an old colonial mansion house, the Cantero Palace, this museum contains many items detailing the city's role in the slave trade. It also gives an account of how the sugar industry prospered and then declined in the area. Trinidad's involvement in the independence struggles is also well documented. Works of art detailing significant moments in the city's development are also given prominence.

Guamuhaya Archaeological Museum
Calle Simon Bolivar No 457
Open: Tuesday to Saturday 09.00–12.00 and 14.00–18.00; Sunday 09.00–13.00; closed on Monday
Situated in a beautiful old rococo building dating back to the late 18th century, this museum details life in Cuba from pre-historic times up to the time of Spanish colonisation. The name, Guamuhaya, was given to the Escambray mountain range overlooking Trinidad by the Taino Indians. The museum reputedly occupies the site of the former home of Hernán Cortés, the Spaniard who conquered and plundered Mexico.

Museum of the Architecture of Trinidad
Calle Desengano No 83
Open: Tuesday to Saturday 09.00–12.00 and 14.00–18.00; Sunday 09.00–13.00; closed on Monday
Situated close to the Plaza Mayor, this museum houses exhibits which reflect the architectural development of the city during the 18th and 19th centuries. The truss roof of the building dates back to *circa* 1738.

Romantic Museum
Calle Fernando Hernandez Echemendia No 52
Open: Tuesday to Saturday 09.00–12.00; Sunday 09.00–13.00; closed on Monday
Set in the Palace of the Counts of Brunet, the museum exhibits furniture and decorative artefacts owned by Trinidad's former economic élite. It contains some beautiful china and silverware as well as a number of fine paintings and sculptures.

Museum of the Struggle against Bandit Bands
Open: Tuesday to Saturday 09.00–12.00 and 14.00–18.00; Sunday 09.00–13.00; closed on Monday
It's worth going to this museum, located on Calle Guinart, just to tell people back home that while you were in Cuba you went to the Museum of the Struggle against Bandit Bands and then repeat yourself as nobody will have the faintest idea of what you're on about. Housed in what was once a convent and church of Saint Francis of Assisi, the museum documents the role the National Revolutionary Army played in combating anti-revolutionary guerrillas who were holed up in the Escambray mountains while attempting to topple the Castro administration during the 1960s. Essentially the exhibits comprise a collection of weapons and photographs, although in the courtyard there is a small gunboat supplied by the CIA who were assisting the guerrillas in their counter-revolutionary efforts.

Plaza Mayor
This, as the name suggests, is slap bang in the middle of the old town. Together with Plaza de la Catedral in Havana, this is one of the most elegant squares in Cuba. It is overlooked on the north by some of the city's most impressive buildings, including most of the important museums, while to the east is **La Santísima Trinidad**, the city's most important church, which dates back to the 18th century. The cobblestones of the Plaza Mayor and the streets surrounding the square are made of ship's ballast brought to the city from New England during colonial times.

Church of Santa Ana
Situated 700m from the central square on Calle José Mendoza, this recently restored church was built during the 18th century and is notable for its beautiful baroque facade and bell tower.

Calle Simon Bolivar
The most interesting street in the city runs alongside the Plaza Mayor and contains Trinidad's most important museums.

Beaches
The best beaches in the vicinity are to be found at Ancon peninsula 10km south of the city. There are some good scuba-diving sites close by the Hotel Ancon and it's possible to hire both windsurfing and fishing equipment if you are a resident at the hotel.

The closest beach to Trinidad is Playa La Boca, 5km outside the city. While less salubrious, this is a good beach to go to at weekends if you want to mingle with the locals.

Accommodation
Category 3
Hotel Ancon (216 rooms), Carretera María Aguilar, Playa Ancon, Trinidad; tel: 419 4011
Situated 10km away from the city on a small but pretty beach, this is a large hotel and, as you would expect, the facilities are good and include a restaurant and bar plus a large swimming pool.

Hotel Costa Sur (111 rooms), Playa María Aguilar, Trinidad; tel: 419 6100 or 2502
This is also around 10km from the city. The facilities are slightly inferior to Hotel Ancon but are pleasant enough to make for a comfortable stay. The hotel has a good restaurant and there is the customary swimming pool to boot.

Chapter Ten

Ciego de Avila Province

Ciego de Avila province is the flattest in Cuba, never rising more than 50m above sea level. Although there are relatively few rivers running through the province, there is a good system of underground irrigation which makes the area fertile and  productive; sugar cane and pineapple plantations make up the bulk of local crops.

The province was once home to a large Indian population and there are several semi-preserved sites which are worth looking up. There are also remnants of the fortifications, built during the late 19th century, which were used to divide up the island during the War of Independence.

CIEGO DE AVILA CITY

History and orientation

There are little in the way of tourist attractions in the city of Ciego de Avila, but many people are obliged to stop off there, especially those en route to the burgeoning tourist resort of Cayo Coco off the northern coast of the province. The city, 460km east of Havana and 110km west of Camagüey, has developed as something of an historical halfway house; travellers used it as an overnight watering hole before continuing on to the islands of Trinidad and Santo Domingo in the 17th century.

The first land grants were made in the vicinity during the 16th century, but the city of Ciego de Avila was not formally founded until the middle of the 19th century.

Getting there and away

Communications to and from the city are good. Both the main road and rail link from Havana to Santiago de Cuba cut through the city. Flights operate from Havana on Wednesdays and Fridays.

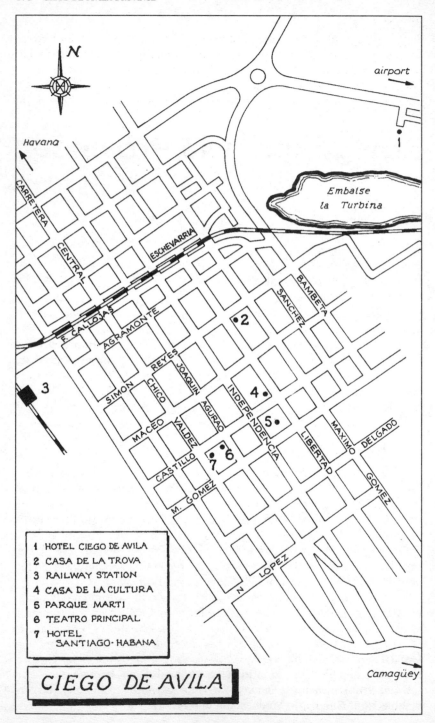

N

Havana

CARRETERA CENTRAL

airport

Embalse la Turbina

ESCHEVARRIA

F. CALLOJAS

AGRAMONTE

SIMON CHICO

REYES

JOAQUIN

AGURAO

MACEO

VALDEZ

CASTILLO

M. GOMEZ

INDEPENDENCIA

SANCHEZ

BAMBETA

LIBERTAD

MAXIMO GOMEZ

DELGADO

N

LOPEZ

Camagüey

2
4
5
7 6
3
1

1 HOTEL CIEGO DE AVILA
2 CASA DE LA TROVA
3 RAILWAY STATION
4 CASA DE LA CULTURA
5 PARQUE MARTI
6 TEATRO PRINCIPAL
7 HOTEL
   SANTIAGO-HABANA

CIEGO DE AVILA

By road
Buses from Santa Clara and Camagüey (often en route to and from Havana and Santiago de Cuba) call at the city daily. The interprovincial bus station is situated 2km east of the city centre on the Carretera Central. Services are invariably full and you are unlikely to have much joy obtaining a ticket in any direction unless you book two weeks in advance.

By train
The *especial* service from Havana arrives at Ciego de Avila daily at 00.30 before continuing on to Santiago de Cuba. You should book a week in advance if possible. *Segunda* services operate on the route but they are long, extremely uncomfortable and wholly unreliable.

Accommodation
To accommodate those en route to more interesting destinations as well as those curious enough to stop over, there are currently two dollar hotels in and around the city.

Category 3
Hotel Ciego de Avila (137 rooms), Carretera de Ceballos; tel: 33 28013
Situated 5km north of the city centre, close by Lake Estanque, this modern hotel is unexceptional though clean. Its facilities are good and include a swimming pool, a decent restaurant and a nightclub.

Hotel Santiago-Habana (76 rooms), Calle Chico Valdez and Honorato del Castillo; tel: 33 25703
Closer to the city centre, the hotel has undergone a recent facelift and is now a designated three-star tourist hotel. It's modern (built in 1957) and without character, but it is convenient and relatively inexpensive. The facilities are not up to much (no swimming pool!).

Eating and drinking
The choice here is limited to the two hotels. The restaurant at the **Hotel Ciego de Avila** has a more extensive menu than the **Hotel Santiago-Habana** but in either case the food tends to be unadventurous, bland and overpriced. The **Casa de la Trova** on Calle Simon Reyes and Calle Libertad is worth visiting.

Things to see and do
There isn't a great deal, unfortunately. You may wish to check out the **Parque Martí** which is not one of Cuba's best parks. The surrounding buildings are mainly uninteresting 20th century constructions; the pick of them is the city hall built in 1911.

A few blocks from the park is the **Teatro Principal,** a 500-seater theatre which is due to undergo further restoration works.

The **Museo Provincial** on Calle José Antonio Eschevarria is worth a visit if you are interested in the area's role in the struggle to overthrow Batista while the **Centro Provincial de Arte** building on Calle Independencia may appeal to some. The **Casa de la Trova** on Libertad No 130 can occasionally deliver a raucous night out.

AROUND CIEGO DE AVILA

Morón

The small coastal town of Morón lies 36km north of Ciego de Avila. Its citizens, known as Moronians, have traditionally made their living from fishing although, with tourism beginning to blossom in the nearby resort of Cayo Coco, the town is looking optimistically towards a new, more lucrative future. A large, modern hotel (144 rooms) has recently been built in the city and the area in general has been earmarked for tourism investment by the Cuban authorities. Close to the city on the northern coast is a strange lagoon called Laguna de la Leche (Milk Lagoon). It derives its name from the lime deposits lying on the bed of the lagoon which have coloured the water a murky white. The lagoon is home to a variety of wildlife, most notably several thousand flamingos. It is a prime fishing lake and consequently is very popular with anglers. It is possible to book fishing and shooting trips to the lake from the **Hotel Morón** (tel: 335 3901/3904). The price of a room at the hotel ranges from $33 for a single to $43 for a double.

During the War of Independence at the end of the 19th century, the Spanish built a series of sentry towers and watch points, stretching from the north coast to the south coast of the province. Some of these towers still remain although most are in a crumbling state of disrepair. The Spanish also built a road called the Trocha ('shortcut'). This links the towns of Morón in the north and Jucaro in the south. The premise behind the construction was for it to act as a fortification point, a dividing line between the east and west of the country which could be defended by the Spanish against Cuban rebels intent on marching westwards. The road and the area in general were the scene of heavy fighting during the war.

Chapter Eleven

Camagüey Province

Set within the broad plains of central Cuba, the land in this area has been compared with Belgium or Montana in the USA because of its similar typography. The panorama is uniformly flat, broken up only by palm trees, whilst the soil, some  of the most fertile in the land, makes it suitable for the growing of sugar cane. The area is also cattle country – home to herds of cattle, primarily Cuban Charolais, which are bred for beef, and Zebu, bred for their milk. The province is also home to one of the most important port towns in the country, Nuevitas, which handles the transportation of the many thousands of tons of sugar produced by the 13 provincial sugar mills. Camagüey province also boasts the up and coming beach resort of Santa Lucía, some 100km north of the city.

CAMAGÜEY CITY
History and orientation
The capital of the province is the city of the same name. Lying some 570km east of Havana, Camagüey is sometimes called the 'City of Tinajónes'. *Tinajónes* are large earthen pots based on a design similar to the sort of vessels the Spanish used when bringing wine across from Spain. Traditionally, Camagüey has been a victim of chronic water shortages and, to counteract this problem, the Spanish potters who were resident in the town made these huge pots with the aim of collecting rainwater from the heavy but infrequent showers the city experienced. The *tinajón* is now regarded as an essential household object in Camagüey and as you walk around the city you can't help but notice them. There is a legend that if a man takes a drink from a *tinajón* offered to him by a woman, he will fall in love with that woman and remain in Camagüey for the rest of his life. The same feeling of permanent residency can be experienced when waiting for a local bus!

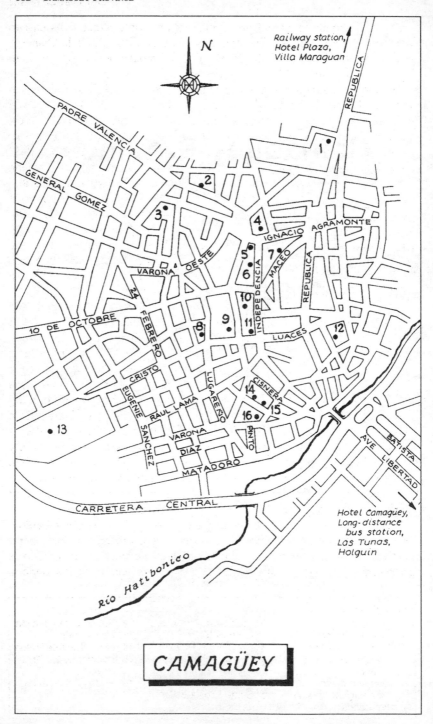

Railway station,
Hotel Plaza,
Villa Maraguan

Hotel Camagüey,
Long-distance
bus station,
Las Tunas,
Holguin

CAMAGÜEY

The city's main street is Calle Ignacio Agramonte which runs east to west into the Plaza de los Trabajadores (Worker's Plaza). Calle Cisneros leads from the north and the Plaza de los Trabajadores connects it to Parque Agramonte, south of the Plaza.

The city of Camagüey (which means 'son of the tree') was founded in 1515 by Diego de Velázquez. It was numbered among the first seven townships founded by the great coloniser. Initially, it was sited on the west bank of Nuevitas bay and was called Santa María del Puerto del Príncipe. However, it was subject to frequent pirate attacks and in 1516, for their own safety, the inhabitants uprooted the township and moved it to the banks of the River Caonao, home at the time to an Indian settlement and venue some years earlier to a massacre of over 2,000 Indians by one of Velázquez's most brutal and notorious lieutenants – Narráez. In 1528, after an uprising by the Indian population against Spanish control, the city was moved inland and finally came to rest in its current position in the centre of the province, at the same time shedding the name Santa María del Puerto del Príncipe (which was a mouthful to people even in those days) and becoming known simply as Camagüey.

Following the move to its inland site, Camagüey developed and prospered, primarily due to its cattle-raising activities, but also because of the growth of the sugar industry and its geographical suitability, which lent itself to the production of the crop. By the mid-18th century almost one third of the city's inhabitants were black African slaves who had been shipped in to work the sugar plantations. The city had already witnessed its first slave uprising in 1616 and, when the Spanish were moving towards the abolition of slavery in the mid-19th century, Camagüey's plantation owners were keen to press for independence as they saw this as the opportunity to retain slavery, a key factor in the growth and prosperity of their industry. In practice things didn't work out quite as they had planned and when a local assembly was established in the town of Vertientes during the Ten-Year War of Independence, one of the first decrees of that body was the calling for the abolition of slavery.

Historically, the city and the province have been a hot-bed of rebellion. One of Camagüey's most famous sons, Ignacio Agramonte, a major-general in the rebel forces who died in the battle of Las Guasimas, is one of Cuba's greatest patriots and a park in the city has been named in his honour.

Key to map

1 Hotel Colon	6 Las Ruinas Restaurant	12 Sagrado de Corazon
2 Teatro Principal	7 Gran Hotel	13 Cementario
3 Iglesia Santa Ana	8 Casa de la Trova	14 La Campana de Toledo
4 Nuestra Senora de la Merced	9 Parque Ignacio Agramonte	15 Paladar de los Tres Reyes
5 Museum of the Birthplace of Ignacio Agramonte	10 La Volanta Restaurant	16 Plaza San Juan de Dios
	11 Santa Iglesia de la Catedral	

Another of the city's great rebels was a woman named Ana Betancourt, who fought against the Spanish and was also a leader in female emancipation, declaring to the women of Cuba during the Guaimaro Assembly in 1869 that 'You have destroyed the slavery of colour by emancipating the slave. The moment of women's liberation has arrived.' Camagüey also witnessed numerous protests against the Batista regime during the 1950s.

After the 1959 Revolution Camagüey prospered, primarily due to the automation of its sugar industry and the resultant increase in production. Today, like the rest of the country it's feeling the pinch of the *Período Especial* and the American embargo.

Getting there and away
By air
As with Trinidad, Cubana Airlines have recently introduced domestic flights from Havana to Camagüey on weekdays. You can also fly here from Santiago de Cuba on Wednesdays and Thursdays.

From	To	Day	Price
Havana	Camagüey	weekdays	$58
Santiago	Camagüey	Wed, Thu	$34

By train
Camagüey is on the main rail link between Havana and Santiago de Cuba and trains stop at the city daily. The local rail link to other cities such as Ciego de Avila, Manzanillo and Santa Clara is poor. Services are scheduled to run daily but are often cancelled. The railway station is situated on the northern edge of the city, 1km from the centre.

By bus
There are buses which connect the city with both Havana and Santiago, but these services are heavily pre-booked. The same applies to the services to Cienfuegos, Santa Clara, Holguin, Sancti Spiritus, Bayamo and Manzanillo, although you probably stand a better chance of getting on one of these. As in other cities, the staff at the booking office often have a scam going whereby they have reserved the odd ticket or two for tourists who are prepared to pay in dollars. The principal bus station is a couple of kilometres southeast of the centre and the timetable (for what it is worth) is pinned up in the ticket office.

Accommodation
Camagüey is well served by good hotels both in the city and on its outskirts. As in other major cities in Cuba, you will be offered the chance to rent private rooms or apartments for around $8–10 per day.

Category 4
Gran Hotel (72 rooms), Calle Maceo No 67; tel: 32 92093
Currently being restored and due to be reopened early in 1998. Its big advantage is its central location.

Category 3

Hotel Camagüey, Carretera Central, Reparto Jayama; tel: 32 71970
About 4km east of the city on the central highway is this modern 1970s eastern
European style hotel which is a monument not only to the close ties Cuba once
had with that part of the world, but also to everything that was bad about modern
socialist architecture. Designed to be functional rather than homely, the facilities
are OK and it does have its own pool which, when you are in a tropical country
65km from the nearest beach, is a big advantage.

Villa Maraguan (37 rooms), Camino de Guanabaquilla, Circunvalante Norte;
tel: 32 72160
Probably the nicest of Camagüey's hotels, this country-style villa is situated
about 5km outside the city centre. It has excellent facilities including a
swimming pool, open-air nightclub and its own small conference centre. The
rooms are air-conditioned and have colour TV and it is set in pleasant gardens
within a lovely part of the countryside. It is also more expensive than the rest of
the city's hotels.

Hotel Plaza (74 rooms), Calle van Horne No 1; tel: 32 82413
Close to the railway station, this is a pleasant hotel with good facilities in general
but, surprise, surprise, no swimming pool. Nevertheless, the staff are friendly and
you will be made to feel very much welcome. There is a decent restaurant and bar
on site.

Eating and drinking

There are several *paladares* in downtown Camagüey. Ask around and you
will be offered the choice of them. **Paladar De Los Tres Reyes** close to
the Plaza San Juan de Dios is good value at around $8 per head.

La Volanta on Parque Agramonte is worth a visit. Set in a beautifully
restored colonial house with splendid carved ceilings and a delightful
Spanish colonial ambience, in terms of setting, this is one of Camagüey's
finest restaurants.

Las Ruinas on Calle Independencia is owned by the Rumbos group and
is one of the newest tourist restaurants in Camagüey. Reasonable food but
not as good value as the *paladares*.

The **Gran Hotel** will offer the most pleasant setting once refurbishment
works are completed. The **Coppelia** in Parque Agramonte is well worth a
visit if you fancy an ice-cream.

The **Casa de la Trova** in Parque Agramonte is the best place to go for
live music although most of the hotels offer some sort of entertainment,
sometimes cabaret. For a spot of late night boogying try the nightclubs at
the **Hotel Camagüey** and **Villa Maraguan**.

Things to see and do

Sightseeing in the city will inevitably bring you to a closer appreciation of
the life of the city's hero, Ignacio Agramonte, as there is both a park and
a museum dedicated to his memory. The city itself is one of the prettiest
in Cuba, full of architectural gems testifying to its colonial past.

Museum of the Birthplace of Ignacio Agramonte

Avenida Ignacio Agramonte No 59
*Open: Monday and Wednesday to Saturday 13.00–18.00; Sunday
08.00–12.00; closed on Tuesday*
Ignacio Agramonte was regarded as one of Cuba's greatest fighters and
military strategists. His favourite trick in battle was to feign retreat, lure
his enemy into a false sense of security, then strike, usually with
devastating results. He tended to use small battalions of men to
accomplish his objectives and his type of guerrilla warfare against the
Spanish served as a model for Castro and Che Guevara during their
struggles against the forces of Batista.

Parque Ignacio Agramonte

Formerly used as the parade ground during the colonial era, this is also the
place where two of the Cuban heroes of the independence struggle,
Joaquin de Aguero and Andrés Manuel Sánchez, were shot and killed in
1826. The park has a bloody history as a further group of revolutionaries
were shot here during the first struggles against the Spanish. The deaths
of these martyrs to Cuban independence were marked by the planting of
palma real trees.

Nuestra Senora de la Candelaria

Situated on the south side of Parque Agramonte, this church was
originally constructed in 1530 and has since been rebuilt twice, once
following a collapse and once after being burned to the ground. The altar
contains the figure of Nuestra Senora de la Candelaria after whom the
church takes its name. This is Camagüey's main cathedral. Other
interesting churches worth a visit are Nuestra Senora de la Merced on
Avenida Agramonte (again rebuilt following a fire in 1906) and Iglesia
Nuestra Senora de la Soledad.

Plaza San Juan de Dios

This square, built in the 18th century, has been declared a national
monument and is typical in style to many found not only in Camagüey but
in Cuba as a whole. It is bordered by the Church of San Juan de Dios and
the San Juan de Dios Hospital. There are also several other colourful and
interesting old colonial buildings surrounding the square.

Teatro Principal

This beautiful theatre (built during the mid 19th century) is a prime
example of classic Spanish architectural influences. The decorative
vitrales (decorative stained glass windows) and sumptuous use of marble
are typical of the era.

AROUND CAMAGÜEY

Nuevitas

Situated around 68km northeast of the city is the town of Nuevitas. Much of the area is blighted by heavy industry and the thermoelectric generating stations, which form part of the industrial complex, are the biggest in Cuba. There are also a number of fertilizer and chemical factories. Although there are some decent beaches close by, swimming in the waters around here isn't recommended as there is a chance that you may emerge with two heads after your dip in the bay. Nobody is too sure how high the pollution levels are as nobody seems to keep an accurate record (and if they did they probably wouldn't tell you).

Santa Lucía

If what you want is a swim followed by a few hours bathing under a hot sun prior to curling up with a good book under the shade of a swaying palm tree, then this is the place to come. Easily the best beach in Camagüey province, it stretches for about 20km along the northern coast of the province to within a few kilometres of the town of Nuevitas. It is fast becoming a popular holiday destination for western package tourists and is an excellent place for scuba diving as there are more than 50 different species of coral in the waters. The sunsets over this area are spectacular. If you want to unwind for a few days there are three good hotels.

Category 4
Villa Caracol (160 rooms), Playa Santa Lucía, Nuevitas; tel: 48302
A four-star establishment consisting of two-storey bungalows. There are excellent on-site facilities and the atmosphere of peace and solitude comes from the place effectively being a small self-contained village. You can eat, drink, socialise and sleep here and the danger is that, before you know it, you will be in a taxi on the way to the airport getting ready to fly home, having seen nothing of Cuba.

Villa Coral (338 rooms), Playa Santa Lucía, Nuevitás; tel: 48236
Situated almost on top of Santa Lucía beach, this, like Villa Caracol, is a self-contained holiday resort village, only it is bigger. Everything you could reasonably expect from a Cuban beach holiday is here and, if you feel a little adventurous and want to do a bit of exploring, you can rent a moped (or a car).

Category 3
Mayanabo Hotel (237 rooms), Playa Santa Lucía, Nuevitas; tel: 48184
Again set on the beach front, the rooms have balconies overlooking both the sea and the nearby lagoon. The setting is picturesque and extremely tranquil. A good place to relax and unwind.

Chapter Twelve

Las Tunas Province

The history of the province is quite colourful, or so legend would have you believe. The story goes that, in 1519, a Spaniard by the name of Alonso de Ojeda lost his ship in the coastal waters to the north of the province. As his ship went  down, Alonso salvaged a statue of the Virgin Mary and, on making land, credited her with aiding him in his miraculous escape from certain death. As he made his way across the land he vowed to offer the statue to the first village he came across, and on reaching the Indian village of Cueyba, he gave it to the local chief, instructing him to build a church in honour of her divinity. Thus it is said, the Catholic religion established its first tangible foothold on the island and the religious instruction of natives became part of the Spanish colonial brief. Within 50 years, however, there wasn't an Indian population left to instruct.

Although tourism isn't yet an integral part of the local economy, the beach areas of Covarrubias and Corella have been earmarked for development and the Gran Caribe hotel chain are currently building a 12-room hotel at Covarrubias, the first tourist installation in the province. The flora and fauna of La Isleta in the municipality of Manati and Monte Cabaniguan in southern Las Tunas could make these areas tourist magnets in the future.

LAS TUNAS CITY
History and orientation
The capital of the province is the city of the same name which lies 662km east of Havana. There is little of any interest in the city for the tourist and most visitors to Cuba either pass through or around it, rarely stopping to make its acquaintance. The city, originally named Las Tunas was, in 1869, renamed Victoria de las Tunas, a title given it by its Spanish governor to commemorate a colonial victory over the Cubans. The name reverted to

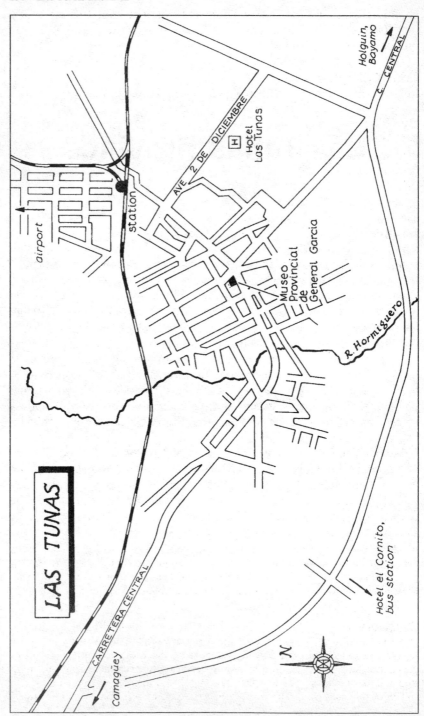

plain Las Tunas in 1895, following the battle in which the Cubans finally took back the city. These days Las Tunas is a centre for trade in the production of sugar and chemicals.

Getting there and away
Flights to and from Havana operate on Mondays, Wednesdays and Fridays.

By train
The trip from Havana takes a scheduled 12 hours on the *especial* service that links Havana and Santiago de Cuba. The service operates daily and the cost from Havana to Las Tunas is $24. One drawback is that you get into the city at the ungodly hour of 04.46. Booking hotel accommodation in advance is a good idea.

By bus
There are no long-distance bus services from Havana to Las Tunas so you'll need to change at Camagüey and continue your journey. The city's bus station is situated around 1km southeast of the city centre. If you are planning to make a valiant attempt at travelling further eastwards by bus towards Santiago de Cuba then your best bet is to get to Holguin and join the scramble for tickets. An even better bet is to give up on the bus service and take the train.

By car
If you are driving, then the road links to both Havana (662km west) and Santiago (160km east) are good. Hitching is difficult although possible, notably between the roads that link Las Tunas to Camagüey and Holguin.

Accommodation
There are two tourist hotels one located on the outskirts of the city, the other 10km southwest.

Category 3
Hotel las Tunas (142 rooms), Avenida de 2 Diciembre and Calle Carlos J Finlay; tel: 31 45014
A modern, white-painted concrete communist construction, the hotel lacks completely any sort of intimate or homely atmosphere but if you're staying overnight in Las Tunas then the chances are it is here you'll be resting your head. Classed as a three-star establishment, its facilities include a swimming pool and a nightclub which is usually empty.

Category 2
Hotel el Cornito (129 rooms), Carretera Central Esta; tel: 31 45015
Located in the countryside outside of the city, the accommodation comprises thatched cabins. There is little of any interest here to recommend an overnight stop and the facilities, sparse as they are, don't lend themselves to a comfortable and enjoyable stay. Better the windswept concrete piazzas of the Hotel Las Tunas.

Eating and drinking

The **Hotel las Tunas** has both a restaurant and a café which serve decent food. Apart from this there is currently little choice for tourists.

Things to see and do

The rooms in the Hotel las Tunas have satellite television! Sadly there isn't a great deal to look at in Las Tunas. A thorough exploration of the city's places of interest can be undertaken in the time it takes to mix a *mojito* and drink it. Cerro Caismimu, a hunting preserve around 18km outside the city, is worth a visit if you're that way inclined. Alternatively, the beaches around Playa Covarrubias on the north coast of the province are good for sunbathing, swimming and scuba diving. The city itself is a friendly place and if you walk around the central square area you are bound to attract attention from curious locals.

Chapter Thirteen

Holguin Province

Travelling from Las Tunas to Holguin, the road, as it sweeps northward after the village of Caridad, takes you through countryside more mountainous and spectacular than the flatlands of Las Tunas province. Holguin province is Cuba's fourth 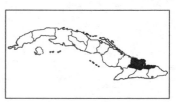 largest. The mountains of the region are home to deposits of nickel and cobalt which have been, and still are being, extensively mined. These industries play an important role in the productivity and wealth of the area. Historically, Holguin was an area more renowned for its farming and cattle raising; however, since the discovery of nickel, these old industries have learned to play second fiddle to a mining industry that now accounts for more than 15% of the country's export revenue. The main nickel mines and processing plants are situated around the town of Moa on the north coast, east of the city of Holguin. Built and owned by American entrepreneurs, they were taken over and nationalised following the Revolution. Sugar plantations and citrus orchards also play a prominent role in the local economy, and the fishing industry of Holguin, although small, complements the province's impressive role as a key producer in the Cuban economy. A new industry has recently taken hold in the province, one that is making a significant contribution to the country's much-needed hard currency reserves – tourism. The north coast has seen a substantial amount of development over the last 10 to 15 years and the beaches of Playa Guardalavaca are now firmly established with foreign tour operators. The province is also home to the biggest bay in the country, the Bahía de Nipe, east of Holguin city.

HOLGUIN CITY
History and orientation
The city of Holguin has been the established capital of the province since 1976. It was founded in 1525 by Captain García Holguin, who sought and obtained a land grant for the area and proceeded to build on it. It is believed that Columbus, after landing in Cuba in 1492, dispatched an expedition as far

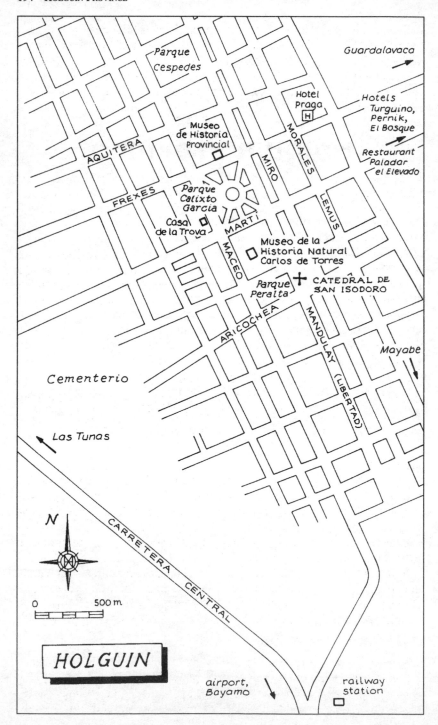

Parque
Cespedes

Guardalavaca

Hotel
Praga
H

Hotels
Turguino,
Pernik,
El Bosque

Museo
de Historia
Provincial

Restaurant
Paladar
el Elevado

AQUITERA

MORALES

MIRO

FREXES

Parque
Calixto
Garcia

LEMUS

Casa
de la Trova

MARTI

Museo de la
Historia Natural
Carlos de Torres

MACEO

CATEDRAL DE
SAN ISODORO

Parque
Peralta

ARICOCHEA

MANDULAY (LIBERTAD)

Mayabe

Cementerio

Las Tunas

N

CARRETERA CENTRAL

0   500 m

HOLGUIN

airport,
Bayamo

railway
station

as Holguin in search of the Japanese emperor's court. His mistake was only realised when his men stumbled across a small Indian village named Cubanacán (centre of Cuba) close to what is now the city of Holguin. In 1752, almost 200 years after Captain García Holguin established the site, the village of Holguin was declared a municipality and from then on prospered and developed into one of Cuba's most important and industrious cities.

Getting there and away
By air
Flights from Havana to Holguin operate daily (except Fridays). Check with Cubana Airlines in Vedado for flight times. The cost of a one-way flight is $70. There are no flights from Santiago de Cuba to Holguin, but there is one flight a week to the town of Moa in Holguin province. The flight leaves from Santiago every Monday at 10.00. A one-way ticket costs $17. Charter flights operate direct to and from Germany and Austria. Sunworld, the UK tour group, also operate a direct charter service from Gatwick airport between 4 May and 23 November. The flight leaves England every Wednesday between these dates at 10.30 and takes nine hours and 40 minutes. Normally you need to book a package holiday although it is always worth checking to see if there are any flight-only deals on offer.

By train
The Havana–Santiago *especial* service calls at Cacocum, 17 kilometres from Holguin (arrival time 03.55). From there you will need to take a bus or taxi into town. The fare from Havana is $30 one way. Some local services and slower long-distance services stop in Holguin itself.

By road
Holguin is served by the main Havana to Santiago road link which, once it reaches the city, drops south towards the city of Bayamo. This is a pleasant journey once across the border from the province of Las Tunas. The two cities are linked by an interprovincial bus route but getting a seat is nigh on impossible. Buses also run from Holguin to Bayamo but the same problems in obtaining tickets apply to this service as with every other in Cuba.

If you are driving and have time to spare, then the road from Las Tunas, which takes you up towards the northern coast through the town of Delicias before cutting south through the villages of Iberia and Auras, is delightful. The mountainous terrain is reminiscent of parts of the province of Pinar del Río.

Accommodation
There are two dollar hotels in the city and several more around the coastal resorts. Finding an available room is usually not a problem although the resort hotels can get booked up during the high season. If in trouble

finding accommodation it may be worth trying a peso hotel, perhaps the **Hotel Praga** on Calle Frexes or the **Hotel Turquino** on Calle Martí.

Category 3

Hotel Pernik (202 rooms), Avenida Jorge Dimitrov and Plaza de la Revolución; tel: 24 481011; fax: 4141.
Situated east of the city centre with good views over the Plaza de la Revolución, the Pernik is a four-star hotel with good facilities. It's a 3km jaunt from here into the city centre proper and the more interesting sections of Holguin. There is a swimming pool, tennis courts and a good restaurant and bar.

Hotel el Bosque (69 rooms), Avenida Jorge Dimitrov; tel: 24 481012
Close to the Pernik is this two-star hotel which is clean and basic with facilities that, while not on a par with its more illustrious neighbour, are adequate enough for a comfortable stay. There is a swimming pool and a disco for late-night revellers.

Category 2

Villa Cayo Cocal (40 rooms), Carretera Central, Holguin; tel: 24 461902
Situated south of the city, 2km from Holguin airport, this is a popular place for package tourists stopping over one night to see the city before moving on to the beach resorts. Small chalet-style accommodation, the facilities are generally good.

Eating and drinking

The best state-owned restaurants are at the **Hotel Pernik** and the **Hotel el Bosque**, both of which serve good, reasonably priced food. As is the case with most of these hotels, the quality of food on offer and the price of a meal has been bettered by the many *paladares* which have opened up in Holguin in recent years. The most central *paladar* is the **El Elevado** on Avenida de los Libertadores. There are, however, many others which Cubans will be happy to show you. There are a few peso restaurants around the Parque Calixto Garcia but it is scarcely worth trying. The bars in both hotels serve good and relatively inexpensive cocktails. There is little action downtown although you can usually get a beer or a cocktail at the **Cocteleria** on Calle Manduley close by Parque Calixto Garcia.

Nightlife

The **Casa de la Trova** on the west side of the Parque Calixto Garcia is a good place to go to meet locals and listen to Cuban music. For a late night out you might consider going to the disco at the **Hotel el Bosque** or the Tropicana-style cabaret at the **Hotel Pernik**.

The city's main theatre is the Teatro Comandante Eddy Sunol on Parque Calixto Garcia.

Things to see and do
Holguin Provincial Museum

Calle Frexes No 198
Open: Monday to Saturday 12.00–19.00; closed on Sunday
This huge building looking out over the Parque Calixto Garcia was once known as La Periquera (the Parrot's Cage) because of the garish coloured

uniforms worn by the Spanish soldiers who stood guard outside during colonial times. The exhibits inside include items once belonging to the aboriginal tribes who populated the area before the arrival of the Spanish. There are also items detailing the role the province played during the War of Independence, including some of the personal possessions of Major General Calixto García, a revered Cuban patriot and hero. His statue is to be found in Parque Calixto Garcia.

Carlos de la Torre Museum of Sciences

Open: Tuesday to Saturday 08.00–18.00; Sunday 08.00–12.00; closed on Monday
This museum is on Parque Calixto Garcia and houses all manner of stuffed birds and mammals along with collections of insects, shells and sponges. The prize exhibits are the two specimens of the royal woodpecker, a rare bird that is almost extinct (a handful live in the Sierra Maestra in the east). There is also a specimen of a manatee (seacow), another endangered species which has been the victim of over-hunting.

Catedral de San Isadoro

Parque Peralta
Holguin's most prominent church is named after the city's patron, San Isidoro. His day, 4 April, is still celebrated in the city.

Loma de la Cruz

To the west of the city is this vantage point which offers wonderful views over the city and across the province. Formerly known as Cerro del Bramadero, a cross was erected on the site in 1790 and a Mass still takes place here every 3 May. Following the service a celebration is held in the form of a lively festival and if you are around the province at the time you should make every effort to see it.

To get to the cross and the vantage point you need to climb the 450 steps which were built in 1950. Once you have made the tiring ascent the whole city becomes visible. The Loma de la Cruz is one of the most visited spots in the city.

Mayabe look-out point

Another popular vantage point, this place, 9km outside the city, offers good views across Holguin and over the valley of Mayabe. The **Villa Mirador de Mayabe** (tel: 24 422160) nearby is a three-star establishment. Difficulties in getting into the city mean that only those who have hired a car tend to stay here. It is, however, a very pleasant place to relax and the setting is superb. The biggest tourist attraction is actually the donkey, Pancho, who lives by the hotel and whose diet includes, when he can get it, beer and pork scratchings.

AROUND HOLGUIN
Villa Blanca de Gibara
The port of Gibara (generally referred to as Villa Blanca) lies 30km north of the city. In the 18th century this place offered the main sea access to the north and eastern regions. These days it is mainly used as a haven for small fishing boats operating in the waters close to the shore. There are cafés close to the waterside which will cook you a good sized fish for only a few dollars provided the local fishermen have had a productive day at sea. The village is small, tranquil and unruffled, with the peace only ever disturbed by the occasional coachload of daytrippers arriving from the nearby beach resorts. One place of interest worth a visit is the **Museum of the 19th Century Cuban Environment** which is located in a large neoclassical mansion house built in 1872. Its decorations and furnishings are all period pieces.

Puerto Bariay
This small port close to Gibara is where Christopher Columbus first landed in Cuba on 28 October 1492. There isn't a great deal to look at but people do visit the town because of its great historical importance.

Farallones de Seboruco
Situated around 6km from the town of Mayari east of Holguin, the Farallones de Seboruco is a large cave of great archaeological importance in Cuba. In 1945 explorers retrieved evidence from the cave that indicated the presence of a people living in the area more than 5,000 years ago. Mayari is on the road to the town of Moa on the north coast, east of Holguin.

Cayo Saetia
Located on the northern shore of the province, Cayo Saetia has been earmarked for tourist development. Its cove-shaped beaches of white sand will, no doubt, soon be peppered by new hotels, but at present it is quiet and relaxed with little around to distract you from sunbathing and swimming. The first hotel, the **Villa Cayo Saetia** has been built although it's a small affair (only seven rooms). Game shooting in the area is popular and you can book tours from the hotel (tel: 24 425350).

Banes
Around 80km northwest of Holguin, the town of Banes was founded on an Indian settlement dating back to the pre-Columbus era. Although quiet and rather run down, the town is home to two of the province's most significant museums. Before the arrival of the Spanish, descendants of the South American Arawack Indians came to the area in their canoes and settled. They were to spread into communities throughout the island of Cuba. The drive from Guardalavaca to Banes (30km) is one of the most scenic in the province.

Bani Cuban-Indian Museum Calle General Marrero No 305, Banes
*Open: Tuesday to Saturday 12.00–18.00; Sunday 14.00–18.00; closed
on Monday*
After arriving at the nearby Puerto Bariay in 1492, the Spanish travelled
inland and came across Bani, a forceful Indian chieftaincy in an area that
was an aboriginal stronghold. The Indian population didn't survive the
Spanish administration too long, but the town of Banes (the name is
derived from the Indian Bani) is a living testimony to their existence. This
museum contains items and former possessions of the local Indian
community that have been found during local archaeological digs. The
gold idol with its Meso-American influence and the aboriginal skull
unearthed a few years back are the two most prized exhibits.
   The museum also tells of the life and history of the pre-Columbus era.

Chorro de Maita Site Museum Chorro de Maita, Banes
*Open: Tuesday to Saturday 09.00–17.00; Sunday 09.00–13.00; closed
on Monday*
In the course of archaeological explorations in the area during the early
part of this century, it became apparent that a large aboriginal
settlement once existed in the area of Chorro de Laita, east of Banes.
Further explorations unearthed human bones and, as the digging
continued, it became obvious that the site was actually a human burial
ground. In all, 198 skeletons were found, making this the largest
aboriginal burial site in the Antilles. Among the aboriginal bones were
found the remains of a Caucasian, believed to be a conquistador whose
death and burial remains a mystery. Another skeleton, a female
believed to have been aged between 18 and 22, was found with a gold
statue by her side, indicating that she was a person of some seniority,
the daughter of the village chief perhaps, or the bride. The site was
declared a National Monument and opened up to the public. A must if
you are in the area.

Moa
A small unattractive seaside town, Moa is where flights from both Havana
and Santiago de Cuba drop off holidaymakers on their way to
Guardalavaca and the coast. Close to the provincial border with
Guantánamo, Moa is connected to the town of Baracoa by a crumbling
coastal road.

Guardalavaca
Situated 53km northeast of Holguin, the name Guardalavaca is actually an
abbreviation of the phrase *Guarda la vaca y guarda la barca* which means
'Watch the cow and watch the ship'. The expression originates from the
days when the locals traded illicitly with pirates and corsairs operating in
the coastal waters, hiding contraband cattle aboard the ships whenever the

local Spanish authorities were checking on the area. Close to Columbus' landing point in Cuba, the area was described by the intrepid explorer as the most beautiful place he had ever seen. Its white sand beaches and rolling hills are indeed very beautiful and its attractiveness has resulted in the invasion of tourism during the last ten years. Today it is home to a burgeoning tourist industry with package holidays now available from England, Canada, Germany and Austria. As yet it is relatively unspoiled as the onset of mass tourism has yet to take hold. That, however, seems to be Guardalavaca's future and, if you are planning to go there, go soon before the rest of the world arrives.

There are plenty of hotels in the resort, but most of them err on the expensive side. Travelling here as an individual tourist can prove costly, but if you come as part of a package tour you can get a two-week deal (including flight and accommodation) for as little as £469.

Category 4

Bahía de Naranjo Marina, Carretera Guardalavaca, Bahía de Naranjo; tel: 25395
Situated on the northern coast close to Estero Ciego, this is a marina purpose-built for boats and pleasure crafts which it is hoped will use the facilities in the more prosperous days ahead. There is chalet accommodation close by and a decent seafood restaurant. Very quiet and secluded and also very expensive. A four-star set up.

Río de Luna Hotel (222 rooms), Estero Ciego; tel: 30202
Situated on the beach of Estero Ciego close to Guardalavaca, this large modern complex (four-star) has all the facilities you would expect in an expensive Caribbean hotel including a very good restaurant. Car and moped hire, which is available in most of the three- and four-star hotels in the area, is also available here.

Category 3

Atlántico Hotel (364 rooms), Playa Guardalavaca, Banes; tel: 30280
This three-star hotel, opened in 1990, is situated almost on top of the beach. There is a large swimming pool (as if you'd need it) and a host of watersports facilities. If you come as a package tourist, you often get free horse riding thrown in with the price; if you come as an individual tourist looking for solitude and tranquillity, you will be disappointed. The hotel is a year-round favourite with package tourists; beach and poolside games and tacky fashion shows are part of the attraction.

Guardalavaca Hotel (261 rooms), Playa Guardalavaca, Banes; tel: 30145
Another recently built hotel complex including 36 bungalows. The three-star facilities include a large sports complex. Package tourists everywhere.

Category 2

Villa Don Lino (145 rooms), Playa Blanca; tel: 20443
Just about the cheapest hotel in the resort, this is in Playa Blanca, just 3km west of Playa Guardalavaca. The facilities are good and for ravers there's a lively disco. Even though it's classed as a two-star establishment, the hotel is used by tour operators and, although often busy, you can still find a piece of secluded beach without too much difficulty and it is certainly good value for money.

Chapter Fourteen

Granma Province

The province of Granma (there isn't a city of the same name) is one of the most geologically diverse of all the island's provinces. Named after the boat which brought Castro and Che Guevara from Mexico in 1956, the province has a long  and colourful history as one of the hotbeds of rebelliousness and independence. The Sierra Maestra mountain range in the east of the province is the most striking section of landscape and contrasts vividly with the flat plains around the Cauto river to the west of Granma. The capital of the province is the city of Bayamo, which has a population of approximately 100,000.

BAYAMO

History and orientation
The city of Bayamo has played an historical role in the shaping of modern-day independent Cuba. One of the seven townships founded by Diego de Velázquez (it was actually the second), it was also the place where Carlos Manuel de Cespedes declared independence from Spain following his freeing of the slaves in his mill and sugar plantation. The first battles of the Ten-Year War of Independence were waged around here and, in 1868, the start of the fight against the Spanish, the city was captured by the independence army and declared capital of the new Republic of Cuba. Sadly, a few months later in January 1869, with the recapture of the city by the Spanish imminent, the rebels took the drastic decision to burn the place to the ground rather than give it up.

Bayamo was once home to a large Indian population who, by Indian standards, were a militant lot and regularly engaged the Spanish in battle. In 1528 there was a major Indian uprising in the area which resulted in substantial Spanish casualties (but more Indian). The Spanish, in a

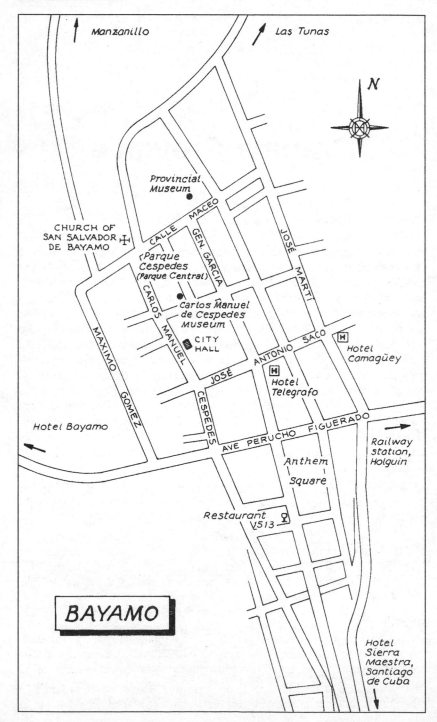

Manzanillo

Las Tunas

N

Provincial
Museum

CHURCH OF
SAN SALVADOR
DE BAYAMO

CALLE MACEO

GEN GARCIA

JOSÉ MARTI

Parque
Cespedes
(Parque Central)

CARLOS MANUEL

Carlos Manuel
de Cespedes
Museum

CITY
HALL

ANTONIO SACO

Hotel
Camagüey

JOSÉ

Hotel
Telegrafo

MAXIMO GOMEZ

CESPEDES

Hotel Bayamo

AVE PERUCHO FIGUERADO

Railway
station,
Holguin

Anthem
Square

Restaurant
V513

BAYAMO

Hotel
Sierra
Maestra,
Santiago
de Cuba

conciliatory effort, offered them the opportunity to farm sections of the land in return for their renunciation of all their traditions and culture including religion, language and dress. They would also be obliged to pay a fee to the Spanish Crown for the privilege. Not surprisingly, the Indians declined and thereafter both the local and national Indian population was swiftly wiped out.

The rebellious nature of the area continued in 1533 when the African slaves working the gold mines of Jobabo, close to Bayamo, took exception to their conditions and treatment and rebelled against their masters. This was the first slave rebellion on the island. The treatment meted out to them rivalled the brutality used against Indians and at least four of the slaves were beheaded, their severed heads displayed in Bayamo as a warning to potential insurrectionists.

Much later in the history of the city, a group of anti-Batista rebels attacked the city's barracks as part of the 1953 Moncada uprisings. Like Moncada, however, the attack was a military flop and those rebels who were not captured were killed in the assault. When Castro returned on the boat *Granma* in 1956, he landed in the province and won huge support almost immediately from the citizens of Bayamo.

Built on a site once known as Las Ovejas, the city prospered, largely as a result of the trade in sugar and coffee. Cattle raising was also an important facet of the local economy. The relative affluence of the city and the province gave rise to a substantial degree of smuggling and black-market trading with foreign freelancers, the waterways around the Cauto river being at the centre of this activity. In 1604, the Bishop of Cuba, Fray Juan de las Cabezas Altamirano, was taken hostage by the notorious French pirate, Gilbert Girón. His request for a large ransom was refused by the Cubans who instead launched an attack against the pirate and his cohorts, killing the majority of them, Gilbert included.

Today the city, like most Cuban cities, is feeling the economic pinch of the *Período Especial*, but it retains a lively air of purpose and optimism. The people here are renowned for their friendliness and hospitality.

Getting there and away
By air
Flights between Bayamo and Havana operate on Tuesdays, Thursdays and Sundays.

By train
Getting here by rail is extremely difficult. There is a station and line that runs between the city and Manzanillo to the west and there is also a rail link to Camagüey. Both are branch lines and about as dependable as a leaking roof. If you must travel here by train, plan your journey meticulously and build in a huge tolerance for unexpected delays.

By car

The most sensible option by far. The road links from both Holguin to the north and Santiago de Cuba to the east are good. If you are travelling in a hired car then you will have no problems. Hitching is more problematic as most people are in the same, dependent position.

Accommodation

At present there are two tourist hotels in or close to the city. Given that Bayamo isn't the biggest draw in Cuba, even if you haven't pre-booked you shouldn't have too many problems in securing a room. There are also a couple of peso hotels, **Hotel Telegrafo** and **Hotel Camagüey**, both on Calle José Antonio Saco.

Category 4

Hotel Sierra Maestra (204 rooms), Carretera a Santiago de Cuba, Bayamo; tel: 23 425013
A modern four-star hotel situated 1km east of the city centre on the main drag to Santiago de Cuba. The facilities, as you would expect in a four-star hotel, are good. The majority of visitors to the city end up staying here.

Category 3

Villa Bayamo, Carretera de Manzanillo, Bayamo; tel: 23 423102
A clean if charmless hotel set about 6km outside of Bayamo city on the main road to Manzanillo.

Eating and drinking

The choice at present is restricted to the cuisine provided by the **Hotel Sierra Maestra**. Bayamo is not the most visited city in Cuba and the ingredients for a lavish night out have yet to materialise. **Restaurante 1513** and the local pizzeria are at present peso establishments not accepting tourists. Perhaps in due course, as the city's reputation for friendliness and hospitality spreads, more tourists will acquaint themselves with the area and cafés and bars will spring up to cater for their needs. The fare in the hotel is adequate but don't expect too many late nights out here.

Things to see and do
Granma Provincial Museum

Open: Tuesday to Saturday 08.00–18.00; Sunday 09.00–13.00; closed on Monday

Situated on Calle Maceo, across from Parque Cespedes (also known as Parque Central) and next door to the birthplace of the Bayamese and Cuban hero, Carlos Manuel de Cespedes, this museum is dedicated primarily to the role of the city and the province in the struggles for liberation and independence. There are relics which survived the destruction of Bayamo by fire in 1869 when the occupying rebels chose to burn the place down rather than hand it back to the Spanish. One of the exhibits is the original score for the Cuban national anthem, which was first sung in the city.

Carlos Manuel de Cespedes Birthplace Museum
Open: Tuesday to Saturday 12.00–19.00; Sunday 09.00–13.00; closed on Monday
By a strange quirk of fate, the house belonging to the independence leader was one of the few to survive the fire of 1869 and it now houses a museum in his honour. The exhibits tell of the life of Cespedes and how, following his decision to free the slaves at his sugar mill at La Demajagua, he set about forming a revolutionary force to take on the Spanish colonists. It tells of his subsequent rise as a revolutionary hero before he died at the hands of the Spanish in 1874 following an ambush at San Lorenzo in Oriente. The museum, which is on Calle Maceo, also has the press which Cespedes used to print the newspaper, *Cubano Libre*, an independent paper he set up after the declaration of independence.

Parque Cespedes
The main square of the city and a focal point for the local community, this is a very elegant plaza with most of the city's places of interest situated around it.

Church of San Salvador de Bayamo
Close by Parque Cespedes, the church was declared a national monument some years ago, not only because of its beauty but also because it was the place where the national anthem was first sung.

City Hall
Overlooking Parque Cespedes, this was the place where the great man declared that slavery in Cuba was to be abolished.

Anthem Square
The first major gathering of the citizens of Bayamo took place here on 20 October 1868 after the rebels had captured the city. The national anthem which had first been aired in the church of San Salvador a year earlier was belted out with much vocal gusto by all present.

Around Bayamo
Dos Ríos
A few kilometres north of Bayamo is the area of Dos Ríos (close to the town of Cauto Cristo). It was here on 19 May 1895 that the national hero José Martí was killed while fighting in the War of Independence. Dos Ríos has been declared a national monument in his honour.

La Demajagua – The Cradle of Independence
Situated midway between Bayamo and Manzanillo are the ruins of Cespedes' manor house and estate. They have now been turned into a museum to commemorate the day when he set free his slaves. On view is

the bell which he used to gather his slaves before releasing them and persuading them to join his revolutionary force.

MANZANILLO
History and orientation
The port city of Manzanillo is situated in the southwest of Granma province, east of the Gulf of Guacanayabo. Although it is the main port in the province, the city is quiet, subdued and has the feel of a place that has spent too long out of the limelight. Whether the port rediscovers more prosperous times (Manzanillo was once a thriving concern particularly popular with smugglers because of its backwater position) only time will tell. Tourism hasn't taken a hold in the city and at the moment very few visitors come here. The city is, however, aesthetically attractive, the most notable architectural features being Moorish in origin. The only hotel at present is the **Guacanayabo** on Avenida Camilo Cienfuegos (tel: 054012). If you are staying over, a single room costs $20 a night and a double $27.

Nightlife is limited in choice although the city does have a strong musical tradition – it is the acknowledged originator of the *son* rhythm. On most nights you will find some form of live musical entertainment taking place.

Around Manzanillo
Las Coloradas
To the south of Manzanillo, hugging the coastline, is the narrow mangrove-covered beach on which Fidel Castro and Che Guevara landed the boat *Granma* on 2 December 1956. Surprisingly, there is no tangible memorial marking what was one of the most significant events in Cuban history, but this place is so inaccessible that, even if there were, it's unlikely that many people would make the considerable effort to see it. For history buffs only.

Marea del Portillo beach
Situated on the south coast of the province 20km from the town of Pilón, this dark sand beach has been earmarked for key tourist development with the first two hotels recently built overlooking the sea.

Category 3
Hotel Farallon de Marea (140 rooms), Carretera Marea del Portillo; tel: 25901
A three-star hotel situated on a hill looking out on the beach with the backdrop of the Sierra Maestra mountains adding to the beauty of the setting. Very secluded.

Marea del Portillo Hotel (122 rooms), Carretera Marea del Portillo; tel: 594201
Situated close to the beach, this has a setting that is both pretty and tranquil. Like the Hotel Farallon, the facilities and set-up are geared to mass tourism but as yet the area hasn't quite taken off.

Sierra Maestra National Park

The Sierra Maestra mountain range stretches across the province of Granma petering out just east of the city of Santiago de Cuba. Famed as the area where Castro and Che Guevara held out, formulating and co-ordinating the Revolution, the area is home to Cuba's largest national park. The mountain range is rich in wildlife and natural vegetation and the scenery is among the most beautiful and spectacular on the island. At the moment its tourist potential is relatively untapped and the area can only be explored practically by car. It is possible to arrange tours from Bayamo and Manzanillo. Definitely an area worth visiting.

Calle Padre Pico, Santiago de Cuba

Chapter Fifteen

Santiago de Cuba Province

The eastern province of Santiago is home
to some of Cuba's most rugged terrain.
Its most dominant geographical feature is
the Sierra Maestra mountain range which
runs from Niquero near the Gulf of
Guacanayabo to east of Santiago de Cuba

past the Gran Piedra National Park. The country's highest elevation, the
Pico Real del Turquino (1,974m above sea level), forms part of this range.
The area is noted, among other things, for its sugar production and is also
an important provider of citrus fruits and tobacco. It is, however, most
famed for its history of rebelliousness, being part of Oriente, an area known
as the cradle of the Revolution. These days it has been earmarked as a prime
tourist destination and, with its beautiful physical setting, it seems destined
to become one of the most popular and visited areas of Cuba.

THE CITY OF SANTIAGO DE CUBA

History and orientation

The city of Santiago de Cuba is a sort of San Francisco in the Caribbean.
Built on a sequence of hills overlooking a large bay with the Sierra
Maestra in the background, it is certainly one of Cuba's most picturesque
cities. Its colourful streets sweep up and down steep hills, making walking
through the city, although pleasant, a little tiring if done in long stretches.

Santiago is the primary city in the area known as Oriente and is also
Cuba's second city (population around 1 million). Founded by Diego
Velázquez in 1515, it was originally sited on the mouth of the Paradas
river before being moved one year later to its current location. Because of
its excellent harbour and strategically important location, it became the
official capital of Cuba, succeeding Baracoa, and home to the Spanish
colonial government during the first half of the 16th century. The city
developed with the assistance of the efforts of thousands of slaves who
were brought in to work in the local copper mine at El Cobre (the

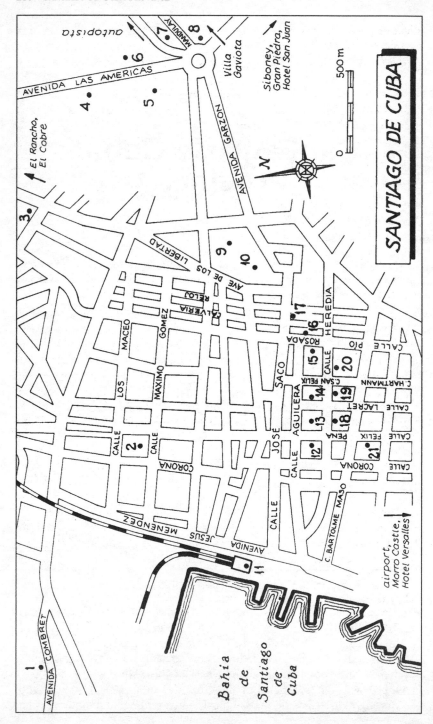

SANTIAGO DE CUBA

discovery of copper was made by chance – the Spanish had in fact been prospecting for gold). The importation of slaves was necessary as the indigenous Indian population had very quickly been wiped out.

Santiago's first mayor, Hernando Cortés, used the city as a base for his conquistadorial forages into Central and South America and his wealth and the wealth of the city in general is reflected in the buildings which were erected around that time, including Velázquez's house with its Moorish style balconies and beautiful stained-glass windows. This was completed in 1520 and eight years later work on the city's cathedral was begun (the Spanish, it should be remembered, were in search of souls as well as gold). All this wealth soon attracted the unwelcome attentions of a host of pirates and corsairs who attacked the city with an almost monotonous regularity. In order to protect against constant attack, the Spanish began to establish an extensive fortification network around the city. Castle Morro, which stands at the harbour's entrance, and the batteries at La Socapa and La Estrella were important elements in this defence and all are still intact today. The city eventually lost its capital status in 1553 when the Spanish decided to move their prime governing functions to Havana.

If Cuba is something of a melting pot, then nowhere is this typified more than in the city of Santiago. Its existence as home to both Spanish colonists and the African slaves they brought in was supplemented in 1791 by around 30,000 French plantation owners who fled Haiti following the successful slave revolution there. The importance of this influx cannot be overestimated as, by bringing with them their advanced technological skills and know-how, the French helped to transform the local economy with sugar and coffee production rising to record levels. In doing so, many more thousands of African slaves were brought in and the city, on the backs of these slaves, continued to prosper and grow.

Santiago has been a victim of several earthquakes down the years although it is the shockwaves of the city's political upheavals which have been more widely felt. In 1836, following external pressure to liberalise the government in Cuba, the Spanish commissioned local government elections, a decree which was countermanded by Havana's governor, Tacon. In a gesture of defiance, Santiago went ahead with local elections, although in the end they were declared null and void. This gesture was the

Key to map

1 Santa Ifigenia Cemetery	7 Restaurante Tocororo	16 Emilio Bacardi Museum
2 Antonio Maceo's Birthplace	8 La Maison	17 Paladar Don Antonio
3 Serrano bus terminal	9 Moncada Barracks	18 Cathedral
4 Tropicana Santiago	10 Coppelia	19 Casa de la Trova
5 Hotel Santiago de Cuba	11 Railway station	20 Casa del Vino
6 Hotel las Américas	12 Casa de Velázquez	21 Museum of Historical Cuban Ambience
	13 Parque Cespedes	
	14 Hotel Casa Grande	
	15 Restaurante Matamoros	

first indication that the city was prepared to assert its own character and values. In October 1868, Carlos Manuel de Cespedes freed all of his slaves from his sugar plantation near Bayamo and called for independence from Spain. There followed the Ten-Year War for Independence during which Cespedes was killed (1874). The *Padre de la Patria* (Father of the Party), as he is remembered, is buried in Santiago cemetery and the city's main square is named after him. Other great leaders who emerged from Santiago include the Maceo brothers and José Martí, Cuba's national hero, who was laid to rest in the city's cemetery, his burial place marked by a grand mausoleum. The city was also the venue for the surrender of the Spanish in 1898 while Fidel Castro, who was born in Oriente, spent much of his time in Santiago and chose Moncada barracks as the focal point of his attempted insurrection on 26 July 1953. Because of the important role the city has played in the shaping of Cuba's history and development it has been granted the official title 'Hero City', the only city on the island to have been awarded this accolade.

City layout
Because of the threat of earthquakes the city has traditionally developed outwards as opposed to upwards, although in recent times there have been a number of developments of multi-storey housing estates as well as the vast and ugly Hotel Santiago de Cuba. The city spreads eastwards from the bay and, in typical Spanish colonial tradition, the streets extend outward from the central square (Parque Cespedes) in a grid pattern. Most of the places of interest are found in and around the central square, the area which constitutes the old town.

Getting there and away
By air
Antonio Maceo airport is 8km south of the city centre. Take the road to Castillo del Morro and after 7km you will reach a roundabout. The airport is well signposted from here. There is a bus service which goes to and from the airport but it is erratic to say the least and, given you will probably not want to chance the wait, you are advised to cough up the $5 for a taxi.

If you need to book a ticket or just re-confirm, the Cubana Airline office is just off the main square, Parque Cespedes. It is a disorganised office with a primitive numbering system and you may have to wait for more than an hour before you are seen. Fortunately Cubana have recently opened an office at the Hotel Santiago de Cuba which is much more convenient. Obtaining a ticket here can normally be done in a matter of minutes. For all flights you need to book around one week in advance although often, as a tourist, you will be given preference over Cubans because you will be paying in much-needed dollars. The aeroplanes which service the Havana route on Friday, Saturday or Sunday are smaller than those which service the route the rest of the time and it is harder to get seats on those flights.

From	To	Day	Cost ($)
Santiago	Havana	Daily	$76
Santiago	Camagüey	Wed & Thurs	$34
Santiago	Baracoa	Tues	$20
Santiago	Moa	Mon	$20

By train

Santiago's railway station is situated at Avenida Jesús Menendez and Sanchez Hechavarria, close to the harbour and less than 1km from Parque Cespedes. If you exit the station, head up the hilly streets straight ahead, turning right at Calle Felix Pena (also called Santo Tomás), you will come out at Parque Cespedes. It is a good hike (around 4km) to the Hotels las Américas and Santiago de Cuba and taking a taxi is a good idea. After a long train journey from Havana, which takes anything between 17 and 22 hours on the fastest *especial* train, you will hardly feel like walking up and down the city's hilly streets. The cost of a one-way ticket to and from Havana is $38, first class. If you need to buy one, the Officina Ladis is situated in the main railway station. It is possible to travel on the 'regular' trains to Holguin (depart 06.25 daily, fare $6) and Camagüey (depart 08.55 daily, fare $13). At the time of writing there was no rail service to Guantánamo, due to major repairs being needed to the line, but it is worth checking to see if these have been carried out.

By bus

Only masochists and Cubans travel by bus and obtaining a ticket to go anywhere long distance is extremely difficult. The waiting lists for bus tickets are astronomical. This is due to a number of factors, the foremost being the scarcity of buses now operational as a result of the petrol shortage and the fact that bus is the cheapest form of inter-city public transport and therefore the most popular. Travelling shorter distances (eg to El Cobre) is slightly easier and if you want to try to get on a bus, the Serrano bus terminal is opposite the railway station by the harbour. Inter-city buses usually depart from Avenida de los Libertadores in the north of the city.

Accommodation

At present there is only one tourist hotel in the city centre, the recently refurbished **Hotel Casa Grande**. As you would expect in the country's second city, there is a good supply of private accommodation offering good value for money. Most likely you will not need to go searching for these establishments. Their agents will normally find you, normally at the airport or the railway station or around Parque Cespedes.

Category 5

Hotel Santiago de Cuba (290 rooms), Avenida de las Américas and Calle M; tel: 226 42612; fax: 226 41756

This is the most prestigious hotel in the city. Built with the assistance of Canadian engineers, the hotel could be described as a startling example of modern architecture or, alternatively, a blot on the Santiago landscape, depending on your taste. The locals call it the 'sugar factory' and, at 15 storeys high, it is easily the tallest building in the vicinity. The hotel foyer resembles an airport concourse. It has five-star facilities including two swimming pools, two jacuzzis, tennis courts, a selection of restaurants and a nightclub. It also has the best stocked dollar shop in Santiago. The 15th floor bar offers stunning views over the city although the drinks are expensive ($3 for a beer, $4 for a cocktail). There is live music every night.

Category 3

Hotel las Américas (68 rooms), Avenida de las Américas and General Cebreco; tel: 226 42011
Probably the best value hotel in the city. The rooms are comfortable and clean (all air-conditioned) and have pleasant balconies. A modern hotel like the Hotel Santiago de Cuba which is across the road, there is a swimming pool, a large restaurant, a café and a poolside bar. There is live music or cabaret most nights. All rooms have colour TVs with satellite channels. The city centre is a 15-minute walk away.

Hotel Casa Grande (55 rooms), Heredia No 201 esq San Pedro; tel: 226 86600; fax: 226 86035
A delightful hotel, ideally positioned overlooking Parque Cespedes. The patio is an ideal place to relax, have a drink and observe city life.

Villa Gaviota (51 rooms), Avenida Manduley 502 between Calles 19 and 21, Vista Alegre; tel: 226 41598
The Vista Alegre district is a quiet, affluent, residential district just east of Hotels las Américas and Santiago de Cuba and about 4km from the city centre. The hotel has excellent facilities including a swimming pool, restaurant and bar and there is even a conference centre.

Hotel San Juan (formerly the Leningrado Hotel) (32 rooms), Carretera Siboney and Parque San Juan; tel: 226 42478
Situated a mile further southeast of Hotels las Américas and Santiago de Cuba, this is as pleasant a place to stay although it has the disadvantage of being out of walking range of the city centre. The modern building is set within its own delightful gardens and, if peace and relaxation at an affordable price are what you're after, the San Juan comes highly recommended. It has good facilities including a swimming pool, restaurant and bar and all the rooms are air-conditioned and have colour TVs.

Hotel Versalles (46 rooms), Barrio Versalles; tel: 226 91123
Very handy for the airport and for the Castillo del Morro but rather impractical if you want to venture freely into the city which is about 6km away. Nevertheless, the facilities are good, but you have a right to expect this as it's not cheap to stay here.

Eating and drinking

The *paladares* which have flourished in the Reparto Sueno area of Santiago, close to the Hotel Las Américas and Hotel Santiago de Cuba now makes it possible to eat well and cheaply in the city. Things in downtown Santiago seem to be on the up as well where a few decent (although pricey) restaurants have recently opened up. The pick of these is the **Don Antonio** on Calle Aguilera between Reloj and Calveria. All the tourist hotels have decent restaurants (the Hotel Santiago de Cuba has three).

Restaurante Tocororo, Avenida Manduley, Vista Alegre; tel: 226 41410
Named after Cuba's national bird, this restaurant is a five-minute walk east of the Hotels Santiago de Cuba and Las Américas. A relatively new establishment, it's set in a delightful old colonial-style house. You can eat either indoors or in the pretty, sheltered courtyard. The menu is extensive and, as in almost all Cuban restaurants, due to the unavailability of the necessary ingredients, some of the dishes are simply figments of the proprietor's vivid imagination. You can get lobster and a bottle of wine but for this you will have to cough up over $30 (the restaurant obtains the lobsters on the black market from local freelancers for $3 each). A prawn dish will cost you between $10–14 and a fillet steak $10–12. If you are on a tight budget you will probably want to avoid this place although the staff are extremely friendly.

La Maison, Avenida Manduley, Vista Alegre
Close by the aforementioned hotels and home to Santiago's small fashion industry, La Maison also has an upmarket restaurant and bar. The setting is beautiful but, again, the prices on the menu are unrealistic. A 'Special Paella' costs $35 (at this price it would have to be so special you'd want to take it home to meet your parents) while lobster tail is a snip at $30. You can have, if you so desire, a lobster pizza for $8.60 or a ham sandwich which will lighten your wallet to the tune of $9. The drinks are more reasonably priced at $1.50 for a beer and $2.50 for a cocktail. If you have a craving for chocolate you can buy a large bar of Nestlé chocolate for $1.50.

Restaurante Matamoras/Cafeteria Matamoras, Calle Pío Rosado
Situated in downtown Santiago, this is one of the best and most popular restaurants/cafeterias in the city. You have a choice of eating in either a candle-lit, intimate restaurant setting or in the more raucous cafeteria at the front of the building. The menu is the same in both, as are the prices. Diners are entertained in the cafeteria by some superb live *salsa* and many people take to their feet for a little dance late in the evening. This place is the liveliest spot in the city at the moment and the food – spaghetti Napolitana $3, rice & vegetables $1.20, fried plantain $1.20 – is good and cheap. The booze is also reasonably priced with Labatts imported from Canada selling for $1.20 and cocktails for around $1.50.

Café Casa Grande, Parque Cespedes
The setting on a balcony overlooking the Parque Cespedes is unrivalled and, even if the food is nothing to write home about, it is still an excellent place to sit sipping a drink while checking out the action in the park below. A meal of fish and rice costs $6 and drinks (beer and cocktails) range from $1.50–2.50. In the daytime the cafeteria is frequented by a deaf and partially dumb magician who calls himself 'Magic Tony', real name Antonio Loyola Rodríguez. His tricks include stealing the watch off your wrist and pouring water in and out of your ear with a rolled-up newspaper. His final trick will involve you handing over a couple of dollars and, if you feel sufficiently entertained, he will be more than happy to keep hold of them. The Casa Grande also sells popcorn from a quaint old dispenser at the back of the building.

Restaurante el Morro, Castillo el Morro; tel: 226 91576
An up-market restaurant close to the grand setting of the old fortress, the fare is typically Spanish and the prices are typically inflated.

El Cayo, *en Cayo Granma, en el centro de la bahía de Santiago*
(on the Granma quay in the middle of the bay)
A pleasant restaurant serving both international and Creole cuisine on the edge of the harbour. Slightly expensive.

Nightlife

Most restaurants and hotels have their own music and cabaret acts and, as is the norm in Cuba, the standard of musicianship is very high. While the nightlife isn't as vibrant as in Havana, you will be well rewarded if you venture outside your hotel and make your way downtown. The origins of Cuban *salsa* can be found in the east of the country and the city retains its tradition of being the home of some of the hottest bands on the island.

Casa de la Trova, Calle Heredia 208 between Calles Hartman and Lacret
Cuba has many *casa de la trovas* but none as famous and with as great a reputation as this one. The ballad form (*trova*) originated in Santiago and is best described as being a synthesis of African percussion and Spanish guitar accompanied by lyrics dealing with the daily struggles of the lives of Cubans. The Casa de la Trova acts as a venue, not only for amateur musicians, but also for established professionals who often return to pay homage to the roots of their music. The weekend is the best time to come, although there also tends to be music playing throughout the week. The walls are bedecked with photographs, dating back decades, of some of the groups and individuals who have played there. When you enter the casa through the dark wooden saloon doors the aura of musical passion and intensity comes up and grabs you by the throat. This place is a must.

Tropicana Santiago, Avenida de las Américas, by Calle M; tel: 226 43445; fax: 226 335209
Like Havana, Santiago boasts its own Tropicana cabaret extravaganza. The costumes and the sets are equally ostentatious and if you like big cabaret nights out then you will enjoy this. The Cubans, it has to be said, do know how to put on an extravaganza. Drinks are a bit pricey (cocktails averaging $4 a piece).

Casa del Vino, Calle Heredia
Only three doors down from the Casa de la Trova this place has only recently opened and is yet to develop any sort of reputation as a place to visit. Worth checking out though given the limited number of bars in the city.

Ciroa, Avenida Manduley, Vista Alegre
This is the place to come for a real hoot, the only problem being that it is supposed to be for Cubans and not for tourists. If you manage to make any friends in Santiago, insist that they bring you here. Essentially it's a cut-price version of the Tropicana with the cabaret acts, the dancing girls and the Cuban crooner in a white suit. The real fun begins at the end of the show, which takes place around a vast swimming pool, when everybody gets up to dance. It is a slightly surreal sight, especially on a moonlit night, to see 200 Cubans dancing around the edge of a swimming pool. By the time the dancing starts, however, you will most likely have consumed the half bottle of Cuban rum that comes with the admission ticket (costing only a few pesos) and things won't seem so strange. Ciroa is an

entertainment complex for the Cuban young and there is a restaurant, bar and discothèque on site. It's the most popular place for local youths to go to let their hair down. Previously the best nightspot was the discothèque at the Hotel Las Américas, but that has now been converted into a games room for tourists who, generally speaking, are not too interested in playing bar football or pool on a tropical Caribbean island. If you can't get a Cuban to take you along, it is worth asking at the reception to see if they'll let you in anyway.

Things to see and do
Santiago has plenty to offer for sightseers, blessed as it is with a host of interesting museums and buildings. The Revolution and the struggles for independence, as you would expect, are well documented in the museums in and around the city. Santiago is proud of the important historical role it has played in the country's fight for independence and is more than happy to let you know it.

Museums
Moncada Barracks, Calle Carlos Aponte (three blocks east of Avenida de los Libertadores)
Open: Monday to Saturday 08.00–18.00; Sunday 08.00–12.00
Following the success of the Revolution in 1959, the barracks were turned into the '26th of July' school and it remains a school to this day. The name marks the date of the attempted storming of the barracks by Castro which is regarded as the birth of the popular insurrection against the Batista regime, eventually leading to his downfall on 1 January 1959. It is probably one of the most famous landmarks in the history of the Revolution, even though the attack itself failed disastrously (three of Castro's men were killed on the spot but more than half of the other 130 were captured and executed in the days following). Castro's idea was to surprise the forces stationed at the barracks who, it was assumed, would be too distracted by the carnival festivities that were happening on the day. He would commandeer weapons which he planned to hand out to the people. The insurrection, he assumed, would then spread like wildfire. In the event this did not happen although the shockwaves Castro's actions sent to Batista and his henchmen in Havana were profound. It was apparent that the days of his dictatorship were numbered.

Today one of the school buildings houses a museum which documents the attack and the historical struggles for independence. The walls of the building are still heavily pockmarked from the firefights that took place on the day of the attack.

Emilio Bacardi Museum, Calle Pío Rosado between Calles Aguilera and Heredia
Open: Tuesday to Saturday 09.00–18.00; Sunday 09.00–13.00; closed on Monday
Originally the Museum and Library of Santiago de Cuba, this is the second oldest museum in the country. It is named after the Santiago

industrialist, Emilio Bacardi Moreau, who contributed many of the exhibits on display in the museum. As well as housing an important collection of Cuban colonial paintings, it is also home to a fascinating archaeological hall which includes among its exhibits a collection of mummies from Egypt and South America. The Egyptian mummy, shipped over from Thebes by Bacardi, is the body of a young woman dating back more than 2,000 years to when Thebes ruled over Egypt. The Peruvian mummies date back to the Paracas culture. There is also a torpedo on display, which is a handmade effort put together by rebels during the war of independence against the Spanish. The intention was to try to blow up Spanish ships moored in the bay.

Museum of Historical Cuban Ambience, Calle Felix Pena No 612
Open: Monday to Saturday 08.00–18.00; Sunday 09.00–13.00
This wins, hands down, the title for the most curiously-named museum in the country. It is housed in what is reputedly the oldest mansion house in Cuba, built during the early part of the 16th century. It is claimed that the top floor of the building was once occupied by Velázquez, although this has never been substantiated. The bottom floor was formerly a smelting house where gold was turned into ingots for shipment back to Spain.

The aim of the museum is to show the development of Cuban architecture exemplified by the decorative elements (the intricate joinery and iron work etc) which are evident in many of the country's buildings. It is well worth a visit if you are interested in learning a bit more about the historical development of Cuban architecture and furnishings.

Antonio Maceo's Birthplace, Calle los Maceo No 207
(entrance Calles Corona and Rastro)
Open: Monday to Saturday 08.00–18.30; closed on Sunday
Antonio Maceo is regarded as one of Cuba's greatest national heroes and this modest house, where he was born on 14 June 1845, has been turned into a museum in his honour.

Maceo had a reputation of being a fearless fighter and his courage and tactical acumen saw him rise rapidly through the ranks of the Liberation Army. At the end of the Ten-Year War of Independence he refused to hand in his weapon, regarding the settlement with the Spanish as unsatisfactory. His role in the east to west invasion during the second period of anti-Spanish hostilities which began in 1885 saw him sweep through the island with a small band of machete-wielding insurgents. This is regarded as a great military and tactical success, although Maceo was never to witness the independence he fought so hard to attain as he was killed in battle on 7 December 1895.

Casa de Velázquez, Calle Felix Pena by Parque Cespedes
*Open: Tuesday to Saturday 08.00–18.00; Sunday 09.00–13.00; closed
on Monday*
Formerly the home of Diego de Velázquez, this mansion house has been
preserved as a beautiful museum with its original furnishing and features
retained. Building was started on the house in 1516 and completed in
1520. Its architectural influences are predominantly Spanish, but much of
the furniture is of English and French design. The stained-glass vitrales,
which are evident everywhere you go in Cuba, are exemplified here and
their beauty is strikingly evident. The Spanish-style kitchen still contains
many of the original ceramics.

Piracy Museum, Castillo del Morro
Open: Tuesday to Sunday 09.00–18.00; closed on Monday
Piracy was a huge problem in the Santiago area from as early as the
16th century until the mid-19th century. The majority of pirates were
actually sanctioned by and working on behalf of the governments of
England, France and Holland, who were envious of the riches the
Spanish were shipping back from the Americas and were prepared to go
to great lengths to get their hands on the booty. Many of these
government-sponsored corsairs recognised the opportunity for a spot of
freelancing and subsequently formed groups which roamed around the
Caribbean (and particularly around Cuba), robbing and killing to their
hearts' content. Their activities were not solely confined to sea and
often they would venture on land to sack cities and generally
misbehave. The city of Santiago itself was the victim of many such
attacks, especially by the French pirate, Jacques de Sores, who once
kidnapped a group of the city's luminaries, demanding 80,000 pieces of
gold as ransom. The cheeky pirate actually remained in the city for a
month waiting for payment.

The exhibits in the museum testify to the role pirates and piracy have
played in the history of Santiago and Cuba in general.

Other places of interest
Parque Cespedes
Situated in the heart of the city and bordered by the cathedral, Hotel Casa
Grande, the Cuban Historical Milieu Museum and the provincial
government headquarters building, this is the where young Cubans
congregate in the evening and parents bring their children to be
entertained on goat-pulled cart rides. The square itself is only small and
for that reason always seems congested. There are stone benches
surrounding it and if you sit here for just a few minutes you will be
approached by curious locals, some of whom will be more interested in
selling you cigars or rum than simply practising their English.

The cathedral
The creamy pink-coloured cathedral now occupying the site on Parque Cespedes is not the original but is, in fact, the last in a line of four which have overlooked the square since 1528. There is a small museum within the building containing some interesting documents relating to the history of the various cathedrals.

Santa Ifigenia Cemetery
Northwest of the city centre, off Avenida Combret, is the resting place for some of Cuba's greatest national heroes, including José Martí, Carlos Manuel de Cespedes and Emilio Bacardi. José Martí is laid to rest in a large but simple mausoleum made of white stone, draped, symbolically, with the Cuban national flag. The mausoleum was positioned so that it would always be in the sun during daylight. At the gates of the cemetery is a sculpture which commemorates those Cubans who died fighting in the war in Angola. At the back of the cemetery are the graves of the poor (prior to the Revolution, the graves of the rich and poor were segregated).

Morro Castle
This fortress in Santiago Bay was built in 1663 and overlooks the entrance to the harbour. The designer was an Italian engineer named Antonelli, the man responsible for the El Morro fortress in Havana. The Piracy Museum is here and the building itself, having been extensively refurbished, is impressive. It's also a good vantage point from which to take in the terrific views of the Caribbean and the beautiful sunsets.

La Maison
Situated on Avenida Manduley in the desirable Vista Alegre area of the city, 3km from downtown Santiago, this elegant house harbours a café, restaurant, bar, dollar shop and clothes shop. It also has regular fashion shows in the evening beginning at 21.30. The design of the house is typically neoclassic and the courtyard café is one of the most delightful settings in the city. The house formerly belonged to one of Santiago's richest families.

Calle Heredia
Named after the 19th century Cuban poet, José María Heredia, this is one of the city's liveliest streets. On weekends, a large section of the street is closed to traffic and becomes purely pedestrianised, encouraging locals to gather and celebrate. There is usually live music and it has a deserved reputation as being the cultural centre of Santiago. The street runs adjacent to Parque Central.

Calle Padre Pico
If you come across a tourist brochure of the city, then you are likely to see a picture of Padre Pico somewhere within it. The stepped street leads into

the higher section of the old city from where you can get a good view of the sweeping bay. This is the neighbourhood of El Tivoli, a place marked by undulating streets bordered by cramped, almost compressed, houses. At the bottom of the steps you will invariably find a group of men gathered around a small table playing draughts, chess or cards.

Other streets of interest
Other interesting streets worth checking out are Calles José Saco, Aguilera and Mármol. Calle Pío Rosado is also worth a visit as it makes for a pleasant and more tranquil stroll away from the bustle around Parque Cespedes. You'll find this street running along the back of the cathedral.

WEST OF SANTIAGO DE CUBA
El Cobre
Eighteen kilometres west of the city, the Sanctuary of Our Lady of Charity El Cobre looms before you like a misplaced Disney prop as you make the descent into the village itself. El Cobre is to Cubans what Lourdes and Knock is to European Catholics. Legend has it that three local fishermen, whose boat was in danger of capsizing in heavy seas in the nearby Nipe Bay, came across a statue of the Virgin Mary floating amidst the swells. The storm subsided and the fishermen's lives were saved. The same statue is now displayed in the sanctuary in a glass case above the altar and has become the patron saint of Cuba. Thousands of pilgrims come here each year from all over Cuba to worship and convalesce.

Even for non-believers, the church is still an interesting place to visit. Curiously, there are a multitude of offerings that have been left or sent to the church and which are displayed in glass cases. They include university certificates, items of clothing, autographed baseball bats and even an empty Coca Cola tin. Pride of place, however, goes to the gold medal Hemingway received when he won the Nobel Prize for Literature in 1954. There are also soil samples from over 20 different countries around the world but as yet none from England, Scotland, Ireland or Wales.

The sanctuary provides rooms and if you have a fistful of pesos burning a hole in your pocket now is the time to get rid of some of them. A double room here costs only eight pesos a night and a triple room a mere 11 pesos. The sanctuary restaurant will serve you up a plate of rice and beans with stewed meat and a dessert for only five pesos.

The village of El Cobre will not detain you for too long as, apart from the church, there is nothing of any interest to see. One blight on the area is the opencast copper mining operation which is going on opposite the sanctuary. It is the one blot (and a major one too) on a very pleasing landscape. When you visit the area you will be approached by kids trying to sell you 'diamonds' which are in fact pyrites churned up during the mining operation.

EAST OF SANTIAGO DE CUBA

The scenery on the road east towards Guantánamo is agreeable but less dramatic than that to the west of the city. If you are wondering about all the strange monuments dotted along the roadside as far as Siboney, they are tributes to those who died in the attack at Moncada. They testify to the names and occupations of those who were killed both during and after the insurrection.

Once out of the city there is very little traffic on the road and the gently undulating hills make cycling in this part of the country quite pleasant. About 5km outside the city is the Abel Santamaría housing estate built after the Revolution. This is an interesting place to look around as it is typical of the sort of self-sufficient housing project that Cuba has been keen to promote during the last 30 years.

Siboney

About 18km from Santiago is the beach resort of Siboney. Tourists tend not to bother too much with the place as there are no facilities to cater for them. It is, however, a popular place for Cubans and it's a good place to come to meet people and make friends – if only on a day trip. The beach itself is black sand and largely unappealing. The hills around the village of Siboney were once a stronghold for anti-Batista rebels.

Siboney Farm

Granjita Siboney, Carretera de Siboney
Open: Tuesday to Sunday 09.00–17.00; closed on Monday
Siboney Farm was the meeting place for Castro and his commandos prior to the attack on Moncada barracks. Over 100 men gathered here the night before the attack to be briefed by Castro on strategy. Castro's last words to his men before setting out were 'We will be free men or martyrs.' Sadly, many of them ended up the latter after the attack.

Today the farm houses documentary evidence of the days leading up to and after the assault including some of the guns, personal effects and clothing worn by the commandos. There are newspaper clippings telling of public outrage following the arrest, torture and murder of many of the commandos.

Bacanao Park

Bacanao National Park has recently been declared a Reserve of the Biosphere by UNESCO due to the importance and fragility of its ecosystem. Incorporating Gran Piedra, the Santiago Zoo, La Siberia Botanical Gardens, the La Isabelica Coffee Plantations and the beaches of

Daiquiri, Sigua, Cazonal and Bacanoa, the park has been earmarked for tourist development and tourist facilities are beginning to spring up throughout the area. Most bizarrely, Bacanao is also home to a pre-historic theme park with a host of life-sized concrete dinosaurs and assorted reptiles. If the Cuban tourist authorities think this sort of thing is going to lure foreigners away from the beaches of Varadero or the architectural splendour of Havana, then they are sadly mistaken.

Accommodation
Category 2
Villa la Gran Piedra (41 rooms), Carretera de La Gran Piedra, Parque Baconao; tel: 226 5224/5913
Set in a spectacular location 1,230m above sea level, this hotel is around 16km outside of Santiago. It's a great place to come if you want to be alone. Popular with romantic couples, there are 19 suites guaranteeing extra privacy and the facilities (including the customary swimming pool) are first class. The views over the Caribbean and west to the city are beautiful. Prices for rooms and suites start at $25 with the most expensive suite costing around $55 per night.

Gran Piedra National Park
A journey 30km east of the city will bring you to some of the best hiking territory in the country. Around 1,300m above sea level, the views over the Caribbean and surrounding province are breathtaking. At the pinnacle of the park is a giant boulder which, it's believed, is a remnant of an ancient volcano that gradually eroded away with the passage of time (the name 'Gran Piedra' means 'giant boulder'). The area is the natural habitat of rare species of birds including the tocororo – the national bird of Cuba. The hills are green and thick with vegetation and it is an excellent setting in which to relax and unwind.

La Isabelica Museum
Carretera de la Gran Piedra (16km east of Santiago de Cuba)
Open: Tuesday to Saturday 09.00–17.00; Sunday 09.00–13.00; closed on Monday
If you are interested in how the French plantation owners revolutionised the coffee-growing industry in Cuba following their settlement in the country after the Haitian revolution, then this is the place to come. There are also exhibits telling of the history of French settlement in the area and the museum has the added advantage of being in a delightful location high up in the Sierra Maestra with good views over the Caribbean.

Daiquiri
This is not the home of the famed cocktail of the same name; that was first mixed in El Floridita bar in Havana. Daiquiri has little to recommend it apart from a small beach and an exotic sounding name.

Sigua

A further 18km east along the coastal road is the village/beach resort of Sigua. This is largely frequented by Cubans, although there are a couple of tourist hotels close by the beach. You are guaranteed to receive a warm welcome if you bother to make the trip out from Santiago. Locals will even offer to catch you a nice fish for your dinner in return for a couple of dollars.

Chapter Sixteen

Guantánamo Province

Cuba's easternmost province is one of the least visited yet most interesting of all the country's municipalities. The city of Guantánamo, located in the south of the province is best known for being the site of the American naval base (actually situated on Guantánamo bay a few kilometres north of the city). Described by Carlo Gébler in his book *Driving Through Cuba* as 'A depressed city of miserable, low houses and railway marshalling yards filled with decrepit rolling stock', its other claim to fame is that it gave its name to the internationally famous song *Guantanamera,* a song from which it is difficult for any visitor to the city to escape. The claim of being cultural capital of the province is, however, justifiably made by the city of Baracoa in the northeast of Guantánamo province. One of the first of the seven townships, the city is the oldest in Cuba and locals regard it as the cradle of Cuban civilisation.

The province is, with the possible exception of parts of Pinar del Río province, the wildest, most uncharted piece of territory in the land. Most visitors tend to bypass Guantánamo city in favour of the more attractive and interesting Baracoa. Very few make the effort to travel further east of this point.

GUANTÁNAMO CITY
History and orientation
Situated 90km east of Santiago and a few kilometres north of the bay of the same name, the city of Guantánamo is pretty much the place Carlo Gébler described. Compared with other major cities, there has been little in the way of urban development in Guantánamo and the place and the people live very much in the shadow of the American naval base. In the mid-19th century there was a thriving sugar industry in and around the city and an estimated 40% of the local population were black slaves who

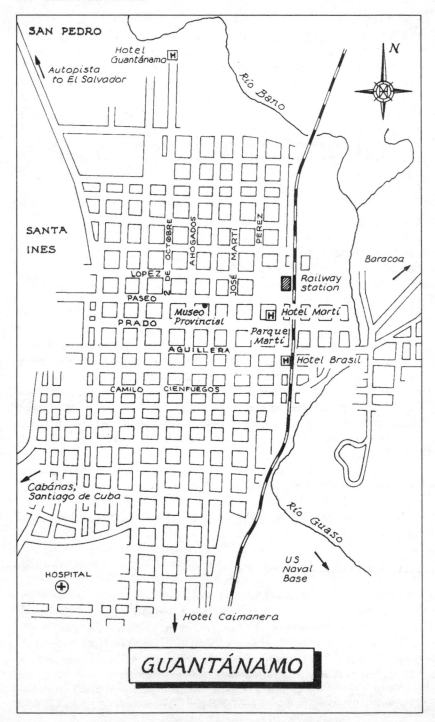

SAN PEDRO

Hotel Guantánamo H

Autopista to El Salvador

Río Bano

N

SANTA INES

2 DE OCTOBRE

AHOGADOS

JOSÉ MARTÍ

PEREZ

LOPEZ

PASEO

PRADO

Museo Provincial

H Hotel Martí

Parque Martí

Railway station

Baracoa

AGUILLERA

H Hotel Brasil

CAMILO CIENFUEGOS

Cabánas, Santiago de Cuba

Río Guaso

US Naval Base

HOSPITAL ⊕

Hotel Caimanera

GUANTÁNAMO

were brought in to work the plantations. Historically rebellious, the city was invaded and briefly captured by Máximo Gómez and his independence fighters in 1871. During the days leading up to 1959, Castro received solid support from the people of Guantánamo.

Until the Revolution, the city was economically dependent on the jobs provided by the American naval base although there was little or no direct investment from the Americans in the local infrastructure. The city became a rest and recreation point for American servicemen and drinking and gambling dens and prostitution were the order of the day. The dependency culture ended in 1959 and today only a handful of Guantánamese are allowed access to the base to work. Although the city is run down and grimy, the people are friendly and hospitable and all visitors are guaranteed a warm welcome. One day here is enough to take in most of the city.

Getting there and away
By air
Flights to and from Havana are currently operating daily. The cost of a one-way ticket is $80.

By road
From Santiago de Cuba there are two routes, the first and most direct being the main highway which connects the two cities and which passes through the small town of Cabanas. The other more scenic and roundabout route is the coastal road that meanders along the coastline through Sigua before veering sharply south towards the city (Guantánamo bay is on your right). This is a delightful route taking you through the towns of Siboney and Daiquiri. The interprovincial bus terminal is located 4km west of the city and services operate to and from Santiago, Holguin and Baracoa. The weekly long-distance bus to Havana is booked up decades in advance.

Accommodation
The only place in the city for tourists to stay is the monolithic **Hotel Guantánamo**, a modern, Soviet-style construction designed by an architect who had obviously had an imagination bypass operation while studying for his professional qualifications! It is located at Calle 13 north between Calles Ahogado and 1 Oeste; tel: 21 36015. It has 124 rooms. A single room here goes for $20 a night and a double for $27 (all year round). The hotel restaurant is the only place in the city where you are likely to get a decent meal. There is the obligatory swimming pool and a nightclub into the bargain for late-night party people. There are also a couple of peso hotels, **Hotel Martí** and **Hotel Brasil**.

Around 20km south in the town of Caimanera, by Guantánamo naval base, is the newly built **Hotel Caimanera** (tel: 21 99414). Only a small

TOURISTS PAY TO 'SPY' ON US BASE
Dalia Acosta

The US Navy's base at Guantánamo – a bone of contention between Cuba and the United States for 35 years – is now being offered as a tourist attraction for would-be espionage agents. For a $100 fee, visitors to this Caribbean island can take advantage of the Gaviota Cuban tourist company's 'Border Scenes' tour to 'spy' on the base.

The tour being offered is a humorous response to a national campaign to develop the leisure industry into the country's main source of foreign exchange and Cubans have turned the bitterly disputed base into a tourist destination. Along with the island's white sand beaches, unspoiled reefs , nature preserves, historic sites, conference facilities and now, views of an 'enemy military base', the government hopes to attract a million tourists to the island by the year 2000. Industry experts say Cuba has the potential to become a leading regional tourist destination by the end of the century...

Tour operators tempt tourists to observe the military base through binoculars, peer at US marines in training and watch 'enemy' ships and aircraft conducting manoeuvres. The offer includes the possibility of contemplating the most densely mined terrain in the world, according to military experts, with a base perimeter surrounded by interminable kilometres of fences and thickets of barbed-wire studded with sentry boxes.

Built in 1903, the Guantánamo naval base is located some 900km from Havana and at the beginning of this decade included some 3,000 military personnel and 4,000 civilians shielded from Cuban territory with 70,000 anti-personnel and anti-tank mines.

Official Cuban sources report more than 12,500 base-side provocations of Cuban troops between 1962 and 1990. Covering an area of 117.3 km^2, only 49.4 of which are on land, the military base includes a refugee camp that sheltered many of the 35,000 Cubans who left the island during the 'boat crisis' of August 1994.

Now tourists are taken to the first Cuban watchpost in a Soviet helicopter and driven by bus another dozen kilometres through semi-desert terrain to Malones, at an altitude of slightly more than 300m. At Malones, the visitor enjoys traditional music and cocktails made with Cuban rum before continuing to ascend through tunnels to the other side of the hill. At the summit is the observation post offering a fascinating panorama of the US military base. The tour package plans to include a visit to Caimanera, a town of 10,000 inhabitants located inside Guantánamo bay and the only place in Cuba with restricted access because of its location on the military border.

Visitors can rest at a three-star hotel with a swimming pool, restaurant, bar, and enjoy water sports in a cove dominated by the tense silence of enemy guards who study each other across a kind of tropical and invisible 'Berlin wall'. It appears that the Cubans aren't the only ones who decided to finish out the century by taking economic advantage of the base. As the Guantánamo refugees gradually leave the base under agreements struck in May 1996, the US authorities have decided to sell off the huge tent city that at one point sheltered more than 40,000 Cubans and Haitians. Now everything appears to be for sale: tents, beds, toilets, trash containers, cushions, complete vehicles and parts, feeding bottles, drapery, clothing and even a transporter. ... Washington's apparent intention is to recover part of the estimated $1 million per day that it cost US taxpayers to support the rescue operation of Haitians and Cubans who attempted to flee to the United States by boat...

establishment (17 rooms), this is a good place to stay if you want to check out the views across the bay and the base. It's a three-star hotel with good, modern facilities. A single room is $24 ($20 low season) and a double $32 ($26 low season).

Things to see and do
Guantánamo Naval Base (USA)

Occupying the two horns at the mouth of the bay and the waters in between, Guantánamo American naval base is the last colonial outpost remaining on the island. The base (49.4km^2 of land) was occupied by the Americans long before the actual signing of a lease in 1934 which granted its possession to the USA until the year 2033. Home to around 7,000 American servicemen, it is a self-sufficient entity with its own TV and radio station, water supply, medical, sports and general recreational facilities. It even has its own McDonald's, the only place in Cuba where you can get a decent burger. American servicemen have been instructed to shoot on sight any Cuban soldier who attempts to breach the perimeter fencing, while Cuban military personnel, ever watchful in the area, have been issued with the same instructions should any American soldier stray out of bounds.

These days the base is of little or no strategic importance to the Americans but the psychological threat it imposes on Castro and the Cuban people makes it worth retaining. Until the recent reversal of the American 'open arms' policy, whereby any Cuban fleeing the island was given automatic political asylum, many Cubans attempted to swim to the base through the surrounding shark-infested waters. More people died in the process than were successful. At the moment the base currently houses around 20,000 Cuban refugees (and a further 15,000 Haitians) who were picked up at sea during the raft exodus in September 1994.

Each year the American navy sends Castro a cheque for $4,085, the annual payment of rent. Each year Castro puts the cheque into a locked drawer, refusing to cash it. Although the base is a thorn in the side of Cuba, who have long protested to the international community against the continued presence of the Americans, the pragmatists in the Cuban authorities have cottoned on to the fact that the base can earn Cuba valuable tourist dollars. Consequently, you can now buy day tours to the base from Santiago and Guantánamo city and although you cannot visit the site you can observe it from a recently built look-out point.

As the press story in the box opposite highlights, the irony of the base as a tourist attraction gives a great deal of amusement to the Cubans.

BARACOA
History and orientation
About 120km northeast of Guantánamo, Baracoa is situated on a bay close to the eastern tip of the island of Cuba where the Caribbean Sea meets the Atlantic Ocean. Columbus discovered the area in December 1492 (he erected a cross on the beach and named it Puerto Santo) and wrote, 'The bay is in the form of a small shield and high up beyond, there is a high and square mountain that resembles a table.' The table in question is the Yunque mountain, the most famous mountain in all of Cuba. In 1512 Diego Velázquez founded a township at the mouth of the Maniguanigua river and gave it the name Nuestra Senora de la Asuncion de Baracoa. It was from here that he set about his conquest of the entire country. Baracoa became the capital of Cuba for the three years following Velázquez's arrival and all manner of tradesmen, fishermen and prospectors flocked to its boundaries as the city prospered under his jurisdiction. In 1515, however, the honour of being capital was switched to Santiago de Cuba, a city with a far superior harbour. Thereafter followed a period of decline in which, with Velázquez now gone, the city fell prey to attacks from motley bands of pirates and corsairs operating in the waters around Cuba's northern coast. The city was flattened, twice, by rebelling Indians and pyromaniacal French pirates before recovering sufficiently to play host to a thriving black-market economy in contraband goods. The Spanish, in an effort to shore up and kickstart the legal economy, introduced coffee and cocoa to the area. Baracoa's stunted development owed more to its geographical isolation than any other factor (the city was only easily accessible by sea) and, despite attempts to promote agricultural growth in the area, its remote location ensured that the city never achieved a meaningful or lasting level of prosperity. The city is often affectionately referred to as the 'Cinderella of Cuba'.

Baracoa, like most of the cities of the east, prides itself in the role it played both in the wars for independence and in the 1959 Revolution. In 1877 Antonio Maceo captured the city for 15 days and in 1895 an expeditionary force landed on the bay to tackle the Spanish. One of Baracoa's most famous fighters, a woman named Luz Palomares, was renowned for going into battle armed only with a machete and a bad attitude. Prior to the Revolution the city had the highest illiteracy rate in Cuba but, thanks to a concerted promotion of education nationwide, Baracoa now boasts, along with the rest of the country, the highest literacy level *per capita* in Latin America.

Getting there and away
By air
Flights from Havana are currently operating on Tuesdays, Fridaus and Sundays. The one-way cost is $80. It is als opossible to fly from Santiago de Cuba. The cost is $19 one way.

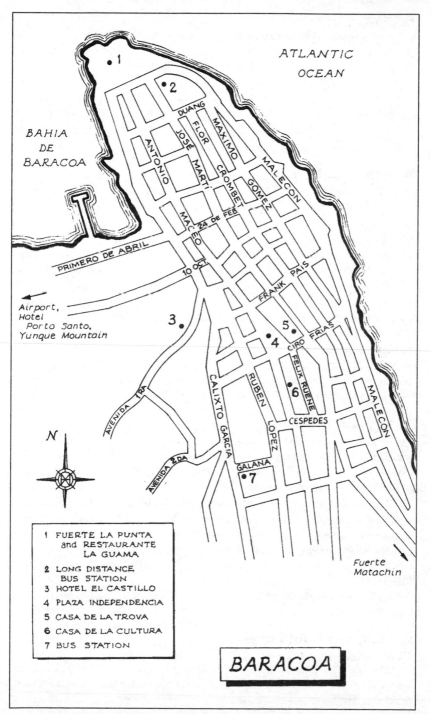

ATLANTIC OCEAN

BAHIA DE BARACOA

Airport,
Hotel
Porto Santo,
Yunque Mountain

N

Fuerte
Matachin

1 FUERTE LA PUNTA
  and RESTAURANTE
  LA GUAMA

2 LONG DISTANCE
  BUS STATION

3 HOTEL EL CASTILLO

4 PLAZA INDEPENDENCIA

5 CASA DE LA TROVA

6 CASA DE LA CULTURA

7 BUS STATION

BARACOA

By road

The journey from Guantánamo takes you along the southern coastline as far as Cajobabo and then north up to Baracoa. There are over 200 bends along the way and, although the road isn't in the best of conditions, it's one of the best drives in the country, taking you up and down rolling hills like a fairground ride. Be sure to travel in daylight hours as it can be tricky and dangerous after dark. The other route is along the northern coast road from Moa. This road is marginally better but the journey isn't as spectacular.

Accommodation

There are two three-star tourist hotels in the city with little to choose between them in terms of facilities and price.

Category 3

Hotel Porto Santo (60 rooms), Carretera del Aeropuerto, Baracoa; tel: 21 43512
Located 1km outside the city, this is a small modern hotel set in green and pleasant surrounds. You can book tours of the surrounding mountains and even rafting trips down the nearby Toa river from here.

El Castillo Hotel (34 rooms), Calle Paraíso, Baracoa; tel: 21 42103
An old fortress which has been modernised and converted, the bar in this place has a spectacular view across to the Yunque mountain.

Category 2

Hotel Rusa (12 rooms), Calle Máximo Gómez; tel: 21 43011
Built by a Russian woman by the name of Magdalena Rovieskuya and patronised in the past (allegedly) by Errol Flynn.

Eating and drinking

The hotels offer the best choice although you may wish to try **Restaurante La Guama** in Fuerte la Punta to the north of the city. The restaurant has a tradition of specialising in Indo-Cuban food, rarely available. A peso restaurant, with the problems of food shortages affecting Baracoa as much as any other city, La Guama is not guaranteed either to be open or have enough food to sell. The local speciality, *cucurrucho,* a sweet made of coconut, cocoa and tropical fruits wrapped in palm leaves, is magnificent if you can get it.

Nightlife

The **Hotel el Castillo** has a discothèque and both hotels have decent bars (especially the El Castillo, simply for the views). The local **Casa de la Trova** is situated on Calle José Martí No 149. There is occasional live *salsa* at the **Casa de la Cultura** on Calle Antonio Maceo. Alternatively, check out the local action at the Plaza Independencia.

Things to see and do
Plaza Independencia
Like most main squares, this is the focal point for community life in the city. Locals gather here to gossip, tell jokes, play games and watch television on the communal screen. The local Indian chief and rebel, Hatuey, is remembered in statue form. Situated in the middle of the plaza, he looks across to the **Catedral de la Nuestra Senora de la Asuncion** which was founded in 1512 at a different location but reconstructed on its present site in 1833. The cathedral contains the Cross of Parra, an important relic said to be the actual cross which Columbus planted upon his arrival in 1492 (a claim which has aroused some scepticism). It is said to be the oldest symbol of Christianity in the Americas. Whether you believe it's genuine or a fake, the Baracoans are intent in promoting this as a tourist attraction and don't take too kindly when you question its authenticity. The cross is said to have miraculous powers. I am still awaiting my win on the National Lottery.

Yunque de Baracoa
So named because its flat top resembles an anvil (*yunque* being Spanish for 'anvil'), the mountain was formerly the site of a multitude of aboriginal communities. One of the more important of these were the Taino Indians, many relics of whose culture (ceramics, icons etc) as well as skeletal remains have been recovered from the area. Because of the remoteness and inaccessibility of the area, many black slaves, fleeing from their masters, took refuge in the mountains. The shape of the Yunque is reminiscent of Sugar Loaf mountain in Brazil.

Baracoa Municipal Museum
Open: Tuesday to Saturday 09.00–17.00; Sunday 09.00–13.00; closed on Monday
Situated in Fuerte Matachin, one of the three forts built by the Spanish to protect the town, primarily from pirates and corsairs, the building has been renovated and now houses a history of the development of Baracoa as well as other exhibits including samples of the local flora and fauna.

The Stone Zoo
Located 10km outside the city, this curious zoo comprises a multitude of stone animals, all apparently the creation of a local coffee farmer who, using his hammer and chisel, has fashioned these exhibits on the strength of photographs he has seen in books. The sculptor has, so the story goes, never seen any of the animals he creates in the flesh.

Chapter Seventeen

Offshore Islands

ISLE OF YOUTH
(Isla de la Juventud)

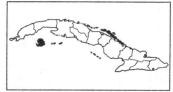

History and orientation
Formerly known as the Isle of Pines, the
island adopted its new name in 1978 as an
acknowledgement of the contribution made by the country's young to the
success of the Revolution. The island is situated about 100km off the
south coast of mainland Cuba and one might imagine the 69,000 people
living on the island have something of an identity crisis as this was the
island's fifteenth name change since 1494 when Columbus first set foot
there. The indigenous Indian population knew the island as Camargo,
Siguanea or Guanajay while Columbus, reputedly after one of his crew
had seen a mysterious white shrouded figure, gave it the name La
Evangelista. To the many pirates who used it as a base for their own
particular brand of skulduggery it was known as the Island of Parrots. It
lies close to the sea lanes used by the Spanish fleets who, after a hard
day's plundering in the Americas, would return to Spain via Havana, and
the pirates, corsairs and general aqua-ne'er-do-wells of England, Holland
and France habitually waylaid these fleets, stealing their cargoes before
nipping back to the sheltered bays of the islands. It is estimated that
around two thirds of all Spanish ships never actually made it back to
Spain, a large portion of them being attacked and robbed from the
sanctuary of the Isle of Youth. Among the most salubrious of names
formerly to have used the island as a launching pad for their caddish deeds
were John Hawkins, Francis Drake and Henry Morgan. As a result of its
piratical past it is also reputed to be the island on which Robert Louis
Stevenson based his novel *Treasure Island* (the topography of the map
used in the book bears a striking resemblance to the Isle of Youth).

It wasn't until 1925 that the island finally became part of Cuban national
territory although Cuba had long since staked its claim. One of the barriers
for its annexation at the time was the Platt Amendment which included a

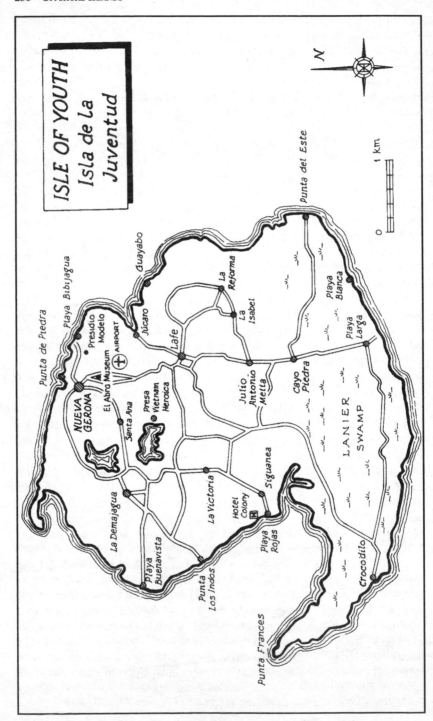

ISLE OF YOUTH
Isla de la
Juventud

clause excluding territorial settlement there. Its history as a penal colony dates back to the days when the Spanish used it as a Devil's Island prison camp, banishing Cuban undesirables and political prisoners to its shores (José Martí was sent here as an 18-year-old having received a six years' hard labour sentence for anti-Spanish activities – he served only three months before being deported to Spain). More famously, or infamously, Fidel Castro and his cohorts who survived the attack on Moncada barracks, Santiago de Cuba in 1953, were imprisoned here in the Presidio Modelo ('model prison').

These days the island is home to some of Cuba's most important agricultural farmland and is a key producer of citrus fruits for export. It is also home to around 10,000 African students given free and subsidised education by the Cuban government, something of which Cubans are justifiably proud. Because of the large presence of African students, the island in general and the capital, Nueva Gerona, in particular, have a more cosmopolitan feel. The standard of living is generally higher, largely due to the preponderance of well cultivated, arable land which makes the problem of food shortages less pronounced than on the mainland.

The island is split into two fairly distinct topographical sections, north and south, and is dissected by a large swamp which runs from the southeast coast to the southwest coast. The north is generally flat and dry although there are a few marble hills near Nueva Gerona and the area is heavily farmed for citrus fruits (especially grapefruit). The harvesting of the grapefruit in January is marked by one of the country's biggest and best festivals. The beaches in the north are black sand and generally disappointing. The same cannot be said of the south for, although its limestone soils are unsuitable for farming and large tracts of the area are covered by dense tropical woodland, there are some superb white sand beaches and the south is much more likely to develop as a popular holiday destination in the future. If you want a holiday centred around palm-fringed beaches and calm crystal-blue seas then the south coast of the Isle of Youth is as good a place as any.

Getting there and away

Getting there is relatively easy and you have two choices – by sea or by air. There are flights daily from Havana to Nueva Gerona and the journey takes less than 30 minutes. Flying there is an experience in itself as the twin-propellered 22-seater Russian-made YAK 40s that operate on the route give you the opportunity to imagine what being airborne was like for your granny. If the idea of sitting in a small, ageing, metal tube suspended 1,500m over the Caribbean Sea is not your idea of fun then you should take the other option of going by sea. Here, again, you have two choices, hydrofoil or ferry. Both depart from the small port of Batabanó on the south coast of the mainland about 70km from Havana. The hydrofoil journey takes just over two hours and the ferry around six and a half hours.

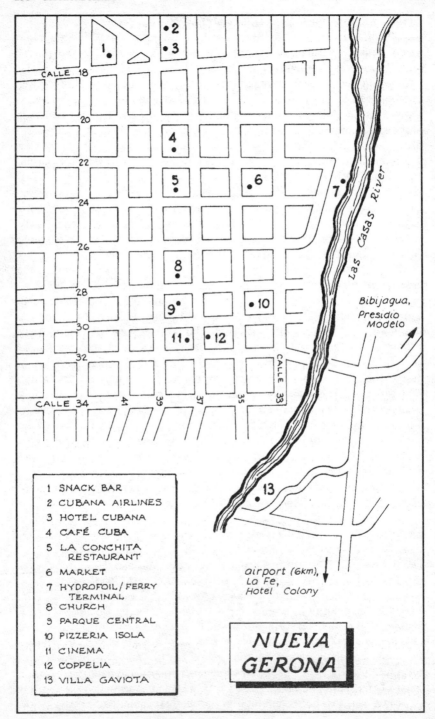

1 SNACK BAR
2 CUBANA AIRLINES
3 HOTEL CUBANA
4 CAFÉ CUBA
5 LA CONCHITA RESTAURANT
6 MARKET
7 HYDROFOIL/FERRY TERMINAL
8 CHURCH
9 PARQUE CENTRAL
10 PIZZERIA ISOLA
11 CINEMA
12 COPPELIA
13 VILLA GAVIOTA

NUEVA GERONA

There are four Cubana flights a day from Havana to the island and the cost is only $16 one way. Aerocaribbean also fly regularly although passengers generally have to travel as part of an organised tour. Similarly, the hydrofoils operate four daily crossings (two in the morning, two in the afternoon). You should check for the latest departure times as these are not always consistent. The cost is $8 one way and the connecting bus link to Havana will set you back another $3. The ferry operates one trip a day, leaving Batabanó at 09.00 and reaching Nueva Gerona at 16.30. The return journey sets off around midnight, getting you back to the mainland for 06.30 at a cost of $4 one way. If you travel on either the plane or the ferry you should book around four days in advance if possible.

The Cubana Airline office in Nueva Gerona is on Calle 39 between Calles 16 and 18. It is open Monday to Thursday 08.00–12.00 and 13.00–16.30; Friday 08.00–12.00 and 13.00–15.30. It is closed on both Saturday and Sunday.

Getting about

There is no internal rail system and the local bus service is erratic. The road network is good, especially in the north of the island and there is a small section of motorway (*autopista*) running between Nueva Gerona and La Fe (mainly deserted). There are plenty of taxis in operation and hitching is also a popular form of getting from A to B, although the fuel shortages have taken their toll on the number of cars in circulation. Arriving at Nueva Gerona airport, 8km from the city, you are met by a bus which transports you into the town and stops off en route at the various tourist hotels and villas. There is also an airport at Siguanea in the south of the island which serves the Hotel Colony and Playa Rojas beach resort in that area. The best way to get around the island is by bike and, if you have brought yours from home and have begun to wonder whether it was really worth all the effort, a visit to the Isle of Youth will convince you it was. As you cruise smugly past other visitors whose time is spent gazing into the horizon looking desperately for a plume of blue smoke signifying an oncoming bus or lorry, the inconvenience of dismantling and reassembling your bike for every journey taken by plane will seem but a mere bagatelle. Sadly there are no bike-hire places on the island yet, although it will only be a matter of time before some entrepreneur sees the obvious opening in the market.

Nueva Gerona

Nueva Gerona is a busy and relatively prosperous town and the small but colourful streets have a provincial Latin American, rather than distinctly Cuban, feel about them. Many of the African students who study on the island are based here and the town has a more cosmopolitan atmosphere than most other towns and cities outside Havana. Parque Central on

Calle 39 in between Calles 28 and 30 is the place where many of Nueva Gerona's young congregate. At weekends it is also home to some excellent live *salsa* and if you are visiting the city this is a good place to start. Of an evening there always seems to be something going on. The main street is Calle 41 which from north to south leads to the General Hospital at the intersection of Calle 18. However, Calle 39, parallel to Calle 41, is where you will find most of the town's cafés and restaurants and is also home to the local tourist information office (between Calles 26 and 28). This shop doubles as a dollar shop selling biscuits, camera film, beer and compact discs. It also has a film-processing facility.

Nueva Gerona is the capital of the island and the only thing that constitutes anything remotely resembling a town, the population being around 30,000. The African students, as well as studying here, also contribute towards the island's citrus fruit industry (as part of the free/subsidised education programme they are obliged to work part-time).

Accommodation

In keeping with what appears on the face of it to be a planned attempt to segregate tourists from the cities, there are at present no hotels which accept tourists in Nueva Gerona. There are several peso hotels in the city and you are at liberty to try to get in, although the chances of success are pretty remote as there seems to be a strict policy of non-acceptance. Even offering to pay your hotel bill in dollars is likely to be met with polite but firm disapproval. This is a great pity as Nueva Gerona is an interesting town and would benefit from the money tourists would be happy to spend there given the chance. For the moment, however, the city becomes largely out of bounds at night as tourists are reluctant to place themselves at the mercy of the Cuban transport system when trying to make it back to the tourist hotels outside the city. If you want to try to get into a peso hotel, the most central and convenient is Hotel Cubana (next door to the Cubana Airline office) on Calle 39 between Calles 14 and 18.

Category 4

Hotel Colony (77 rooms), Carretera de Siguanea; tel: 61 98181
This is the island's number one hotel situated in the southwest of the Isle of Youth around 50km from the airport. It has both terraced rooms and individual bungalows and is set within pleasant tropical gardens. It is popular with tourists on scuba-diving holidays as there are over 50 deep-water diving sites close by. You can hire equipment and take lessons if you want to make a voyage to the bottom of the sea. Being so far from Nueva Gerona or any other tourist hotel you are pretty much a captive of the hotel and its facilities and the prices are not exactly cheap. Watch out for the mosquitoes in the evening as they are exceptionally bad-tempered and like nothing more than a nibble on unsuspecting and unprepared tourists. Take plenty of repellent.

Category 3
Villa Gaviota (26 rooms), Autopista Nueva Gerona, La Fe; tel: 61 23290
Situated about 2km outside Nueva Gerona, this is probably the best value hotel on the island. Set out in a fairly ugly complex, the modern chalets (over two floors) are clean and comfortable. All have balconies looking out on to the swimming pool. The restaurant is good and the bar serves a mean cocktail. The Cuban practice of blaring out music over the PA system is maintained here and, if it continues, it can only be hoped that the cassette deck, currently on its last legs and capable of omitting the most appalling distortions, is replaced. There is a tourist office on site and the staff both here and in the restaurant are extremely friendly and helpful. This hotel is currently the closest one to the island's main city which accepts foreigners – Nueva Gerona is just a 15-minute walk.

Eating and drinking
Unfortunately, outside of the hotel there are few opportunities to indulge yourself, but if you are looking for action then Nueva Gerona is the place you are most likely to find it. There are several cafés and restaurants along Calle 39 including **La Conchita** at the junction of Calle 24 and **Café de Cuba** on Calle 22. La Conchita seems to be operating a policy of Cubans only at present, but Café de Cuba is more open and is a good place to meet young locals who come here to dance and socialise. There is a small wooden stage in the courtyard which functions as a dance floor and as a foreigner you will most likely be asked at some stage of the proceedings to exhibit your own special brand of dancing skills. **Coppelia Ice-cream** on Calle 37 between Calles 30 and 32 still does a good *helados* while the **Pizzeria Isola** on Calle 35 at the junction of Calle 30 serves pizzas for Cubans but not tourists. With the recent decision to allow farmers to sell any produce over and above what they need to provide to fulfil government quotas, the market at Calles 24 and 35 should soon be a good place to pick up goodies such as fruit and vegetables.

Cinema
There is a small cinema situated on Calle 37 at the junction of Calle 32. The films shown include many you will probably have seen back home about ten years ago. When open (the cinema seems to close for long periods) this is a good place to mix with the locals.

Outside Nueva Gerona
Presidio Modelo (Model Prison)
Five kilometres east of Nueva Gerona is the infamous Model Prison. Built between 1926 and 1931 on the insistence of the then dictator, President Machado, it was modelled on the Joliet Prison, Illinois, USA. The Isle of Youth was chosen to house such a prison as it was considered far enough from the mainland to make any attempts at escaping unattractive. Originally designed to house 6,000 inmates, there were a total of four circular buildings over five storeys. Each floor had 93 cells which were each

designed to accommodate two inmates. The central area is occupied by a two-storey circular building which once housed the store room and kitchen as well as a mess room for 5,000 prisoners. The grand and impressive administrative building in front of the five circular blocks has recently been refurbished and redecorated and is now home to the Model Prison Museum which includes a pictorial documentary of the history of the museum as well as details of the time Castro was detained here after the attack on Moncada barracks in 1953. Following the arrest of Castro and those who survived (including his brother Raoul) and their detention in the Presidio Modelo, the political prisoners were kept away from other inmates for fear of them spreading their revolutionary enthusiasm and beliefs. Batista must have hoped that the detention would have broken their resolve, but instead Castro and his comrades used their time in prison to prepare for a further assault on the dictator. The prisoners formed a group known as the Abel Santamaría Academy (named after one of the student leaders who had died during the attack on Moncada) and compartmentalised their days into periods of study, recreation and cultural pursuit. Castro, whilst there, wrote a famed pamphlet, *History Will Absolve Me*, which was smuggled out of jail and effectively became the manifesto of the July 26th Movement calling for a return to the 1940 constitution and honest and just government.

El Abra Museum

About 4km south of Nueva Gerona is the farm of El Abra, formerly the home of José Martí who stayed here after he was released from prison on the mainland. A friend of José Martí's father, named José M Sadre, a Catalonian landowner, managed to convince the Spanish authorities to release Martí (then aged 18) from his six-year sentence in prison to a term on his farm on the Isle of Youth. Martí arrived here on 13 October 1870 and remained here until December before leaving for exile in Spain.

Today the museum is a national monument and the exhibits include a pictorial and documentary portrayal of the life of Martí and many of his personal belongings.

Bibijagua (Beach of Black Sand)

A local tourist brochure describes this place as 'resembling an unreal paradise'. Formed by the process of sea erosion on the local black marble rock, the beach is in reality a seaweed and litter-strewn piece of rather uninviting coastline with not a great deal to recommend it. There is a peso resort for Cubans next to the beach but it has limited facilities and, like so many places on the Isle of Youth, they are reluctant to allow foreigners to stay, preferring to encourage them to use the more exclusive facilities of Playa Rojas which are designed specifically for tourists. If you have a bike it is an easy ride out and, as the Model Prison is en route, you may wish to combine the two in one visit.

Punta del Este Caves

Prior to the arrival of the Spanish colonists, the Isle of Youth was inhabited by Indian settlers and one of their settlements, a series of caves in the area of Punta del Este, is regarded as an important historical and archaeological find. Discovered by a sailor, Freeman P Lane, whose vessel was shipwrecked in the vicinity in 1910, the caves are considered unique in the Antilles and contain 235 pictographs – paintings of a celestial and tribal nature which have been replicated and are exhibited in the Natural Science Museum in Havana. There are seven caves in all. Reaching them at present has to be undertaken as part of an organised tour. You can book this through the tour desk at your hotel.

Sports

Some of the best scuba diving in the Caribbean can be found off the southeast coast of the Isle of Youth. The 6km stretch between Punta Francés and Punta Pedernales contains an area known as the Costa de los Pirates, so called because many pirate ships are thought to have plied the area and legend has it that there are many shipwrecks laden with treasure sitting at the bottom of this part of the Caribbean. There are nearly 60 internationally recognised diving sites in the area and the Gulf Cliff, which runs parallel to the coast, overlooks the calm waters that are home to a multitude of tropical fish, corals and molluscs. There is an international diving school based at the Hotel Colony nearby.

Although fishing is forbidden in this area (it is a protected area which operates a ban on any activity which might affect the region's sensitive ecosystem) there are other parts of the south which offer excellent sea-fishing opportunities. The Hotel Colony operates specialist tours for any would-be fishermen.

Crocodiles

The Lanier Swamp in the south of the island is still home to a small crocodile population. It is possible to visit the local crocodile farm by booking an organised tour. It is advisable not to undertake solo explorations for crocodiles even if you have adequate medical cover.

CAYO LARGO

History and orientation

Situated 60km south of Zapata peninsula and 190km southeast of Havana, Cayo Largo occupies a position east of the Isle of Youth in the Caribbean Sea. Although only a relatively small island (around 28km long) it is blessed with an almost continuous stretch of beach, notably along its south coast. The area is being developed into a prime tourist destination with its eyes fixed firmly on up-market package tours, particularly from Europe and Canada.

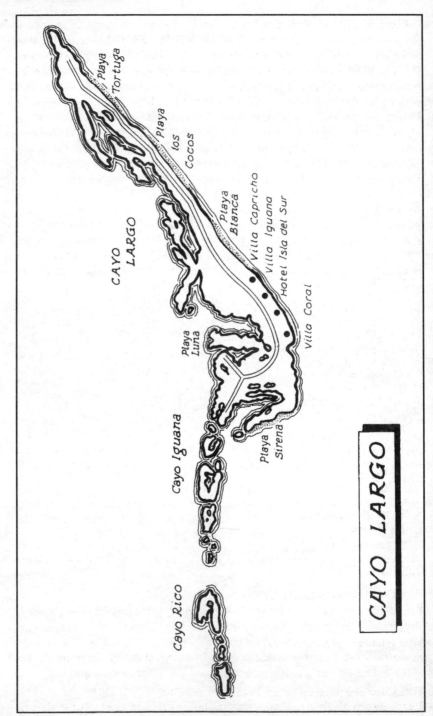

Playa Tortuga

Playa los Cocos

Playa Blanca

Villa Capricho

Villa Iguana

Hotel Isla del Sur

Villa Coral

CAYO LARGO

Playa Luna

Playa Sirena

Cayo Iguana

Cayo Rico

CAYO LARGO

There is little written about the island's history, although it is known that it was favoured by pirates during the 17th and 18th centuries and there are several shipwrecks in the vicinity. These days the only pirates you are likely to find on the island are the people who run the hotels. Accommodation here is very expensive, as is food and drink. Given that you are a captive market on the island, there is little you can do about it except pay up or leave. The beaches are pretty and it is an idyllic setting. There is also an abundance of natural wildlife including iguanas and giant sea turtles. Staying here, however, is about as much a Cuban experience as lying under a sunbed with a bottle of rum at your side. There is little to do apart from sunbathe and indulge (although there are some good scuba-diving sites around the island). There are six beaches all of which will be able to satisfy your sun and sand lust. They are: Playa Sirena, Playa Lindaman, Playa Blanca, Playa los Cocos, Playa Tortuga and Playa Luna.

Getting there and away
At present you normally have to travel to Cayo Largo as part of an organised tour, either as part of a day trip or package lasting a week or more. Flights leave from both Havana and Varadero on a daily basis (check locally for details). A day trip will set you back around $115 and for that you are flown in, ferried around the island, fed, refreshed and taken to a tourist shop where your dollars will be levered from you in return for tourist tat (maracas, wall-mounted shells etc). If you are going to make any day trips you could pick far more interesting and rewarding places than this. If you want to take your chance and go freelance then you should be able to persuade your tour agent or tour operator to sell you a flight-only ticket. Once there, however, you will find yourself paying a small fortune for accommodation and food. It is much cheaper to go as part of an organised tour.

Accommodation
Category 4
Hotel Isla del Sur (59 rooms), tel: 794215; fax: 332108
Situated between Lindaman beach and Blanca beach, this is a four-star modern hotel.

Villa Coral (64 rooms), tel: 794215
The newest of the resort's hotels designed in pseudo-colonial bungalow style. Situated close to the sea.

Villa Iguana (114 rooms), tel: 794215
Newly-built two-storey bungalow accommodation situated in the centre of the island.

Villa Capricho (60 rooms), tel: 794215; fax: 332108
Thatch-roofed bungalow accommodation situated in a pine forest close to the sea.

Eating and drinking

You are a captive market on Cayo Largo and food here is expensive. The only places to eat are the tourist hotels and, while the food tends to be superior to most places in Cuba, you are entitled to expect that given the cost. Lobster is in abundance on the island and you can have it for breakfast if you want. At an average price of around $40, you may wish to opt for something a little less extravagant.

Nightlife

Most hotels have their own cabaret and live music shows and the **Hotel Isla del Sur** has a nightclub/disco. The island is not a place for swingers; the people who come here tend to be looking for peace and tranquillity rather than raucous nightlife.

Things to see and do
Cayo Iguana

Close to Cayo Largo's western tip is a small group of islets, the best known of which is Cayo Iguana. So named because of a large resident iguana lizard population, you can visit here by boat on a day trip. The cost is usually no more than $25. The lizards also live on Cayo Largo although not in such great numbers.

Cayo Rico

Home to a lobster farm, white sand beaches and a lot of palm trees, Cayo Rico is the furthest west of the group of islands. Currently unspoiled, it has been earmarked for future tourist development. You can get here by boat from Cayo Largo.

Scuba diving

The protected coral reef around the island makes for good diving. The reef itself stretches for more than 30km and includes the rare and protected black coral.

CAYERÍA DEL NORTE

History and orientation

Situated off the northern coast of the provinces of Ciego de Avila, Villa Clara and Camagüey is an archipelago which seems destined to become one of Cuba's principal tourist attractions. Made up of five islands – Cayo Coco, Cayo Guillermo, Cayo Sabinal, Cayo Santa María and Cayo Romano – the Cayería del Norte is still largely underdeveloped and is an ideal place for those looking for a peaceful and relaxing beach holiday. Presently only Cayo Guillermo and Cayo Coco have facilities that cater for tourists but all that is set to change. Don't be surprised to find hotels springing up regularly throughout the islands over the coming years. Joint projects with the Cuban government and foreign investors have already been signed.

The most impressive construction is the causeway which links the northern coast of Ciego de Avila province and Cayo Coco, a 30km road that was built by hundreds of men working around the clock. Simply driving (or cycling) the route is an experience in itself. The link has been extended so it is possible to hop between islands without having to travel by boat.

Cayo Coco

Earmarked for tourist development, this is currently a haven of peace and tranquillity. With a land area of 360km^2, it is one of the biggest islands and its beaches of powder white sand span over 20km of the coastline. The best beaches (and the ones where you'll find accommodation – sadly, very expensive) are on the north side of the island. It is also a haven for wildlife with hummingbirds, Cuban cuckoos and lizards numbering among the varied species.

Cayo Guillermo

A series of small islets, Cayo Guillermo is the most developed in tourist terms. Within a land area of only 13km^2 there are currently five hotels (others are in the pipeline) catering primarily for Canadian and German package tourists. The beaches are delightful and stretch for more than 5km of the coastline. The islets are home to a local population of flamingos.

Cayo Sabinal

Situated off the northern coast of the province of Camagüey rather than Ciego de Avila, Cayo Sabinal is actually joined to the mainland by a thin strip of land close to the city of Nuevitas. To the east of Cayo Sabinal is the more popular and developed resort of Santa Lucía which is now linked to the island by an extension to the causeway that threads through Cayería del Norte. There are restaurants close to the link route that cater primarily for tourists popping across from Santa Lucía. The island is home to a variety of wildlife including thousands of flamingos which gather in the inland streams and marshes. Egrets and cranes are also indigenous to the area.

Cayo Santa María

The furthest west of the islands and actually off the north coast of the province of Villa Clara, Cayo Santa María is the least visited, most secluded of the five islands. Linked by the longest stretch of causeway it is only a matter of time before that changes.

Accommodation
Cayo Coco
Category 5
Hotel Guitart, Playa Larga, Cayo Coco; tel: Central Reservation 33 3202
A five-star hotel with five-star facilities and prices to match. You are a captive market on Cayo Coco so if you plan on staying here you'll simply have to bite the

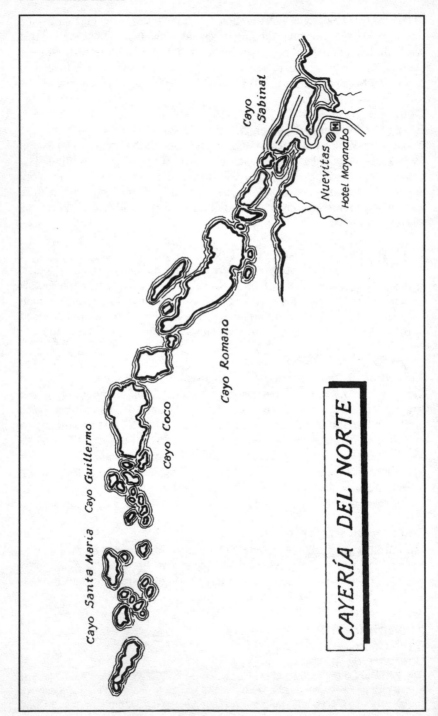

bullet and cough up the money. If you come as part of a tour group or as a package tourist, things will work out considerably cheaper.

Cayo Guillermo
Category 4
Villa Cojímar (60 rooms), Cayo Guillermo; tel: 053044; fax: 3044
The bungalows that constitute this little resort are named after characters created by Ernest Hemingway. Had they been named after elements of his own character you might have had the Villa Macho, the Villa Heroic or the Villa Drunk. Situated on a palm-fringed, white sand beach this is the stuff of which picture postcards are made.

Category 3
Villa Flotante (Floating Villa) (12 rooms), Cayo Guillermo; tel: 053044; fax: 3044
A strange, ugly building which, for some reason (perhaps novelty value), is moored just off one of the island's beaches. Perhaps somebody told the Cuban tourist authorities that rich westerners love sleeping in hotels floating in a 1m deep stretch of water. Classed as a three-star establishment, the facilities are moderate. There is no need for a swimming pool. Simply open your bedroom window and fall out.

Villa Oceano (8 rooms), Cayo Guillermo; tel: 053044; fax: 3044
Bungalow-style accommodation almost on top of the beach. Clean, pleasant and quiet. Facilities include car hire which is available in most of the hotels on the island.

Category 2
Hotel el Paso, Cayo Guillermo; tel: 25343
A two-star hotel popular with package tourists.

Hotel el Último Paraíso, Cayo Guillermo; tel: 22352
The other two-star establishment on the island. Clean, spartan and, like the El Paso, popular with tour groups.

Language

General conversation

Yes	*Sí*
No	*No*
Hello	*Hola*
Goodbye	*Adiós, Hasta luego, Ciao*
My name is	*Me llamo*
What is your name?	*¿Como se llama?*
Do you speak English?	*¿Habla usted inglés?*
I don't speak Spanish	*No hablo español*
I don't understand	*No entiendo*
Excuse me	*Permiso*
Please	*Por favor*
Thank you	*Gracias*
Good morning	*Buenas días*
Good afternoon	*Buenas tardes*
Good evening	*Buenas tardes*
Good night	*Buenas noches*
Pleased to meet you	*Mucho gusto*
How are you?	*¿Qué tal?*
I am hungry	*Tengo hambre*
I am thirsty	*Tengo sed*
I am well	*Muy bien*
I am ill	*Muy enfermo*
I am hot	*Tengo calor*
I am cold	*Tengo frío*

Useful words

Big	*Grande*	Open	*Abierto*
Small	*Pequeño*	Closed	*Cerrado*
How many?	*¿Cuántos?*	Man	*Hombre*
How much?	*¿Cuánto?*	Woman	*Mujer*
What?	*¿Qué?*	Mother	*Madre*
Where?	*¿Dónde?*	Father	*Padre*

Who?	*¿Quién?*	Sister	*Hermana*
Which?	*¿Cuál?*	Brother	*Hermano*
When?	*¿Cuándo?*	Son	*Hijo*
Why?	*¿Por qué?*	Daughter	*Hija*
Fast	*Rápido*	Children	*Niños*
Slow	*Lento*	Married	*Casado*
Right (direction)	*Derecha*	Single	*Solo*
Left (direction)	*Izquierda*		

Numbers, days, months and time

Zero	*Cero*	Monday	*Lunes*
One	*Uno*	Tuesday	*Martes*
Two	*Dos*	Wednesday	*Miércoles*
Three	*Tres*	Thursday	*Jueves*
Four	*Cuatro*	Friday	*Viernes*
Five	*Cinco*	Saturday	*Sábado*
Six	*Seis*	Sunday	*Domingo*
Seven	*Siete*		
Eight	*Ocho*	January	*Enero*
Nine	*Nueve*	February	*Febrero*
Ten	*Diez*	March	*Marzo*
Twenty	*Viente*	April	*Abril*
Thirty	*Trienta*	May	*Mayo*
Forty	*Cuarenta*	June	*Junio*
Fifty	*Cincuenta*	July	*Julio*
Sixty	*Sesenta*	August	*Agosto*
Seventy	*Setenta*	September	*Septiembre*
Eighty	*Ochenta*	October	*Octubre*
Ninety	*Noventa*	November	*Noviembre*
One hundred	*Cien(to)*	December	*Diciembre*
Time	*Tiempo*	Today	*Hoy*
What time is it?	*¿Qué hora es?*	Yesterday	*Ayer*
Minute	*Minuto*	Tomorrow	*Mañana*
Hour	*Hora*	Morning	*Mañana*
Day	*Día*	Afternoon	*Tarde*
Week	*Semana*	Evening	*Tarde*
Month	*Mes*	Night	*Noche*
Year	*Año*		

Eating and drinking

Food	*Comida*	Cheese	*Queso*
Drink	*Bebida*	Egg	*Huevo*
Water	*Agua*	Omelet	*Tortilla*
Beer	*Cerveza*	Rice	*Arroz*
Rum	*Ron*	Salad	*Ensalada*

Coke	*Cola*	Butter	*Mantequilla*
Milk	*Leche*	Bread	*Pan*
Coffee (black)	*Café solo*	Sandwich	*Emparedado*
Coffee (white)	*Café con leche*	Toast	*Tostado*
Wine (white)	*Vino blanco*	Steak	*Bistec*
Wine (red)	*Vino tinto*	Ham	*Jamón*
Meat	*Carne*	Bacon	*Tocino*
Fish	*Pescado*	Salt	*Sal*
Lobster	*Langosta*	Pepper	*Pimienta*
Shrimps	*Gambas*	Sugar	*Azucar*
Soup	*Sopa*	Ice cream	*Helados*
Chicken	*Pollo*	Lemon	*Limon*
Beef	*Rosbif*	Banana	*Banana*

Nationality

England	*Inglaterra*	English	*Inglés*
Scotland	*Escocia*	Scottish	*Escocés/esa* (male/female)
Wales	*País de Galés*	Welsh	*Galés/esa*
Ireland	*Irlanda*	Irish	*Irlandés/esa*
Great Britain	*Gran Bretaña*	United States	*Estados Unidos*
Canada	*Canadá*	Australia	*Australia*
New Zealand	*Nueva Zelanda*	Germany	*Alemania*
Netherlands	*Países Bajos*		

Appendix Two

Further Reading

General

Anderson, John Lee, *Che Guevara – A Revolutionary Life*, Bantam Press 1997

Azicri, Max, *Cuba, Politics, Economics and Society*, Pinter Publishers Ltd 1988

Barclay, Juliet, *Havana, Portrait of a City*, Cassell Villiers House 1993

Bethell, Leslie, *Cuba – A Short History*, Cambridge University Press 1993

Betto, Frei, *Fidel and Religion*, Pathfinder 1986

Borge, Tomás, *Fidel – Face to Face with Castro*, Ocean Press 1993

Chomsky, Noam, *Year 501, the Conquest Continues*, Verso 1993

Evans, Walker, *Havana 1933*, New York Pantheon Books 1989

Garcia, Cristina, *Dreaming in Cuban*, Flamingo 1992

Gébler, Carlo, *Driving through Cuba*, Abacus 1988

Geldof, Lynn, *Cubans*, Bloomsbury Publishing Ltd 1991

Greene, Graham, *Our Man in Havana*, Penguin Books 1958

Hemingway, Ernest, *The Old Man and the Sea*, Arrow Books 1952

Hemingway, Ernest, *To Have and Have Not*, Macmillan 1962

Lewis, Barry and Marshall, Peter, *Into Cuba*, Zena Publications Ltd 1985

Marshall, Peter, *Cuba Libre: Breaking the Chains*, Victor Gollancz 1987

Martí, José, *Our America*, Monthly Review Press 1897

Mericía, Mario, *The Fertile Prison – Fidel Castro in Batista's Jails*, Ocean Press 1980

Miller, Tom, *Trading with the Enemy*, Atheneum 1992

Otero, Lisandro, *Disidencias y Coincidencias en Cuba*, José Martí Publishing House (1987)

Perez, Louis A Jr, *Cuba – Between Reform and Revolution*, Oxford University Press 1988

Infante, G Cabrera, *Infante's Inferno*, Faber and Faber 1979

Stubbs, Jean, *Cuba: The Test of Time*, Latin America Bureau 1989

Sapieha, Nicolas, *Old Havana, Cuba*, Tauris Parke Books 1990

Sarduy, Perdo Perez and Stubbs, Jean, *Afro Cuba,* Ocean Press 1993
Timerman, Jacob, *Cuba – a Journey,* Picador 1990
Williams, Stephen, *Cuba – the Land, the History, the People, the
Culture,* Multimedia Books Ltd 1994

Health
Wilson-Howarth, Dr Jane, *Healthy Travel: Bugs, Bites and Bowels,*
Cadogan 1995
Wilson-Howarth, Dr Jane, and Ellis, Dr Matthew, *Your Child's Health
Abroad: A manual for travelling parents*, Bradt 1998

OTHER BRADT GUIDES TO CENTRAL & SOUTH AMERICA

Guide to Belize (2nd edition)
Alex Bradbury
'An informative guide to help you discover the natural beauty of Belize' *Woman's Journal*
Now updated with additional information on diving areas and wildlife reserves.
336pp   8pp colour   25 maps   £10.95   1 898323 48 8

Guide to Brazil – Pantanal, Amazon and Coastal Regions (2nd edition)
Alex Bradbury et al
'Invaluable' *The Sunday Telegraph*
For those especially interested in the nature and wildlife of Brazil, this guide is the most detailed available.
256pp   8pp colour   16 maps   £11.95   1 898323 59 3

Backpacking in Central America
Tim Burford
Belize, Guatemala, El Salvador, Honduras, Nicaragua, Coast Rica, Panama. This guide emphasises the region's wildlife and protected areas.
336pp   43 maps   £10.95   1 898323 25 9

Central and South America by Road
Pam Ascanio
'Advice about the best vehicle and equipment to take, route-planning details of border formalities, and country-by-country profiles.' *Geographical Magazine*
256pp   16pp colour   24 maps   £12.95   1 898323 24 0

Backpacking in Chile and Argentina (3rd edition)
Hilary Bradt et al
'This travel guide is a must.' *S A Explorer*
The best and most enjoyable way to see these countries and experience spectacular mountain scenery, well-run national parks, excellent food and wine, good transportation and safe cities.
208pp   45 maps   £10.95   1 898323 04 6

Climbing and Hiking in Ecuador (4th edition)
Rob Rachowiecki, Mark Thurber and Betsy Wagenhauser
'An excellent, informative guide for anyone venturing on to the high mountain climbs and treks of Ecuador.' *Joe Simpson*
The ultimate guide to the volcanoes, mountains and cloudforests of Ecuador.
288pp   45 maps   £12.95   1 898323 54 2

Backpacking in Mexico
Tim Burford
A comprehensive and practical guide to Mexico's long- and short-distance hiking trails and volcanoes, covering Yucatán, Chiapas, Baja, California and Copper Canyon.
256pp   20 maps   £11.95   1 898323 56 9

Backpacking and Trekking in Peru and Bolivia (6th edition)
Hilary Bradt
'Informative, diverting, encouraging and inspirational' *High Magazine*
Hiking trails around Inca ruins and through magnificent mountains. Natural history and Indian culture, plus advice on low-impact travel.
336pp   32 maps   £10.95   0 946983 86 0

Guide to Venezuela (2nd edition)
Hilary Dunsterville Branch
'Information which is vital to the newcomer or prospective traveller … is all here.' *RAC*
From horse-trekking in the Andes to choosing a desert island on which to be 'marooned'.
Emphasis on the national parks and wild areas, but with plenty of city information too.
400pp   8pp colour   83 maps   £12.95   1 898323 31 3

258

CUBA

UK Specialists to Cuba since 1976

Direct Flights from London and Manchester

Car Hire and Hotel Bookings throughout Cuba

Experienced and knowledgeable staff

Holidays for thinking people

DETAILED BROCHURE AVAILABLE FROM:
Regent Holidays (UK) Ltd, 15 John Street, Bristol, BS1 2HR.
Tel: (0117) 921 1711 (24 hours) Fax: (0117) 925 4866
Email 106041.1470@compuserve.com
http://www.regent-holidays.co.uk

COMPLETE LIST OF GUIDES FROM BRADT PUBLICATIONS

Africa by Road   Bob Swain/Paula Snyder   £12.95
Albania: Guide and Illustrated Journal   Peter Dawson/Andrea Dawson/Linda White   £10.95
Antarctica: A Guide to the Wildlife   Tony Soper/Dafila Scott   £12.95
Australia and New Zealand by Rail   Colin Taylor   £10.95
Belize, Guide to   Alex Bradbury   £10.95
Brazil, Guide to   Alex Bradbury   £11.95
Burma, Guide to   Nicholas Greenwood   £12.95
Central America, Backpacking in   Tim Burford   £10.95
Central and South America by Road   Pam Ascanio   £12.95
Chile and Argentina, Backpacking in   Hilary Bradt et al   £10.95
Cuba, Guide to   Stephen Fallon   £11.95
Eastern Europe by Rail   Rob Dodson   £9.95
Ecuador, Climbing and Hiking in   Rob Rachowiecki/Betsy Wagenhauser   £10.95
Eritrea, Guide to   Edward Paice   £10.95
Estonia, Guide to   Ilvi Cannon/William Hough   £10.95
Ethiopia, Guide to   Philip Briggs   £11.95
Greece by Rail   Zane Katsikis   £11.95
India by Rail   Royston Ellis   £11.95
Laos and Cambodia, Guide to   John R Jones   £10.95
Latvia, Guide to   Inara Punga/William Hough   £10.95
Lebanon, Guide to   Lynda Keen   £10.95
Lithuania, Guide to   Rasa Avizienis/William J H Hough   £10.95
Madagascar, Guide to   Hilary Bradt   £12.95
Madagascar Wildlife   Hilary Bradt/Derek Schuurman/Nick Garbutt   £14.95
Malawi, Guide to   Philip Briggs   £10.95
Maldives, Guide to   Royston Ellis   £11.95
Mauritius, Guide to   Royston Ellis   £11.95
Mexico, Backpacking in   Tim Burford   £11.95
Mozambique, Guide to   Philip Briggs   £11.95
Namibia and Botswana, Guide to   Chris McIntyre/Simon Atkins   £10.95
North Cyprus, Guide to   Diana Darke   £9.95
Peru and Bolivia, Backpacking and Trekking in   Hilary Bradt   £10.95
Philippines, Guide to   Stephen Mansfield   £12.95
Poland and Ukraine, Hiking Guide to   Tim Burford   £11.95
Romania, Hiking Guide to   Tim Burford   £10.95
Russia and Central Asia by Road   Hazel Barker   £12.95
Russia by Rail, with Belarus and Ukraine   Athol Yates   £13.95
South Africa, Guide to   Philip Briggs   £11.95
Spain and Portugal by Rail   Norman Renouf   £11.95
Spitsbergen, Guide to   Andreas Umbreit   £12.95
Sri Lanka by Rail   Royston Ellis   £10.95
Switzerland by Rail   Anthony Lambert   £10.95
Tanzania, Guide to   Philip Briggs   £11.95
Uganda, Guide to   Philip Briggs   £11.95
USA by Rail   John Pitt   £10.95
Venezuela, Guide to   Hilary Dunsterville Branch   £12.95
Vietnam, Guide to   John R Jones   £11.95
Zambia, Guide to   Chris McIntyre   £11.95
Zanzibar, Guide to   David Else   £10.95

Bradt Guides are available from bookshops or by mail order from:
Bradt Publications, 41 Nortoft Road, Chalfont St Peter, Bucks SL9 0LA, England.
Tel/fax: 01494 873478. Email: bradtpublications@compuserve.com
Please include your name, address and daytime telephone number with your order and
enclose a cheque or postal order, or quote your Visa/Access card number and expiry date.
Postage will be charged as follows:
UK: £1.50 for one book; £2.50 for two or more books
Europe (inc Eire): £2 for one book; £4 for two or more books (airmail printed paper)
Rest of world: £4 for one book; £7 for two or more books (airmail printed paper)

INDEX